HOUSING LAW

Second Edition

London • Sydney

HOUSING LAW

Second Edition

David Burnet, BA, LLM
Lecturer in Law
Cardiff Law School

Cavendish
Publishing
Limited

London • Sydney

Second edition first published 1999 by Cavendish Publishing Limited, The Glass House, Wharton Street, London WC1X 9PX, United Kingdom

Telephone: +44 (0) 20 7278 8000 Facsimile: +44 (0) 20 7278 8080

E-mail: info@cavendishpublishing.com

Visit our Home Page on http://www.cavendishpublishing.com

First edition 1996

Reprinted 1998

Second edition 1999

British Library Cataloguing in Publication Data

Burnet, David

Housing Law. – 2nd ed.

1. Housing Law – Law and Legislation – England 2. Housing – Law and Legislation – Wales

I. Title II. Burnet, David

344.4'2'06'3635

ISBN 1 85941 489 3

Printed and bound in Great Britain

To my parents

ACKNOWLEDGMENTS

I am grateful to Tony Caffel for generous advice about the mysteries of word processing.

Above all, I am very grateful to my wife Viv for her support and encouragement throughout.

CONTENTS

TABLE OF CASES

TABLE OF STATUTES

INTRODUCTION

> Housing problems cast a long shadow across British society. Homelessness is now at record levels ... More than two million households are thought to be in negative equity. The tax system, meanwhile, provides deep tax concessions to owner occupiers, rents have risen sharply in real terms, there is a lack of effective choice between housing tenures for most households, and the poorest are caught in a severe poverty trap of which housing benefit is a major contributor.
>
> (Goodlad and Gibb (ed), *Housing and Social Justice* (1994))

It is instructive to retain and re-examine this quotation, which headed the introduction to the first edition of this book. The emphasis in the second edition on a contextual approach to housing law and policy is unchanged, but how far has housing law and policy itself been transformed or, more realistically, modified, since the end of 1996, when the Housing Act of that year was beginning to bite? The change of administrations from Conservative to Labour in 1997 has not led to a significant reduction in the 'shadow' cast by the housing problems, although some of the political rhetoric of the new era, particularly that defining and deploring 'social exclusion', might lead an uncritical observer to a different conclusion. The levels of homelessness have been remarkably constant over the last few years. A partial revival of the housing market has led to some escapes from negative equity, but many are still suffering. There has been some readjustment of the tax system away from favouring mortgagors with the phasing out of MIRAS, but there is still a lack of effective choice between housing tenures. The poverty trap still exists for many households, although there have been fiscal measures to facilitate the return of single parents to the labour market. Housing benefit has been on the agenda for reform for some time, but no concrete proposals have yet emerged. The statistics on the state of UK housing show no substantial improvements in the last decade. Therefore, the quotation, as is sometimes conceded by policy makers in the new Labour administration, still largely holds good.

So far as the 'big' ideas for housing renovation and urban regeneration are concerned, the emphasis on privatisation through various mechanisms has continued and a New Deal for disadvantaged communities has been announced. The long awaited release of capital receipts from the sale of council housing has meant some further injection of funds into regeneration, but the ageing housing stock and demographic forecasts of household formation make the task of housing renewal just as Sisyphean as ever. So far as the means of effective privatisation of housing stock are concerned, local housing companies do not seem to be as popular as previously and have been rejected as an option by tenants in some recent high profile instances. The renewed emphasis on tenant empowerment has led in some directions uncongenial to the new Housing Minister. The private finance initiative is now increasingly looked to as a means of levering in finance, but it probably has more detractors and sceptics than did local housing companies.

What other significant changes in policy direction have taken place? Compulsory competitive tendering is to be replaced by 'best value' and there is greater emphasis on tenant involvement on decision making. There is much greater co-operation between various government departments, such as housing and health, when it comes to the formulation of what are infuriatingly described as 'joined up' solutions to 'joined up' problems, such as rough sleeping or social exclusion. In July 1998, the Social Exclusion Unit produced a report on rough sleeping in England which pointed to difficulties with hostel provision and lack of policy co-ordination. It also set the target of reducing the numbers of rough sleepers by two-thirds by the year 2002.

So far as long term capital investment in housing is concerned, in October 1998, the government issued a consultation paper, *Proposed Single Allocation to Local Housing Authorities for Capital Investment in Housing*, designed to enhance local authority discretion in resource allocation and to target finance on areas in greatest need. The 'single housing pot' is not, however, without its critics who fear that the eventual disappearance of a distinctive housing element in a general pot will be compatible with reduced investment in housing.

The major components of the 1996 Housing Act survive largely intact. The rights of homeless people have not been dramatically advanced by the incoming Labour Government beyond the easily achieved stroke of the pen restoration of the full duty homeless to reasonable preference status when it comes to general allocation criteria. The legislation itself does not seem to have come under much judicial scrutiny through litigation. The latest straws in the wind are that there is dissatisfaction with the prioritisation of certain needy groups when it comes to access to social housing, since this inhibits the laudable policy of achieving a better social mix and balance in communities. In addition, ironically, the spectre of changing housing provision for single mothers has recently re-appeared some years after the proposals for hostels for such individuals were dropped by a previous administration. So far as the private rented sector is concerned, there is no enthusiasm for re-introducing some form of regulation and redressing the balance tilted towards the landlord interest by new improved informally created assured shortholds. All that has happened is a belated attempt to curb some of the excessive rises in 'fair rents' for long standing occupants under the Rent Act 1977.

What other legislative developments might be on the horizon? There is increased pressure for rationalising and equalising the bundles of rights enjoyed by secure and assured tenants, since discrepancies in rent rights or security can apart from their intrinsic apparent unfairness also be damaging to initiatives to persuade tenants to foresake their local authority for some other form of tenancy. An influential policy document in this connection is *One for All – A Single Tenancy for Social Housing*, by Marianne Hood, which states:

> The basic idea of a single tenancy for the social housing sector is simple. It would reconcile the differences between secure and assured tenancies, combining the best features of each. In particular, from the secure tenancy, it would use the principle that important basic rights and obligations are enshrined in statute, and therefore common to all tenants. From the assured tenancy it would borrow the flexibility of additional rights and obligations (for both parties) that can be established by contract and incorporated in tenancy agreements.

According to the Housing Minister, Hilary Armstrong, the main emphasis in future is to integrate housing policy into a broader framework of 'strengthening the family, tackling social exclusion and meeting welfare to work objectives'. The inadequacies of present housing provision have in fact been acknowledged very recently by the Deputy Prime Minister, in April 1999, commenting on the Budget:

> Britain's current housing system is failing those in need. It is time we modernised housing policy to ensure the opportunity of a decent home for everyone and promote social cohesion, well being and self reliance.

The full significance of the Woolf reforms of civil procedure, which came into force on 26 April 1999, have yet to be felt in the context of housing. The 'overriding objective' of handling cases economically, fairly and expeditiously is, of course, to be welcomed, but there are concerns that, for example, the rights of defendants in possession proceedings could be eroded if they are channelled into the small claims procedural track where legal aid will be unavailable.

A Housing Policy Green Paper is expected shortly. A modernised housing policy could take a little longer. This book is intended to be up to date until the end of June 1999, but it has been possible to smuggle in some subsequent developments.

> Housing problems cast a long shadow across British society. Homelessness is now at record levels ... More than two million households are thought to be in negative equity. The tax system, meanwhile, provides deep tax concessions to owner occupiers, rents have risen sharply in real terms, there is a lack of effective choice between housing tenures for most households, and the poorest are caught in a severe poverty trap of which housing benefit is a major contributor.
>
> (Goodlad and Gibb (ed), *Housing and Social Justice* (1994))

It is instructive to retain and re-examine this quotation, which headed the introduction to the first edition of this book. The emphasis in the second edition on a contextual approach to housing law and policy is unchanged, but how far has housing law and policy itself been transformed or, more realistically, modified, since the end of 1996, when the Housing Act of that year was beginning to bite? The change of administrations from Conservative to Labour in 1997 has not led to a significant reduction in the 'shadow' cast by the housing problems, although some of the political rhetoric of the new era, particularly that defining and deploring 'social exclusion', might lead an uncritical observer to a different conclusion. The levels of homelessness have been remarkably constant over the last few years. A partial revival of the housing market has led to some escapes from negative equity, but many are still suffering. There has been some readjustment of the tax system away from favouring mortgagors with the phasing out of MIRAS, but there is still a lack of effective choice between housing tenures. The poverty trap still exists for many households, although there have been fiscal measures to facilitate the return of single parents to the labour market. Housing benefit has been on the agenda for reform for some time, but no concrete proposals have yet emerged. The statistics on the state of UK housing show no substantial improvements in the last decade. Therefore, the quotation, as is sometimes conceded by policy makers in the new Labour administration, still largely holds good.

So far as the 'big' ideas for housing renovation and urban regeneration are concerned, the emphasis on privatisation through various mechanisms has continued and a New Deal for disadvantaged communities has been announced. The long awaited release of capital receipts from the sale of council housing has meant some further injection of funds into regeneration, but the ageing housing stock and demographic forecasts of household formation make the task of housing renewal just as Sisyphean as ever. So far as the means of effective privatisation of housing stock are concerned, local housing companies do not seem to be as popular as previously and have been rejected as an option by tenants in some recent high profile instances. The renewed emphasis on tenant empowerment has led in some directions uncongenial to the new Housing Minister. The private finance initiative is now increasingly looked to as a means of levering in finance, but it probably has more detractors and sceptics than did local housing companies.

What other significant changes in policy direction have taken place? Compulsory competitive tendering is to be replaced by 'best value' and there is greater emphasis on tenant involvement on decision making. There is much greater co-operation between various government departments, such as housing and health, when it comes to the formulation of what are infuriatingly described as 'joined up' solutions to 'joined up' problems, such as rough sleeping or social exclusion. In July 1998, the Social Exclusion Unit produced a report on rough sleeping in England which pointed to difficulties with hostel provision and lack of policy co-ordination. It also set the target of reducing the numbers of rough sleepers by two-thirds by the year 2002.

So far as long term capital investment in housing is concerned, in October 1998, the government issued a consultation paper, *Proposed Single Allocation to Local Housing Authorities for Capital Investment in Housing*, designed to enhance local authority discretion in resource allocation and to target finance on areas in greatest need. The 'single housing pot' is not, however, without its critics who fear that the eventual disappearance of a distinctive housing element in a general pot will be compatible with reduced investment in housing.

The major components of the 1996 Housing Act survive largely intact. The rights of homeless people have not been dramatically advanced by the incoming Labour Government beyond the easily achieved stroke of the pen restoration of the full duty homeless to reasonable preference status when it comes to general allocation criteria. The legislation itself does not seem to have come under much judicial scrutiny through litigation. The latest straws in the wind are that there is dissatisfaction with the prioritisation of certain needy groups when it comes to access to social housing, since this inhibits the laudable policy of achieving a better social mix and balance in communities. In addition, ironically, the spectre of changing housing provision for single mothers has recently re-appeared some years after the proposals for hostels for such individuals were dropped by a previous administration. So far as the private rented sector is concerned, there is no enthusiasm for re-introducing some form of regulation and redressing the balance tilted towards the landlord interest by new improved informally created assured shortholds. All that has happened is a belated attempt to curb some of the excessive rises in 'fair rents' for long standing occupants under the Rent Act 1977.

What other legislative developments might be on the horizon? There is increased pressure for rationalising and equalising the bundles of rights enjoyed by secure and assured tenants, since discrepancies in rent rights or security can apart from their intrinsic apparent unfairness also be damaging to initiatives to persuade tenants to foresake their local authority for some other form of tenancy. An influential policy document in this connection is *One for All – A Single Tenancy for Social Housing*, by Marianne Hood, which states:

> The basic idea of a single tenancy for the social housing sector is simple. It would reconcile the differences between secure and assured tenancies, combining the best features of each. In particular, from the secure tenancy, it would use the principle that important basic rights and obligations are enshrined in statute, and therefore common to all tenants. From the assured tenancy it would borrow the flexibility of additional rights and obligations (for both parties) that can be established by contract and incorporated in tenancy agreements.

According to the Housing Minister, Hilary Armstrong, the main emphasis in future is to integrate housing policy into a broader framework of 'strengthening the family, tackling social exclusion and meeting welfare to work objectives'. The inadequacies of present housing provision have in fact been acknowledged very recently by the Deputy Prime Minister, in April 1999, commenting on the Budget:

> Britain's current housing system is failing those in need. It is time we modernised housing policy to ensure the opportunity of a decent home for everyone and promote social cohesion, well being and self reliance.

The full significance of the Woolf reforms of civil procedure, which came into force on 26 April 1999, have yet to be felt in the context of housing. The 'overriding objective' of handling cases economically, fairly and expeditiously is, of course, to be welcomed, but there are concerns that, for example, the rights of defendants in possession proceedings could be eroded if they are channelled into the small claims procedural track where legal aid will be unavailable.

A Housing Policy Green Paper is expected shortly. A modernised housing policy could take a little longer. This book is intended to be up to date until the end of June 1999, but it has been possible to smuggle in some subsequent developments.

CHAPTER 1

THE PRIVATE SECTOR AND THE RENT ACTS

THE PRIVATE RENTED SECTOR

Introduction

The recent White Paper on housing, *Our Future Homes, Opportunity, Choice, Responsibility*, 1995, identifies the following main features of the modern private rented sector. First, a buoyant private sector can act as an essential stepping stone for people leaving home, can assist with labour mobility in the economy in an era of short term employment contracts and accommodate those who wish to rent rather than own property. Secondly, private sector tenants tend to be young and single and to move homes frequently. There is, however, a substantial group of older tenants.

History of the Rent Acts

The law affecting short term residential occupiers in the private rented sector is as complex as it is controversial. Since 1915 and the pioneering Increase of Rent and Mortgage Interest (War Restrictions) Act, with some gaps for deregulation, a variety of legislative techniques has been used to intervene in what were traditionally idealised as arms length free market transactions between landlord and tenant. The most recent Rent Act, still of some practical importance, is the Rent Act 1977. The underlying justification for intervention was aptly stated by Lord Simon of Glaisdale in *Johnson v Moreton* [1980] AC 37 where he said 'the constriction of the market and the inequality of bargaining power enabled the landlord to dictate contractual terms which did not necessarily operate to the general benefit of society'.

Against this, there is no shortage of criticism of the pervasive phenomenon of interference through rent control and the imposition of security of tenure. As one early commentator put it, 'Rent control has been blamed for the fall of France, the fall in the democratic government of Austria, the decrease in birth rate and a good many other things' (Willis, 'A short history of rent control laws' (1950) 36 Corn LQ 87). The most frequent accusations are that it deters new building and investment, drives housing off the rental market, discourages the adequate maintenance of property, encourages underoccupation and hinders flexibility in the job market. As will be seen later, in recent years, there has been an attempt in Britain to restore market forces in the shape of the Housing Act 1988. Previous attempts at deregulation occurred in 1923 and, notably, in 1957, with the Rent Act of that year.

It is not proposed here to give the usual brief chronological, whistle stop account of successive Rent Acts, but instead to pinpoint particular legislation where appropriate. What is, however, apparent from the history of social legislation of this type is that it has haphazardly developed a twofold emphasis, initially, on rent control and, subsequently, on security of tenure. The practical interdependence of these two aspects is obvious, since rent rights with insecurity are as useless as security at unaffordable rates. In the view of one analyst (Honore, *The Quest for Security, Employees, Tenants, Wives*, 1983), security of tenure was originally regarded as an adjunct of rent control, but successive Acts have increased the preoccupation with security of tenure, including statutory successions to tenancies, with the result that, ultimately, it has become a case of 'the tail wagging the dog'.

The private rented sector has steadily and, indeed, spectacularly declined from its zenith in the early 20th century when it constituted 90% of household occupation and appears now to have bottomed out at around 10%. To some, the decline is wholly attributable to the impact of successive Rent Acts, but they, in turn, have to acknowledge that the Housing Act 1988 is phasing out the Rent Acts and there is no sign of a renaissance of the private sector. The recent White Paper, *Our Future Homes,* claimed that there has been a 17% rise in the number of households renting from private landlords in England between 1988 and 1994 (p 21), but much of this could be frustrated sales of freeholds leading to renting rather than a genuine revival.

Predecessors of the 1988 Act, such as the 1957 Rent Act, also failed to have the desired effect and may even have been counterproductive. Monocausal explanations of a predictable type, blaming everything on the Rent Acts, have some punch as ideological weapons in the interminable debate about the merits and demerits of intervention in the market, but should be displaced by more modest, tentative and multifactorial explanations, such as the drive for owner occupation and other economic and fiscal measures putting landlords at a disadvantage. However, another striking fact about the history of the Rent Acts is the ease with which they have been avoided or evaded, in which case assumptions about the oppressive weight of legal regulation are unjustified if the Acts have been more honoured in the breach than in the observance.

The latest statistics from the OPCS survey, Private renting in England 1993–94, demonstrate that there is still life in the Rent Act 1977 categories. Around 20% of agreements were regulated tenancies and 8% resident landlord and other limited security agreements, whereas the 1988 Act creatures, assured and assured shorthold, weigh in at 17% and 38% respectively.

Another significant attribute of the legislation over the years, apart from its unnecessary complexity, is the combination of cultural lag, incompetence or inertia which has dictated that regulatory formulae, which might initially have had some precise impact and justification, quite rapidly become artificial and anachronistic. A classic example of this sort of linguistic hangover is the original insistence in 1915, because of unrest among munitions workers, on targeting a particular unfurnished sector towards the lower end of the market. A criterion appropriate to emergency wartime legislation survived decades of social and demographic change, including change prompted by the terms of the legislation itself, to be despatched only in 1974. Viewed dispassionately, as the housing market alters, there is no particular merit in privileging unfurnished accommodation if the net results are to encourage landlords to discover the delights of 'Rent Act' linoleum and junk shop furniture and severely to limit the potential of protective legislation. To quote from the minority report of the Committee on the Rent Acts (Cmnd 4609, 1971, p 233):

> This distinction has given rise to a marked switch of accommodation from unfurnished to furnished in stress areas, particularly in London, and has deprived of security those tenants most in need of it, the young couples starting a family who would move to more permanent homes if they could, the immigrants to the cities and those families least able to manage their affairs.

Against this, is the argument put forward by Martin, *Residential Security*, 1989, p 67, that the Acts 'should always provide for a class of unprotected tenants in order to encourage letting'. However, it would seem sensible to choose a class in such a way that there is something for the Rent Acts still to bite on rather than to undermine them altogether. It is difficult to view the Rent Acts from some rationalist resource allocation perspective when other anachronisms, such as board and attendance, have survived even longer than furniture, from 1915–88. Martin does concede that the ease with which furniture could be used by landlords to circumvent the Acts necessitated more rational demarcation of the protected and unprotected. It is a balancing act that the law has never satisfactorily achieved in the lifetime of the Rent Acts.

The lease/licence distinction

Why has the lease/licence distinction been so important? The basic answer is that the Rent Acts have, throughout their history, privileged leases and not licences, mainly because the original emergency legislation in 1915 naturally did not go in for sophisticated avoidance conscious drafting and subsequent Acts reproduced certain legal classifications, more through inertia than anything else. The prescribing of a tenancy is built into all the definitional sections in succeeding Rent Acts and, indeed, in cognate legislation for social housing, but what can be done to transcend this preoccupation with tenancies is illustrated by the formula employed successfully in protection from eviction legislation since 1964 – that of 'residential occupier', which cuts across both lease and licence.

Although the deregulation clumsily imposed in the Housing Act 1988 has largely negated the need to anatomise the lease/licence distinction, by offering assured shorthold tenure as a panacea for landlords, there is still a need to explore the distinction in some contexts. Much effort has been expended by judges and analysts in attempting a clear demarcation, but, unfortunately, the dividing line is often as elusive as ever. It is striking that, while certain judges have striven to elucidate different senses of awkward cluster concepts, like exclusive possession, others, notably Lord Denning, have happily operated with mysteriously undefined and malleable notions. It is not helpful to be told, for example, that exclusive possession is not decisive if the meaning of exclusive possession is itself indeterminate. Using exclusive possession and exclusive occupation interchangeably does not assist matters. Lord Templeman is a recent exponent of this conflation, but is by no means the first.

It is possible that, in the general analysis of important principles, too much attention has been paid to judicial statements made at the highest level and too little to the day to day judgments in the county court. Nevertheless, it makes sense to analyse the development of doctrine in the knowledge that changes of course at the appellate level are bound, sooner or later, to be reflected at ground level. It is difficult to imagine, for example, the higher courts persistently accepting non-exclusive occupation agreements as licences, rather than tenancies, and the opposite trend prevailing among the lower orders.

Defining characteristics?

The classic definition of a licence is less problematical than that of a lease. A licence legitimises what would otherwise be a trespass and is fundamentally a personal privilege, as opposed to an interest in land. In the archaic language of Vaughan CJ in *Thomas v Sorrell* (1673) Vaughan 351: 'A dispensation or licence properly passeth no interest nor alters or transfers property in any thing, but only makes an action lawful which, without it, had been unlawful.' If exclusive possession is taken to mean the right to exclude the landlord and others from premises, that exclusionary sense seems *prima facie* inconsistent with the quintessence of a licence: its personal and precarious character. Some analysts have juggled with a compromise solution of a revocable personal privilege of exclusive possession, but without much success. As one Australian judge pithily put it:

> To say that a man who has, by agreement with a landlord, a right to exclusive possession of land for a term is not a tenant is simply to contradict the first proposition by the second [Windeyer J, in *Radaich v Smith* (1959) 101 CLR 209, p 222].

If some other sense of exclusive possession is intended, such as sole occupancy with no hint of exclusionary right, then exclusive possession and licences are not so incompatible. However, as we shall see, changes in the law are more readily effected by developing and exploiting the ambiguity of legal notions than by a full frontal conceptual assault.

The traditional characteristic of a lease is that it does confer on the occupant the right to exclude all other persons, including the landlord, from the premises. This could be called the exclusionary sense. Of course, there is a danger of circularity of reasoning here in that tenancies are recognised by the existence of exclusive possession and exclusive possession is the upshot of a tenancy. There is a related difficulty with any control test: is control the consequence or the cause of exclusive possession? Nevertheless, it is perfectly possible to have exclusive possession and a tenancy and be controlled through covenants in the lease, rather than having complete control. It is quite common for landlords to stipulate that tenants cannot have people, especially children, to stay and to regulate by remote control in great detail, whilst accepting that they have parted with possession and need permission to enter the property to view the state of repair. The detail can go so far in the writer's experience as 'Not to use any form of spray or silicone based furniture polish to clean the furniture, but only proper, high quality furniture cream'. Some of the detailed regulations imposed on tenants makes them look more like licensees.

At any rate, in the case of *Lynes v Snaith* [1899] 1 QB 486, the orthodoxy was apparent; if a person entered into exclusive possession (undefined), then that created a tenancy, albeit sometimes a tenancy at will, and was inconsistent with the existence of a licence. Exclusive possession was, therefore, before the era of protective social legislation, both a necessary and sufficient condition for the existence of a lease. The lack of conceptual precision in definition was mirrored by the lack of difference in practice between leases and licences, as both were equally insecure.

A matter of intention?

Analysts have detected a trend in the law away from reliance on intention to a more paternalistic approach, dictating the nature of an agreement through the operation of assumptions. Focusing on intention is fraught with difficulty. Is the intention to be found within the confines of a written agreement, or are surrounding circumstances to be taken into account? And whose intention is it? Commonly, it will be the intention of the landlord that is reflected in the terms, without any room for negotiation or construction of a composite or compromise intention. There is the further difficulty that, if intention is to be respected, does that mean that an intention to avoid the Rent Acts has to be implemented? Such an idea meets head on the established proposition that parties are not allowed to contract out of the Rent Acts.

The development of doctrine: exclusive possession and occupation

Although prior to the Second World War, the judiciary tended to be sympathetic to the supposed aims of the Rent Acts, after 1945, there was a gradual change of policy and a willingness to fudge definitional matters further or even to alter established common law doctrine to avoid the burden of social legislation. Before the Second World War, the tendency was to shape the common law in accordance with a purposive view of the legislation.

The early days of the Rent Acts

It is a commonplace that the Rent Acts began as a temporary measure – indeed, the law report summaries are at pains to stress the 'emergency' character of the early Acts, but the basic history lesson to be learnt is that, 'although Rent Act protection was initially designed to concentrate on housing occupied by the poorest tenants only, there was a gradual, if haphazard, extension to more and more types of property' (Partington and Hill, *Housing Law: Cases, Materials and Commentary*, 1991, p 115). Intervention in the free market was a common feature in policy of other combatants in the Great War. It is generally accepted that the immediate stimulus for the 1915 Act was unrest among munitions workers, especially in Glasgow, at landlords profiting from increased rents in conditions of wartime scarcity. The Act was hurriedly drafted and naturally focused on freezing rents by reference to those obtaining at the outbreak of war.

This legislative background offered some relatively easy scope for interpretation in the early years, but, with the subsequent extension of control without sophisticated drafting, the judges were always struggling to identify the aspirations of the latest provisions when it came to basic issues, such as joint tenancies. Characteristically, in the early years, the judiciary were able to adopt a generous approach to the perceived spirit of the legislation, in marked contrast to the approach of most judges in later years.

A classic illustration of judicial sensitivity in the early years is found in what is probably the first ever case on the Rent Acts: *Rees v Marquis of Bute* [1916] 2 Ch 64. In pardonable ignorance of the 1915 measures, the Marquis offered for sale by auction in early 1916 some 150 cottages he owned, on terms of 99 years, on payment of a premium. Unfortunately, under the terms of the 1915 Act, the exaction of such a lump sum was outlawed by s 1(2) in relation to 'a tenancy of any dwelling-house to which this Act applies' and there was nothing to exclude the cottages from the Act. The judge, Younger J, who presided over many Rent Act cases, subsequently offered the following encapsulation of the purposes of the 1915 Act:

> The Act in question is plainly an emergency Act designed to meet an exceptional crisis. It is intituled an Act to restrict, in connection with the present war, the increase of the rent of small dwelling-houses and the increase of the rate of interest on, and the calling in of, securities on such dwelling-houses and it is to remain in force during the continuance of the war and for a period of six months, thereafter, and no longer. The Act is doubtless specially intended to meet difficulties occasioned in munition districts by the large influx of population into these areas which has taken place and by the difficulty or impossibility of making adequate housing provision for the new comers in war time.

The judge reasonably felt unable to ignore the plain wording of the statute, in spite of the obvious functional differences between long and short tenancies. He went so far as to praise the Marquis' offer of the long leases, arguing that, if the premium were averaged out over the whole 99 year term, the lessees would be better off financially than they were under existing weekly tenancies. The actions of the Marquis 'had been greatly appreciated in South Wales'. Veneration for such philanthropy and acceptance of the crude financial reckoning in favour of the tenantry should have been moderated by awareness that responsibility for rates, taxes and repairs – including, presumably, a covenant to yield up the premises in good repair at the end of the term – had deftly been transferred from freeholder to leaseholder, making the status quo rather more attractive to well advised occupants and, in fact, creating for leaseholders the sort of problems that, ultimately, enfranchisement and other notorious social legislation – the Leasehold Reform Act 1967 – attempted to alleviate.

The upshot was that the premiums were reluctantly found to be unlawful and, since Rees had not taken possession, the Marquis was relieved of the obligation to perform the contracts upon repayment of money received. A striking footnote to this first casualty with interpretation was the speedy introduction of the Courts (Emergency Powers) (No 2) Act 1916, enabling county courts to authorise the grant of leases in excess of 20 years, including a premium, if 'satisfied that the terms of the tenancy are, on the whole, not less favourable to the tenant than the terms on which the dwelling-house was previously let'. One can only speculate how heavily the concomitant transfer of repairing and other obligations figured in such an assessment.

As the scope of the early legislation was enlarged, this expansion was not, as might be anticipated, met with increased hostility by the judiciary in the ensuing decades. Judges, such as Lord Justice Scrutton, were scrupulous about focusing on the broad purpose of the legislation and adapting doctrine with a view to facilitating that purpose. Concepts such as exclusive possession and exclusive occupation were largely taken for granted and there was no judicial eagerness to find that some arrangement other than a tenancy existed, even if, on the facts, the occupant might look more like a lodger. It was not until the Second World War that the judges started to chisel away at legislative protection by such means as stressing the requirement for a 'separate dwelling' as means of excluding sharers.

The judicial approach to the Rent Acts after the Second World War

In the aftermath of the Second World War, perhaps as part of a more general trend among judges to 'substantive formalism', there were some disturbing cases in terms of judicial enthusiasm for sanctioning circumvention of the Acts, even if, in 'floodgate' terms, the repercussions were not immediately apparent, as when marginal cases, such as apparent acts of generosity to existing occupiers, come under judicial scrutiny. However, it is important to remember that the cumulative effect of, for instance, undermining the notion of exclusive possession as conclusive of the existence of a tenancy could well be manifested in doctrinal upheaval after some decades as, when, in the crucial period in the mid-1970s, the judiciary were able to use a highly intuitive and impressionistic set of inherited criteria in the name of legal principle. It will therefore be necessary to consider some post-war cases in detail and attempt to relate them to broader justificatory principles.

Foster v Robinson [1951] 1 KB 149 has been accurately characterised as a disturbing decision, where an employer 'effectively bought his freedom from the Rent Act at minimal cost' (Gray and Symes, *Real Property and Real People*, p 423). After many years of service on a farm at a rent of £6.50 a year, the tenant became too old and ill to work and accepted an offer from the landlord terminating the existing tenancy and permitting him to live rent free in his cottage for the rest of his life. He died after only four years of this new dispensation and his daughter, who had lived with him for nine years before his death, was anxious to stay on and rely on the former tenancy. The landlord insisted she should leave.

The Court of Appeal were unanimous in finding that the arrangement with the landlord merely conferred a licence on the defendant's father and, hence, fell outside the stringent conditions in the 1939 Act stating the circumstances in which possession could be granted against a tenant. Lord Evershed rejected without further argument any idea that the effect of the arrangement was to create some form of tenancy at will which would have fallen within the Rent Acts. Albeit with some show of reluctance, he endorsed the view in Megarry on the Rent Acts that 'there is nothing to prevent the parties from so arranging matters that there is nothing to which the Act can apply'. He abhorred:

> ... any suggestion that a decision in the plaintiff landlord's favour would open the door to devices whereby a landlord could go to a sick tenant and get him to agree to some

> arrangement which was really to the advantage of the landlord and the grave disadvantage of the tenant.

Somewhat optimistically, he relied on the good sense of county courts as a means of protecting occupants, presumably, in instances of strong evidence of undue influence underlying any purported surrender of a tenancy. In this instance, the meeting of minds consisted of the landlord announcing that the existing tenancy would cease and the tenant saying – with hand not far from forelock – 'Thank you very much'.

The doctrinal implications of decisions of this type are that 'genuine' transactions must be upheld and there is no need to re-interpret the traditional rules on surrender by operation of law in the shadow of the Rent Acts. This respect for (convenient) common law principle can quickly be contrasted with the judicial approach in the cognate case of *Marcroft Wagons v Smith* [1951] 2 KB 496, a classic instance of manipulation of inconvenient established principle. Consistency, as is well known, is the hobgoblin of little minds.

Marcroft was an early classic case of judicial legislation, which tended to be the province of the Court of Appeal. A Rent Act protected tenant died and his widow and daughter remained in occupation, paying rent. When her mother died, the landlords let the defendant stay on paying rent for six months after 50 years of family occupation, although they wanted the property, ultimately, for one of their employees. If a second statutory succession had been operative at the time, her occupation would have been safeguarded, but that had to wait until 1965. Lord Denning analysed the transaction in the following way.

According to traditional common law doctrine, the continued occupation with the consent of the landlords would have been initially a tenancy at will and then a weekly tenancy on payment and receipt of rent. But, Denning's attitude was that it was improper to consider the common law position separately from the new circumstances created by the Rent Acts. This sounds suspiciously like allowing the Rent Acts to enter into the construction of the agreement, a tactic usually frowned on. Denning continued:

> It must be remembered that, at common law, the landlords would have had a clear, indisputable right to turn the defendant out; and, even if they did allow her to stay on and accepted rent from her, the consequences would not be serious because the landlords could always get rid of her by giving her a week's notice to quit. In that state of affairs, it was very proper to infer a tenancy at will, or a weekly tenancy, as the case may be, from the acceptance of rent. But, it is very different when the rights of the landlords are obscured by the Rent Restriction Acts. Seeing that the house was within the Acts, the landlords had no clear right to turn the defendant out. They could not have done so except by proving to the county court that she was not protected by the Acts. And, the consequences of granting her a contractual tenancy would be very far reaching because, then, she would be clothed with the valuable status of irremovability conferred by the Rent Restriction Acts. In these circumstances, it is no longer proper for the courts to infer a tenancy at will, or a weekly tenancy, as they would previously have done from the mere acceptance of rent.

This reasoning is worth quoting at length because it encapsulates typical post-war judicial attitudes to the Rent Acts; indeed, the ideological slip shows clearly when he talks of landlords rights being 'obscured' by the legislation. Traditional individual proprietary right is revered and any legislative encroachment on it resented. Established principles of interpretation, such as the presumption that statute makes minimal alteration in the common law or that judges are bound to interpret words as originally intended when the legislation was passed, are swept aside in favour of forthright reconstruction of common law to circumvent the Rent Acts. On another occasion, Lord Denning voiced misgivings about an articulated vehicle being driven through the Rent Acts, but he has often been behind the wheel himself.

This decision, and many subsequent ones where Denning was active, led to the demise of exclusive possession as a conclusive indicator of a tenancy. Lord Denning pulled himself up by his own bootstraps and busily collected his own decisions to establish an impressive pedigree for the proposition that licensees can also enjoy exclusive possession – that exclusive possession is not decisive. Exclusive possession was, carefully, never defined. Indeed, ironically, in *Marcroft,* the very existence of a statutory tenancy conferring exclusive possession on the occupant without the estate in land indispensable for a tenancy was used by Lord Evershed to add strength to the proposition that exclusive possession was not decisive. This involved use of the Rent Acts to undermine the Rent Acts.

A more honest route which would have avoided the obfuscation of exclusive possession would have been to argue that the act of generosity inherent in the arrangement negated any intention to create a tenancy and, thereby, obviated the existence of exclusive possession, hence the occupant was merely a licensee. Lord Denning himself pinpointed this possibility in *Facchini v Bryson* [1952] 1 TLR 1386, where he identified 'something in the circumstances, such as a family arrangement, an act of friendship or generosity, or suchlike, to negate any intention to create a tenancy'. This categorisation of exceptional circumstances negating the existence of a tenancy still represents the law. It was at this point, in the early 1950s, that Denning produced his celebrated remarks about articulated vehicles in the following way:

> It is not necessary to go so far as to find the document a sham. It is simply a matter of finding the true relationship of the parties. It is most important that we should adhere to this principle or else we might find all landlords granting licences and not tenancies and we should make a hole in the Rent Acts through which could be driven – I will not, in these days, say a coach and four, but an articulated vehicle.

Ironically, at this point in Denning's jurisprudence, the focus on the true relationship (however that is to be determined) and the downgrading of exclusive possession were already well established and they were instrumental in undermining the Rent Acts.

In tracing the further development of the doctrinal distinctions between lease and licence, there are several cases to be analysed before we reach the heyday of *laissez faire* in the 1970s. *Heslop v Burns* [1974] 1 WLR 1241 is an example of another unconventional transaction readily relegated to licence status by operation of the *Facchini v Bryson* exclusion categories. The facts were that someone formed a 'romantic attraction' for a lady cleaner and provided her and her family with housing for many years. He visited them almost daily and the impression created was that they could not have been intended to have the right to exclude him from the various properties he paid for. So, the inference of a licence was not difficult.

However, the reasoning is more sophisticated than many of the exclusive possession bashing cases presided over by Lord Denning. Lord Justice Stamp was scrupulous in attempting to explore the range of meanings inherent in 'the effect of exclusive possession'. He stated:

> As Somervell LJ indicated in *Cobb v Lane* [1952] 1 All ER 1199, the expression 'exclusive possession' in relation to the occupier of a property may be used in more than one sense. It may, as I see it, be used to mean that, as a factual matter, the occupant, alone or together with his family, occupies the premises and does not share them with any other person. Such a situation is not inconsistent with the occupation being enjoyed under a mere licence. Or the expression may be used to mean that the occupant has a right to exclude the owner from the premises. Where the expression is used in the latter sense as describing a situation where the occupier has the right to exclude the owner, it is clearly more difficult to reconcile it with the existence of a mere licence to occupy.

Such scrupulosity might have given Lord Denning pause for thought when constructing his lineage of cases undermining exclusive possession as a dispositive factor. But, it resurrects the further question of how it is possible to tell when exclusive possession and, hence, a lease has, in fact, been granted. As will be seen in *Somma v Hazelhurst* [1978] 1 WLR 1014, there can be no Archimedean point that will enable an observer to determine the existence of exclusionary rights, whether from narrow construction of a document or analysis of the surrounding factual matrix.

Lord Justice Scarman's judgment in *Heslop v Burns* is also instructive as it attempts some sort of overview of doctrinal development and also introduces, although he is apparently oblivious to this, another source of conceptual difficulty – that the use of exclusive occupation is apparently interchangeable with exclusive possession. The proliferation of terminology is particularly unfortunate as 'occupation' at first sight would appear to encroach more on the factual side of exclusive possession. 'Occupation', on its own, appears a more neutral term and does not necessarily carry the connotations of proprietary right that 'possession' does. Confusion is confounded if it is recognised that, in *Luganda v Service Hotels Ltd* [1969] Ch 209, Lord Denning established a special and distinct sense of exclusive occupation which involved less than the full exclusionary rights sometimes associated with exclusive possession: simply the status of having a room to oneself, even if one cannot exclude the landlord.

In *Luganda,* the plaintiff (a law student, hence, perhaps, the mandatory injunction reinstating him) had his own room in a 'hotel' in London for nearly three years. He had the key to his bedsit and made his own meals. Chambermaids made the bed and cleaned the room every day and changed the linen every week. Lord Denning was satisfied, without explaining why, that the plaintiff was a contractual licensee, even though he was described as a tenant. The question then arose as to whether the plaintiff had 'exclusive occupation' as specified by the relevant statute and, hence, the right to go to a rent tribunal for a reasonable rent and limited security.

In the case, Denning said: 'I am quite satisfied that "exclusive occupation" does not mean 'exclusive possession" in the technical sense in which it is sometimes used in landlord and tenant cases.' He continued: 'A person has a right to "exclusive occupation" of a room when he is entitled to occupy it himself and no one else is entitled to occupy it.' Tantalisingly, he did not elaborate on what the special technical sense of exclusive possession might be, but to make sense of the distinction, it would have to be something close to exclusionary rights.

Lord Scarman in *Heslop* noted the decline of exclusive possession (and occupation) from dispositive to inconclusive of the existence of a tenancy and then continued:

> What on earth had happened between 1899 and 1952? Are we witnessing judicial legislation without the assistance of Parliament? The answer is 'No'. The law, as I understand it, is precisely the same today as it was then. The legal question is a question as to the intention of the parties. The legal balance still shows a tilt in favour of a tenancy at will; for once an exclusive occupation had been established, a tenancy at will is presumed unless there are circumstances which negative it. What has happened, of course, is not that the law has changed, but that society has. To deal with changed social conditions, the Rent Restrictions Acts since 1914–15 have introduced a new dimension to the law of landlord and tenant and there has also emerged into prominence the licence to occupy.

His commentary, involving the supposition that the law has remained unchanged, is remarkably disingenuous, in view of the intellectual gymnastics already observed in cases like *Marcroft*, changing the common law because uncongenial social legislation has been clumsily superimposed on it. The legal balance, in fact, seems usually to tilt in precisely the opposite direction to that imagined. Lord Justice Scarman's analysis also raises the spectre of the tenancy at will, a nebulous form of tenancy sharing nearly all characteristics with licences, being personal and precarious. It is a defining characteristic of a tenancy at will that the tenant has no estate in the land and can be evicted at any time. How is it possible to distinguish between creatures that are virtually identical save that one belongs, by definition, on the proprietary and the other on the personal side of the juridical line? And how is the quality of that proprietary status to be detected? The next case, *Marchant v Charters* [1977] 3 All ER 918, provides some instructive answers. Basically, judicial intuition and an ouija board are the appropriate mechanisms.

Marchant v Charters was a landmark case following the upgrading of furnished tenancies to the possibility of fully protected status in the Rent Act 1974 after decades of artificiality. In other words, as the Court of Appeal were well aware, conceding that an individual had a tenancy would not have assisted him prior to 1974 because of the furniture element, but was a damaging finding for a landlord after 1974.

Mr Charters had a furnished bedsit in 'attractive bachelor service apartments'. There was a degree of self-catering involved and the rooms were cleaned every day. Lord Denning reviewed some previous cases where licences had been discovered and produced the following summary, often reproduced in textbooks as though it were the authoritative closely argued last word on the subject:

> Gathering the cases together, what does it come to? What is the test to see whether the occupier of one room in a house is a tenant or a licensee? It does not depend on whether

> he or she has exclusive possession or not. It does not depend on whether the room is furnished or not. It does not depend on whether the occupation is permanent or temporary. It does not depend on the label which the parties put on it. All these are factors which may influence the decision, but none of them is conclusive. All the circumstances have to be worked out. Eventually, the answer depends on the nature and quality of the occupancy. Was it intended that the occupier should have a stake in the room or did he have only permission for himself personally to occupy the room, whether under a contract or not, in which case he is a licensee? Looking at the position, in this case, in my opinion, Mr Charters was not a tenant of this one room. He was only a licensee.

It is obvious from this that intuition is the only approved basis for settling the question of the nature and quality of the occupancy. This approach of saying that the answer lies in the nature of the transaction, in looking for signs of a personal privilege and in disparaging exclusive possession as a criterion, was frequently used by Denning before this particular case, for instance, in *Shell-Mex v Manchester Garages* [1971] 1 WLR 612. In *Marchant,* he merely reformulated the question – by mentioning the stake in the room, as opposed to personal privilege – instead of offering a way out of the impasse and repeated the defining characteristics without offering any way of discriminating between leases and licences. Incidentally, the flimsiness of this set of criteria was noted by Lord Templeman in *Street v Mountford* [1985] AC 809, where he said:

> But, in my opinion, in order to ascertain the nature and quality of the occupancy and to see whether the occupier has or has not a stake in the room or only permission for himself personally to occupy, the court must decide whether, upon its true construction, the agreement confers on the occupier exclusive possession. If exclusive possession at a rent for a term does not constitute a tenancy, then the distinction between a contractual tenancy and a contractual licence of land becomes wholly unidentifiable.

What did decide the issue? Surely, opinion or intuition derived from a long standing view that landlords' rights are imperilled by the Rent Acts. This outlook may be too sweeping; if what is meant by a stake in the room is a degree of independence and control associated with tenancies, then, as a factual matter, it should be possible to locate people along a continuous spectrum, ranging from the overnight stay in the hotel at one end, through the sort of 'hotel' occupation enjoyed by Mr Luganda, to something that is incontestably a tenancy. With hindsight, some analysts, following the classifications attempted in *Street v Mountford*, have attempted to reclassify Mr Charters as a lodger and, hence, a licensee, but the element of intuition remains. Is it really the case that, on the facts of Mr Charter's occupation, the owner genuinely required unrestricted regular access to the premises, as opposed to limited incursions for specifically defined purposes every day? The very fact that the Rent Acts contemplate tenancies with substantial attendance would seem to indicate that tenancies should not be so easily undermined. It would have been possible for the Court of Appeal to emulate the first instance judge and find a tenancy, albeit one disqualified from full protection because of attendance. Instead, the court preferred the more devastating approach of demolishing the notion of a tenancy arising at all in the extremely common case of bedsit agreements of this type.

Non-exclusive occupation agreements

Although the evidence regarding the impact of the 1974 Act and the upgrading of furnished tenancies is inconclusive, by the late 1970s, the pressure to establish another judge proof means of circumventing the Rent Acts grew. Space does not permit analysis of all the ingenious agreements that proliferated, but *Somma v Hazelhurst* [1978] 1 WLR 1014 is the classic case.

A couple signed separate licence agreements spelling out non-exclusive occupation. They each agreed to share with another person, to be determined by the licensor, and the licensor reserved the right to determine a successor if one moved out and also to move into the room with them at any time. The Court of Appeal were confronted by arguments that they should adopt a purposive view of the Rent Acts and be suspicious of avoidance/evasion devices. They were faced with non-exclusive occupation agreements whose *raison d'être* was to undermine any assumption that exclusive possession in the exclusionary sense had been granted and also, even, to overshoot the more limited notion of 'exclusive occupation'; one of the defining characteristics of the intermediate level of protection in the shape of restricted contracts. The process of establishing the nature of the transactions involved could be short circuited by narrow concentration on the terms of any written agreement on the assumption that that necessarily expressed the intention of the parties. Alternatively, a broader view of the circumstances surrounding the transaction and, indeed, the state of the housing market could have produced an approach more protective of occupants' interests, since people will sign anything in order to obtain shelter.

In the event, the Court of Appeal opted for the narrow constructionist approach wedded to the wording of the documents in question, however bizarre the arrangements actually contemplated. This approach therefore involves the legalistic assumption that the substance of an agreement is in what is agreed in the documents and that it would subvert the intention of the parties if anything else were supposed. The typical wording of such arrangements is the following:

> Whereas the licensor is not willing to grant the licensee exclusive possession of any part of the rooms hereinafter referred to and whereas the licensee is anxious to secure the use of the rooms notwithstanding that such use be in common with the licensor and such other licensees or invitees as the licensor may from time to time permit to use the said rooms. By this licence the licensor licences the licensee to use (but not exclusively) ...

On the approach favoured by the strict constructionist, there is no difficulty if the wording of the agreement all points in the same direction. But, if the document is self-contradictory, avoiding use of the terminology of tenancies, but including details as to the substance of the relationship – for instance, repairing obligations on the occupier or reservation of a right of re-entry – then the label of a licence has to be ignored. *Addiscombe Garden Estates v Crabbe* [1958] 1 QB 513 is the classic approach here, although it involved business, rather than residential, user. It was also significant, in that case, that Lord Justice Jenkins attempted to hold the line against the downgrading of exclusive possession as indicative of a tenancy and argued that the fact of exclusive possession was, at all events, a consideration of the first importance.

It might be thought that, in these circumstances, where the licence drafting is so emphatic, a landlord is protesting too much that a licence is contemplated; however, in *Somma,* the court accepted that simultaneously signed separate agreements of this type removed any imputation of a tenancy. This was so, even though the two occupiers were a couple sharing the room in 'quasi-connubial bliss'. The reasoning of the Court of Appeal, as in some previous cases, is not over elaborate or based on clear principle. The following dictum from Lord Justice Cumming-Bruce is the closest the court came to a justification:

> Counsel for the respondents, basing himself on the judgment of Denning LJ in *Facchini v Bryson* and the reasoning in *Marchant v Charters*, submits that, in a 'Rent Act' situation, any permission to occupy residential premises exclusively must be a tenancy and a licence, unless it comes into the category of hotels, hostels, family arrangements or service occupancy or a similar undefined special category. We can see no reason why an ordinary landlord not in any of these special categories should not be able to grant a licence to occupy an ordinary house. If that is what both he and the licensee intend and if they can frame any written agreement in such a way as to demonstrate that it is not really an agreement for a lease masquerading as a licence, we can see no reason in law or justice why they should be prevented from achieving that object. Nor can we see why their common intentions should be categorised as bogus or unreal or as sham merely on the grounds that the court disapproves of the bargain.

It is not clear that the court did disapprove of the bargain and the Court of Appeal approach to agreements of this type has usually been deferential. The exceptionally narrow legalistic approach applied does have the consequence of encouraging landlords to operate in the private sector free from anxieties about security of tenure or rent control, so the *laissez faire* attitude does, perhaps, maintain supply, although at market and not necessarily affordable rates. The opposed approach, a more interventionist, welfarist attitude committed to the maximisation of tenancies, has its justification in making life as comfortable as possible for those trapped in the private sector, irrespective of any deterrent effect on landlords. This latter perspective could be linked to the view that private sector provision is not ideal and that other forms of tenure, including public sector provision, are more appropriate.

The return to orthodoxy

Until the mid 1980s, non-exclusive occupation agreements were extensively used and the Rent Acts were, therefore, more honoured in the breach than in the observance. Such agreements were only vulnerable if there was some strong contra-indication, such as a conflicting prior oral agreement, or a careless admission, such as 'it is just a legal formality and there is no danger of anybody else being put in' (*Walsh v Griffiths-Jones* [1978] 2 All ER 1002). But, the divide and conquer method of dismantling the elements of a tenancy was abruptly halted in the case of *Street v Mountford* [1985] AC 809, which is still the authoritative House of Lords decision in this problematical area.

The facts of *Street v Mountford* were, however, different to the non-exclusive occupation type agreement, since this was a case of sole occupancy. The agreement between the parties contained a number of restrictions on user, including prohibition of guests without prior permission and the assertion that it was a non-assignable personal licence. The owner reserved a right of access at all times for various purposes and the agreement concluded with the formula: 'I understand and accept that a licence in the above form does not and is not intended to give me a tenancy protected under the Rent Acts.'

The owner must have felt confident that the strict constructionist approach favoured by the Court of Appeal over the years would entail a finding of a licence, since that is what the document assiduously proclaimed. However, in the absence of multiple occupation, how should he have approached the proposition that the occupier enjoyed exclusive possession? With multiple occupancy, as in *Somma*, there is no problem in arguing, on the face of the documents, that, individually, the occupants have, at best, certain sharing rights with a person or persons unknown and are a world away from enjoying the right to keep the rest of the world out. They cannot even say that this is their room and that they do not have to share it with any others. So, exclusive possession appears to be a non-starter, let alone exclusive occupation in the *Luganda* sense. However, the very vagueness of the notion of exclusive possession as harnessed by the courts over the years contributed to a reversal of fortune for many landlords. Mr Street conceded that the agreement granted exclusive possession to Mrs Mountford, probably accepting and implying that she enjoyed sole occupancy as a factual matter, rather than contradicting the terms of the agreement and self-destructively acknowledging that she had exclusionary rights. He also had the benefit of the line of cases carefully stage managed by Lord Denning in which the concession of exclusive possession was not to be seen as the concession of a tenancy, since exclusive possession was compatible with certain forms of licence.

Lord Templeman gave the sole judgment in the House of Lords and succeeded in scotching the growth of licences without placing the law on a clear conceptual footing. The basic intention, apparently, since little background explanation was given, was to return the law to the deceptively simple orthodoxy prevalent before the 20th century complications – the orthodoxy that exclusive possession with certain clearly defined exceptions was conclusive of the existence of a tenancy. Perhaps, naively, he said:

> In the case of residential accommodation, there is no difficulty in deciding whether the grant confers exclusive possession. An occupier of residential accommodation at a rent is either a lodger or a tenant. The occupier is a lodger if the landlord provides attendance or services which require the landlord or his servants to exercise unrestricted access to and use of the premises. A lodger is entitled to live in the premises, but cannot call the place his own. If, on the other hand, residential accommodation is granted for a term at a rent with exclusive possession, the landlord providing neither attendance nor services, the grant is a tenancy.

Lord Templeman also indicated that the wording of any document was not conclusive and that it was legitimate to explore the surrounding circumstances to establish what legal relationship was in fact created. However, at a later stage in the judgment, he asserted that a lodger enjoyed exclusive possession and cast doubt on the validity of his analysis. The drift of the judgment, though, was clear: that non-exclusive occupation agreements and many other licences, in fact, created tenancies. Lord Templeman also made the point that:

> ... although the Rent Acts must not be allowed to alter or influence the construction of an agreement, the court should, in my opinion, be astute to detect and frustrate sham devices and artificial transactions whose only object is to disguise the grant of a tenancy and to evade the Rent Acts.

It is not clear, however, how it is possible to achieve this immunity from influence when the focus is necessarily on more or less transparent attempts to get round the Rent Acts.

The decision came as a profound shock to landlords cushioned for years from any intervention into the free market and freedom of contract. Naturally, the emphasis then switched to other forms of avoidance/evasion, some specifically sanctioned by statute, like holiday lets and board arrangements, and others suggested by the statutory terminology, such as company lets and deferred purchase agreements. In addition, the judgment of Lord Templeman, despite its robustness of approach, left open a number of crucial questions, not least the applicability of his criteria in the common situation of multiple occupation, especially with a floating population.

There remains the further question: why should the Rent Acts and the attendant policy of fair rents be suddenly supported after years of judicial non-intervention? Here again, intuition and an ouija board may help, since there was no clear articulation of any underlying justification. A desire to return to old orthodoxy and apparent simplicity does not seem a powerful motivating factor, any more than some sudden conversion to a purposive approach and a commitment to maximise the scope of the Rent Acts. It is, however, true that the record of the House of Lords in Rent Act cases over the decades is more tenant friendly than the contribution of the Court of Appeal. One suggestion which appears more plausible is that spiralling rents in the deregulated market following *Somma* put pressure on housing benefit to keep up and prompted a return to fair rents and lower housing benefit for basically fiscal reasons. Housing is always ripe for cuts in public expenditure.

At any rate, a few years later, the House of Lords had the opportunity to clarify the law and tackle the problems of multiple occupation. In *AG Securities v Vaughan* [1990] 1 AC 417, typical circumstances of more casual sharing had to be evaluated. A series of licence agreements was entered into with four occupants at different times for different amounts. The right to exclusive possession of any part of the flat was specifically excluded. There was a steady turnover of occupants and the practice was for the continuing occupants to move around when any bedroom was vacated and leave the least popular bedroom to the newcomer.

It might be thought that, on a robust approach, comparable to the view taken in *Street* on *Somma*, it would be possible to discern individual rather than joint tenancies in this arrangement and to argue that the occupants had exclusive possession of whatever room they were currently occupying and some shared rights over communal parts. This would involve arguing that their rights crystallised at the point when they applied for a fair rent. Another tortuous justification for a finding of a tenancy would be that of surrender and re-grant – that, every time one of the occupants moved on, there was a surrender of existing rights and a re-grant of the next pattern of room occupation.

The House of Lords, however, this time with Lord Templeman and colleagues, determined that the four occupants were, in fact, licensees, thereby making quite a hole in the general propositions advanced in *Street v Mountford* [1985] AC 809 about the predominance of tenancies. The underlying justification was, in the words of Lord Bridge (p 1207) that the bargain was 'a sensible and realistic one to provide accommodation for a shifting population of individuals who were genuinely prepared to share the flat with others introduced from time to time'. It is true that individual rather than collective responsibility is easier for some occupiers, as there is always the risk of one joint tenant disappearing, leaving the remainder liable for his contribution. Or, as presciently argued by Yates and Hawkins, *Landlord and Tenant Law*, 2nd edn, 1986, p 470, 'the arrangement enables changes in the group to be made with less formality and greater flexibility and also relieves both parties of the need to find someone prepared to undertake the obligations contained in a formal agreement for a fixed period'.

The reasoning advanced in the House of Lords is not very compelling, particularly if it is accepted that floating populations of this type are common in urban areas and, therefore, not a negligible part of the private rented sector. In practical terms, and the more recent House of Lords decisions are often reliant, in part, on pragmatic considerations, there does not seem to be much to choose between strangers who happen to approach a landlord as a unit, as with house sharing students with no previous connections, and the *Vaughan* type floating population. There was also the worry that, following the decision, unscrupulous landlords would construct a floating population from a pre-existing group by requiring signatures on different days for marginally different amounts and would have no difficulty in persuading the courts that no sham was thereby involved.

Lord Templeman began his analysis with a laborious exposition of the content of the Rent Acts and the inequality of bargaining power that necessitated them. He noted that opinion on the Acts was polarised and claimed that:

> ... the court lacks the knowledge and the power to form any judgment on these arguments which fall to be considered and determined by Parliament. The duty of the court is to enforce the Acts and, in so doing, observe one principle which is inherent in the Acts and has long been recognised – the principle that parties cannot contract out of the Acts.

Lord Templeman proceeded to make the analytical switch from exclusive possession to exclusive occupation without saying why he favoured a change of terminology. The test then became whether the enjoyment of exclusive occupation for a term in consideration of periodical payments creates a tenancy. On the appeal before them, the question was whether the occupiers were tenants or licensees of the whole of the premises. The analysis, therefore, did not touch on the most fruitful possibility – that they were tenants of individual rooms. Instead, it was a comparatively easy matter to demolish the supposition that they were joint tenants, since, on the death of one, there was no question of the remaining three being entitled to joint and exclusive possession as they could not keep out the next nominee of the landlords.

This reasoning and the related argument that it is not possible to construct joint tenancies out of disparate agreements lacking the four unities of possession, interest, title and time, seems to be *prima facie* compelling, but reckons without the possibility that the occupants could be considered to be tenants in common instead and, hence, still within the purview of the Rent Acts. Tenants in common need only possess one of the four unities: possession. The problem of attempting to reconcile common law doctrine with apparent statutory intention is as old as the Rent Acts themselves and, in the early years, was resolved more sympathetically to the obvious purposes behind the Acts, as when it was concluded in *Remon v City of London Real Property Co Ltd* [1921] 1 KB 49 that 'tenant' must also mean 'ex-tenant' to make sense of the protective ambitions of the legislation. Latterly, the Court of Appeal, in particular, has capitalised on the traditional doctrine of the unities to rule out the existence of tenancies.

The case of *Antoniades v Villiers* [1988] 3 WLR 139, decided concurrently with *Vaughan,* involved revisiting the strange world of non-exclusive occupation agreements explored in *Somma.* The only material differences in the agreements and surrounding circumstances were that, in principle, there was more room in the later case for the landlord to execute his declared option of moving in as many other persons as he chose. The landlord also required both of the occupiers to sign anti-matrimony agreements, although what he hoped to gain by this is unclear. On the authority of the robust approach to shams (or pretences, as Lord Templeman would latterly prefer to characterise them), the written agreement belied the true nature of the arrangement. The couple enjoyed exclusive possession of the flat and were, therefore, joint tenants.

As stated earlier, the use of assured shorthold tenancies under the Housing Act 1988 dispenses with security of tenure and rent rights for occupants and offers a statutory guarantee for landlords. The official booklet promoting the 1988 Act is called *Now it's Worthwhile Being a Landlord.* Indeed, the 1996 Housing Act will extend the scope of assured shortholds and make the criteria even more landlord friendly. Statutorily guaranteed insecurity is an advance on licences which were always subject to the vagaries of judicial reasoning. However, the lease/licence distinction remains of importance for agreements predating the 1988 Act. A factor to be taken into account is the extent to which the courts will accept the spirit of *Street v Mountford* and find tenancies, even if there are signs that some of the unities may be lacking. There are also difficulties in applying the principles enunciated by Lord Templeman in other contexts, such as management of short term accommodation by local authorities and housing associations.

Conclusion

The desire in *Street* to maximise the scope of tenancies in the shadow of the Rent Acts is clearer than the constituent reasoning. There is a presumption that those let into exclusive possession are tenants, but, how exactly, exclusive possession or exclusive occupation is established remains unclear. Any exceptions are likely to be the obvious categories formulated in *Facchini,* family arrangements, acts of generosity and the like. Service occupancy where the occupation is for the better performance of employment duties is another. In these circumstances, there is still uncertainty about whether exclusive possession was granted, but is referable to the existence of something other than a tenancy, or whether there was no grant of exclusive possession at all.

It seems that, in the last few years, the advent of assured shortholds has driven away the more convoluted form of licence agreement. Their further promotion in the 1996 Housing Act should assist the process. There are, however, in theory some unresolved questions about the existence of joint tenancies in circumstances where the landlord has carefully made occupants separately liable for rent. Despite the arguments in *Antoniades* about the interdependence of separate licence agreements, there could be occasions as in *Mikeover v Brady* (1989) 21 HLR 313 where the court, particularly the Court of Appeal, holds that there can be no joint tenancy because there is no unity of interest as occupiers are only individually liable for their own share of the rent. Any element of a sham will be harder for the court to detect than in other cases, such as *Aslan v Murphy* [1989] 3 All ER 130, where the occupier was mysteriously barred from using the room for 90 minutes (between 10.30 am and noon) each day. The lease/licence distinction and the general significance of *Street* will also be discussed in the context of public sector tenancies.

TENANCIES REGULATED UNDER THE RENT ACT 1977

Introduction

Although one of the purposes of the Housing Act 1988 is to phase out the Rent Acts, the method of despatching them is more to allow them to expire through natural causes like the passing of time, migration and exhaustion of statutory succession, rather than at a single stroke. Those responsible for the 1988 Act claimed that they had learnt their lessons from the sweeping deregulation of the Rent Act 1957 which supposedly precipitated Rachmanism and other problems. The 1988 Act was not to be retrospective and the rights of existing tenants were not to be jeopardised. Tenancies regulated by the Rent Act 1977 and existing prior to 15 January 1989 would stay protected.

Indeed, there are elaborate transitional provisions specifying the circumstances in which protected tenancies can still be created after the 1988 Act commencement date. These include where there has been prior agreement (pre-15 January 1989) to create such a tenancy or where it is a grant to a person who, immediately before the tenancy was granted, was a protected or statutory tenant and is so granted by the person who, at that time, was the landlord under the tenancy (s 34(1)(b) of the Housing Act 1988). The statute is, therefore, silent on the fundamental point as to whether or not the new tenancy has to be of the same or virtually identical premises as the old. In *Goringe v Transectra* [1994] CL, 29 April, the tenant had been occupying a dwelling since 1960 and had succeeded to a statutory tenancy in 1977. In April 1989, the tenant moved into other property owned by the landlord. In 1992, the landlord sold his interest in the premises to new owners who decided that the tenant was an assured tenant under the 1988 Act and served a notice of increase of rent under s 13 of that Act. The tenant sought a declaration that he was still protected by virtue of s 34(1)(b). The court, at a low level in the hierarchy, decided to consult Hansard to resolve the ambiguity following the breakthrough in *Pepper v Hart* [1993] AC 593. In this instance, there were clear pronouncements by the promoters of the legislation that there was to be no requirement of same or similar premises as such a stipulation would permit unscrupulous landlords to escape security provisions merely by shuffling tenants around. So, the declaration was granted.

The upshot is that there are still many agreements predating the relevant date of 15 January 1989 still in existence and the framework of security of tenure, rent and other rights will have to be described and contrasted with later legislation.

The definition of the 'protected' tenancy

The essence of the 1977 protective framework is to split the original contractual agreement, the 'protected' tenancy, from its subsequent incarnation, the 'statutory' tenancy, which is the status of irremovability imposed by statute at the end of the protected tenancy. As has been stated in relation to the protected tenancy, 'the gates of the Rent Act do not open wide to all comers'. The definitional section within s 1 of the 1977 Act will have to be considered in some detail, followed by the exclusions from protection – both those contained in the legislation itself and those implied by it.

Section 1 of the Rent Act 1977

The prerequisite is: 'a tenancy under which a dwelling-house (which may be a house or part of a house) is let as a separate dwelling.'

Tenancy

The requirement of a tenancy is as old as the Rent Acts themselves and, as already shown, has generated problems by inviting the growth of licences. Subtenancies are included and no differentiation between types of tenancy is made, so some of the more exotic tenancies, like tenancies at will or by estoppel, are covered in principle. It seems bizarre that tenancies at will, which are virtually equivalent to licences, should be honoured in this way.

House

As there is no further definition beyond part of a house, which could be a single room, the outer limits of the criterion have had to be explored in relation to caravans and houseboats and even caves. The problems with caravans were discussed in *R v Rent Officer of Nottingham Registration Area ex p Allen* (1985) 17 HLR 481, where the common sense point was made that it depended on the degree of mobility. Total immobility would be the most likely indicator of a dwelling-house and the rent officer should be on the look out for sham mobility. On the facts, the caravan in the *Allen* case, because it was moved periodically and services were disconnected for that purpose, was held not to be a 'house'.

Another recent case, *Elitestone Ltd v Morris* [1997] 2 All ER 513, demonstrates the difficulties at the margin and also involves analysis of the law of fixtures. Wooden chalets which had originally been holiday homes in the 1930s had thereafter been in permanent occupation. There was no dispute about whether the written agreements created tenancies, but the issue was whether the chalets were within the Rent Acts or the wrong side of the line as something less than fixtures on the land. At first instance the judge held that the chalets were suitably attached to the land, but the Court of Appeal disagreed and said there had been no annexation. The House of Lords (1 May 1997), took a different view to the Court of Appeal, perhaps, partly, because they were shown photographs of the chalets in question, a high tech facility denied to the Court of Appeal. They were also influenced by the approach taken in the Australian case of *Reid v Smith* [1905] 3 CLR 656, which also involved wooden structures supported on brick piers, rather than fixed by cement. The properties in question were not easily transportable, like Portakabins, but would have to be dismantled and rebuilt elsewhere. So far as the law of fixtures was concerned, there was some ambivalence in the leading judgments in the House of Lords about the relevance of such doctrine, since, in the words of Lord Lloyd, 'One would not ordinarily think of the building itself as a fixture'. The traditional fixtures jargon of degree and purpose of annexation was not deemed particularly helpful, but was, nevertheless, used to justify the outcome, although 'the answer is as much a matter of common sense as precise analysis'. Judicial appeals to common sense are not always commonsensical, but this decision can surely be supported on the grounds that the Rent Acts are designed to protect occupiers in their homes and it would be artificial to distinguish the abodes 'in what was represented as being an idyllic rural environment' (to quote Lord Clyde) from other homes within the Rent Acts, especially if immobilised caravans can qualify.

Let as a separate dwelling

In this context, sharing arrangements, whether with the landlord or other occupiers, are the sort of factor that could prevent qualification under the statute. We have already analysed 'total' sharing of a room or rooms leading to a finding of a licence. However, there are other forms of sharing where there is partial exclusive possession, but sharing of other elements of accommodation.

An elaborate jurisprudence grew up in the 40s and 50s about the types of sharing that would destroy the supposition of a 'separate' dwelling. Certain rooms came to be regarded as essential living accommodation, generally those associated with sleeping, cooking and eating. In *Neale v Del Soto* [1945] KB 144, a tenant did not have a separate dwelling and, hence, a protected (controlled) tenancy because he only had exclusive possession of two rooms and shared the kitchen and other rooms with the landlord. The argument for the occupier was that such sharing of amenities would become an avoidance device if no separate dwelling were found, but the court were more impressed by the enforced proximity counterargument for the landlord. A nightmare vision was produced of generations of landlords having to share the whole of the rest of a house with the occupants of an attic, 'almost in perpetuity' (p 146). Thus, kitchens are living rooms, but bathrooms and lavatories are not.

Some aspects of sharing are specifically covered by ss 21 and 22 of the 1977 Act, which go back several decades. Under s 22, where a tenant is sharing accommodation with other tenants, as in the common occurrence of house sharing with individual rooms exclusively occupied, the separate accommodation is protected and the tenant cannot be evicted from the shared accommodation unless the order also affects the separate accommodation. Section 21 makes similar circumstances of sharing with a landlord into a restricted contract, provided the tenancy was granted on or after 14 August 1974 and before 15 January 1989.

Separate dwelling can sometimes be read in the plural, in the sense that more than one unit of occupation if let together can constitute 'a' dwelling. Thus, in *Langford Property v Goldrich* [1949] 1 KB 511, two flats on the same floor of a building qualified. However, a flexible and purposive approach has been adopted to this formula, so that there was no difficulty in *Horford Investments v Lambert* [1976] Ch 39 for the court to rule out the activities of an entrepreneur bent on profit maximisation by claiming protection for two sublet houses. He was applying for a fair rent for his head tenancy, but not proposing to pass the savings on to his tenants. Lord Scarman, typically, was more forthright than his colleagues about policy considerations and said:

> The policy of the Rent Acts was, and is, to protect the tenant in his home, whether the threat be to extort a premium for the grant or renewal of his tenancy, to increase his rent or to evict him. It is not a policy for the protection of an entrepreneur, such as the tenant, in this case, whose interest is exclusively commercial, that is to say, to obtain from his tenants a greater rental income than the rent he has contracted to pay his landlord. The Rent Acts have, throughout their history, constituted an interference with contract and property rights for a specific purpose – the redress of the balance of advantage enjoyed in a world of housing shortage by the landlord over those who have to rent their homes. To extend the protection of the Acts to tenancies such as these, in this case, would be to interfere with contract and property rights beyond the requirement of that purpose.

The purpose of the letting

The realistic approach of the courts to the question of purpose is well captured by the headnote to *Wolfe v Hogan* [1949] 2 KB 194:

> Where the terms of the tenancy provide for or contemplate the user of the premises for some particular purpose, that purpose will *prima facie* be the essential factor. Thus, if the premises are let for business purposes, the tenant cannot claim that they have been converted into a dwelling-house merely because someone lives on the premises. If, however, the tenancy agreement contemplates no specified user, then the actual user of the premises at the time when possession is sought by the landlord, must be considered.

On the facts, since the initial letting was of a large room for antique and junk dealing, the fact that the occupier had subsequently used the premises as a dwelling did not bring her within the Rent Acts.

TENANCIES EXCLUDED FROM PROTECTION

References to sections below are to the 1977 Act unless otherwise stated.

Tenancies above the rateable value limits

The limits set in the 1977 Act are fairly high, as they reflect the veering of policy back to extensive protection in the 1960s following the impact of deregulation in the 1957 Act. The luxury end of the market is excluded because the traditional problems of scarcity and overcrowding and disrepair are not prevalent at that end of the spectrum. The rules are ferociously complicated and made worse by the rating revaluation in 1973 and by the need to adapt the criteria with the advent of the community charge to replace residential rates.

Where the tenancy was entered into before 1 April 1990, and that necessarily takes in almost all of them, s 4 of the 1977 Act specifies that the tenancy will be excluded if the property exceeded the rateable value limits on the 'appropriate day'. The limits are:

(a) Class A. If the appropriate day is on or after 1 April 1973, the limits are £1,500 (Greater London) and £750 (elsewhere);

(b) Class B. If the appropriate day is on or after 22 March 1973, but before 1 April 1973, the limits are £600 (Greater London) and £300 (elsewhere) on the appropriate day and £1,500 and £750 respectively on the 1 April 1973;

(c) Class C. If the appropriate day is before 22 March 1973, the limits are £400 and £200 on the appropriate day, £600 and £300 on 22 March 1973, and £1,500 and £750 on 1 April 1973.

Tenancies at low rent: s 5

This mysterious looking section has the simple purpose of excluding long leases from Rent Act protection and leaving their characteristics to be met by other codes such as the Landlord and Tenant Act 1954. Long leaseholders characteristically pay a premium and then a low annual ground rent. As with other areas of the Act, the possibility of avoidance/evasion is raised by the drafting and, in *Samrose Properties v Gibbard* [1958] 1 All ER 502, an attempt was made to exploit this exclusion by the use of a premium and subsequent low rent. The Court of Appeal took a robust view of the transaction and endorsed the summary made at first instance:

> In my judgment, if the agreement and the lease are viewed together, it becomes clear that the real substance of the transaction is the landlord's demand of £39 for a year's occupancy, and that this is simply divided into an immediate payment of £35, and the balance by quarterly instalments of £1 each. I regard the £35 as commuted rent, which in my view, together with the quarterly rent, is the true consideration for the letting. If I am right, this tenancy is one protected by the Acts.

Where the relationship is not the traditional arms length, but the tenant co-occupies and works for the landlord, the position becomes complicated. In *Barnes v Barratt* [1970] 2 QB 657, it was held that, although, at common law, services could constitute rent, the position was different under the Rent Acts if there could be no quantification of the value of the services rendered. So, even if there was a tenancy, it was not protected by the Rent Acts.

Shared ownership leases: s 5A

This exception was introduced by s 18 and Sched 4 of the Housing and Planning Act 1986 and relates to leases granted under Pt V of the Housing Act 1985 in connection with the right to buy and other long tenancies granted by housing associations with provision for the tenant to obtain additional shares. The purpose seems to be to prevent any recourse to the fair rent system under the 1977 Act.

Dwelling-houses let with other land: s 6

This is another arcane section, the purpose of which has been more accessibly expressed in s 2 of the Housing Act 1988 for assured tenancies. Under s 6, a tenancy is outside protection if the dwelling-house is let together with land other than the site of the dwelling-house. It has to be read in conjunction with s 26 which states that land or premises let together with the house are to be treated as part of the house unless it is agricultural land of more than two acres. A 'dominant purpose' test has been developed to solve the basic conundrum: is this a house let with land or land let with a house? In *Feyereisel v Turnidge* [1952] 2 QB 29, a bungalow on a campsite was excluded because it came with the land rather than vice versa.

Payments for board and attendance: s 7

This section reads:

> (1) A tenancy is not a protected tenancy if under the tenancy the dwelling-house is *bona fide* let at a rent which includes payments in respect of board or attendance.
>
> (2) For the purposes of sub-s (1) above, a dwelling-house shall not be taken to be *bona fide* let at a rent which includes payments in respect of attendance unless the amount of rent which is fairly attributable to attendance, having regard to the value of the attendance to the tenant, forms a substantial part of the whole rent.

This is an important section of disconcerting vagueness attributable to the circumstances of its origin in 1915, when certain lettings were excluded for specific purposes which were clear enough at the time and related to long outmoded housing conditions. It is worth remembering that it was tenancies with these elements that were excluded. According to one reading of *Street v Mountford*, Lord Templeman presumed that nearly all board or attendance agreements created lodgers. As with their contemporary, the furniture exception, these two criteria have survived interminably only to be laid to rest in the Housing Act 1988. As will be seen, a tenancy can still be assured, even if board and attendance are provided.

Board

This factor has never been defined since its inception in 1915. Initially, the idea must have been to focus on unfurnished and unattended houses and to exclude the common phenomenon of digs or lodgings where meals were provided by a resident landlord. Indeed, it is surprising that it was not until 1974 that a resident landlord exception was devised. At any rate, the provision of board has latterly taken on various guises. Cornflakes through the letter box is the caricature, but the provision of a weekly box of groceries as part of the agreement is not unknown. Vending machines on the premises and vouchers for meals in cafés down the road have also been encountered. What, however, has been subjected to judicial scrutiny at the highest level is the more orthodox provision of a meal or meals, as in *Otter v Norman* [1989] AC 129.

The occupants of 36 bedsits in a large house were also paying for the privilege of enjoying daily a continental breakfast in a communal dining room in the basement. There was no hint of anything like lodger status or Mr Charters' mere personal privilege of occupation. The House of Lords reviewed the early history and dictionary definition of board and the opinion in *Wilkes v Goodwin* [1923] 2 KB 86 that any board above *de minimis* would be sufficient. It was noted that, although the definition of board was not altered in the Rent and Mortgage Interest Restrictions Act 1923, some substantiality test was introduced for attendance and furniture, generating the assumption that the omission of reference to board had been deliberate.

There was, therefore, a lack of any recent precedent, but the received wisdom that the line was to be drawn between the cup of tea and the continental breakfast, a meal classifiable as board by Europhiles. There is a Scottish case, *Holiday Flat Co v Kuczera* 1978 SLT 47 to the effect that a continental breakfast is sufficient. The reasoning of the House of Lords in *Otter v Norman* is encapsulated in the following statement from Lord Bridge:

> My Lords, I think we must assume that for many years many landlords and tenants have regulated their relationships on this basis, and, even if I thought that a different construction could reasonably be placed on s 7(1) of the Act of 1977, I would not think it right to adopt it now and to upset existing arrangements made on the basis of an understanding of the law which has prevailed for so long.
>
> The courts have consistently set their face [*sic*] against artificial and contrived devices whereby landlords have sought to deny to tenants the protection intended to be conferred by the Rent Acts. I do not believe that anything of that kind is involved here. A *bona fide* obligation by a landlord to serve even such a modest daily meal as the continental breakfast with which this case is concerned is hardly likely to appeal to the unscrupulous landlord as a soft option. It will necessarily involve not only the cost of the food and drink provided but also all the housekeeping chores which must be undertaken in shopping for provisions, preparation and service of meals on the premises and clearing and washing up after meals. If a landlord and a tenant genuinely contract on terms which impose such obligations on the landlord, it would, to my mind, be surprising if the legislature had provided for the perpetuation of such a contract in favour of the tenant when the landlord wishes to terminate it.

This surprise of Lord Bridge is indeed surprising if it is considered how far removed the practice of provision of board was in the late 1980s from the original context which produced the exception. Just as it is reasonable to ask why a floating population of occupiers should enjoy fewer rights than a slightly more organised group, why should a few bread rolls seriously affect rights? And how strong is the usual rationale for the exception that it would be unfair to oblige a landlord to provide bread rolls for generations of occupants with security of tenure? The obligations on the landlord, easily delegated at little expense, are hardly onerous. Where does this leave arrangements that are less than *bona fide*? If board is not provided as agreed, then the agreement could be deemed a sham. The weekly provision of a box of groceries would appeal to unscrupulous landlords as a soft option in the absence of other avoidance devices. On the authority of *Otter*, such provision would appear to be genuine and unexceptionable.

Attendance

Although signs for 'rooms with attendance' can still be seen occasionally, the notion seems incongruous nowadays and appears to be a relic of a more spacious age. However, it does figure in tenancy agreements involving cleaning and laundry and associated services, and it could have made life awkward for Mr Charters if he had been found to be a tenant rather than a licensee. The flavour of it is captured in this definition from *Palser v Grinling* [1948] AC 491:

> It means service personal to the tenant performed by an attendant provided by the landlord in accordance with his covenant for the benefit or convenience of the individual tenant in his use or enjoyment of the demised premises. 'Service' is a wider word than attendance. Attendance, being personal in its nature, may be dispensed with by an individual tenant at his pleasure, though it is not on that account excluded from what the tenant pays for when the landlord has covenanted to supply it. But services common to others (for example, the heating of a communal water supply, or the cleaning of passages, hall, etc, outside the demised premises) will not constitute attendance. It follows from the above that a landlord's covenant to supply someone to carry down refuse from the flat is a covenant to provide attendance. Similarly, the provision of a housemaid or valet to discharge duties in connection with the flat would be the provision of attendance, but a covenant by the landlord to provide a resident porter or housekeeper for a block of flats would not.

The difference between attendance and board is that the amount of rent attributable to attendance has to be substantial to take the tenancy out of full protection and make it a restricted contract, whereas any board above *de minimis* will disentitle a tenant to full protection, and substantial board will overshoot restricted contract status. Although attendance sounds anachronistic and is uncommon there have been recent instances of exclusion on such grounds. In *Nelson Developments Ltd v Taboada* (1992) 24 HLR 462, daily cleaning of the room and laundry and other services were deemed substantial enough.

A recent case in the Court of Appeal showed nostalgia for the old days of the heyday of licences. In *Huwyler v Ruddy*, 18 January 1996, the services involved in an agreement dating from 1985 were laundry of bed linen and cleaning the room, requiring around 20 minutes a week. Theoretically, a two stage analysis is required here, first to determine whether or not a tenancy exists and then assess, if a tenancy were found, how much of the rent is attributable to attendance. A substantial element would deprive the tenant of Rent Act protection, less than substantial would preserve such rights.

On first impression, it might seem that the agreement was a tenancy and the element of rent insubstantial, given the minimal services. However, both at first instance and in the Court of Appeal a licence was detected, removing the necessity to consider further the operation of s 7. How was the finding of a licence justified? Lord Justice Gibson produced a very creative interpretation of the 'unrestricted access' formula used in *Street v Mountford* by Lord Templeman to differentiate tenant and lodger. The formula is 'The occupier is a lodger if the landlord provides attendance or services which require the landlord or his servants to exercise unrestricted access to and use of the premises'. On a commonsensical reading of such a formula, 20 minutes a week when the tenant is out hardly constitutes such access, or tenants with attendance would be very thin on the ground. However, Lord Justice Gibson endorsed a definition of 'unrestricted' given by Ralph Gibson LJ in *Crancour v Da Silvaesa* (1986) 18 HLR 265, at p 273:

> I take the meaning of the word 'unrestricted' in this context to be primarily concerned with the landlord's need to go into and out of the lodger's rooms at the convenience of the landlord and without the lodger being there to let the landlord in.

On the facts, the Lord Justice was satisfied that access was so unrestricted, since the plaintiff was obliged to get into the room as and when necessary, whilst respecting the privacy of the defendant. So, since no notion of frequency or unpredictability is built into this judicial interpretation, one limited incursion at a set time suffices to turn what would otherwise be a tenancy into a licence. If, at any stage in the future, avoidance devices against protective legislation are desired, this case offers rich pickings. In terms of present liabilities, the decision means that other pre-1988 Act agreements on similar facts are also licences, with the attendant consequences for rent rights and security of tenure. So, the vacuum cleaner can damage your rights as much as a few bread rolls.

Student lettings: s 8

Although some solicitors and landlords in the author's experience (that this is a common misconception is confirmed by a passage in Colbey, *Residential Tenancies*, 3rd edn, 1996, citing the example of a private landlord granting a 'student tenancy') believe that students are *ipso facto* disentitled to protection irrespective of the identity of the landlord, this exception relates only to lettings by specified educational institutions. The section has the obvious purposes of freeing universities and other institutions from problems with rent challenges and obstacles to vacation letting. Rent strikes in halls of residence where the students are self-catering are obviously more problematical than those where meals and other services are provided, since the latter group would fall outside protection through board and attendance anyway.

Because of difficulties of supply, universities and other institutions sometimes lease property from private sector landlords and sublet to students. In *St Catherine's College v Dorling* [1980] 1 WLR 66, such an arrangement was held not to confer a protected tenancy on the College, who were interested in having a fair rent registered. The reasoning was that the premises were not let to the college as a separate dwelling, but as 'a tenancy of a building which contained a number of units of habitation'. There was some judicial hostility to the College for applying with indecent haste for a fair rent only five days after agreeing to the contractual amount.

Holiday lettings: s 9

This exception dates from 1974 and its original aims were the modest ones of protecting seaside landladies and others from losing the right to repossess properties. Prior to 1974, the furnished letting exception from full protection would have disqualified most holidaymakers anyway. The section states that a tenancy is unprotected 'if the purpose of the tenancy is to confer on the tenant the right to occupy the dwelling-house for a holiday'. Although, as we have seen, avoidance devices such as licences have had their moments, the use of holiday lettings in unlikely places for people in work has been widespread over the years. Unlike board and attendance, no effort was made to phase out or redefine this exception in the Housing Act 1988, so holiday lets cannot be assured tenancies either. They can not even be restricted contracts. In view of the lapse of time since the commencement of the Housing Act 1988 in January 1989, it is very unlikely that there are any genuine surviving holiday lets governed by the earlier code, but it is convenient to analyse them at this point.

The authority on holiday lets is *Buchmann v May* [1978] 2 All ER 993 and is unsatisfactory for two main reasons. The first is that, on the facts, the arrangement was a very temporary one, although she had previously been a tenant for two years, with the short term arrangement apparently designed to give the defendant the flexibility she needed before going abroad to join her husband. It did not look like a holiday arrangement, but cl 6 of the agreement stated baldly 'that the letting hereby made is solely for the purpose of the tenant's holiday in the London area'. The Court of Appeal, whilst professing to maintain vigilance against shams, decided that the onus of establishing protection and refuting the presumption of a holiday lay with the tenant. This clearly ignores the reality of the characteristic dictation of terms by the landlord. The second reason for some scepticism about the approach is that the tenor of the judgment in the subsequent case of *Street* is much less disposed to take agreements at face value.

In 1980, there was a decision which is more in line with the later *Street* approach, although the decision was at a lower level. In *R v Rent Officer for London Borough of Camden ex p Plant* (1980) 257 EG 713, some student nurses took a tenancy of a flat and the agreement stated that the occupation was 'for a holiday'. However, the landlord was aware from previous transactions that the tenants were nurses and the judge was satisfied that the express purpose misrepresented the true nature of the agreement. The significance of the *Plant* case is, therefore, that there was patently no misconception on either side about the possibility of a holiday; to that extent it is distinguishable from the *Buchmann* case where the evidence was less clear cut. Since holiday lets survive as an exception in the 1988 Act, and fall outside some of the Protection from Eviction Act safeguards, there may be some reliance on them to this day, despite the attractions of assured shortholds. The difficulty with shortholds is their vulnerability to quick repeal or imposition of security (unlikely with 'new' Labour), not to mention procedural complexity. By contrast, it is not exactly difficult to insert some formula, such as 'it is agreed that the premises are let solely for the purpose of a holiday' in an agreement. Holiday lets have been a source of successful avoidance, as well as a genuine safeguard for certain landlords for over 20 years, and have never been successfully challenged at appellate level.

Agricultural holdings: s 10

A tenancy is not a protected tenancy if the dwelling-house is part of an agricultural holding and is occupied by the person responsible for the control of the farming of the holding. The object of this exclusion is to indicate that dwelling-houses on farms are to be regulated by a separate code such as the Agricultural Holdings Act 1986.

Public houses: s 11

For fairly obvious reasons, a tenancy is not protected if the dwelling-house consists of or comprises premises licensed for the sale of intoxicating liquors for consumption on the premises. Such tenancies are likely to be covered by the business tenancy rules in the Landlord and Tenant Act 1954.

Resident landlords: s 12

This is one of the more important and impenetrable exceptions, created in 1974 to offset the upgrading of furnished tenancies, and designed to be a simple way of encouraging individual landlords into the market, secure in the knowledge that they could recover possession relatively easily. Unlike factors, such as holiday lettings, it is quite likely that tenants of a resident landlord have been in occupation since before 1988 and are, hence, subject to the 1977 Act rules. The OPCS survey suggests a figure of 8%, which includes those with even more limited security.

Conditions

(1) The basic precondition is that the tenancy must have been granted on or after 14 August 1974.

(2) Is the building in question a purpose built block of flats?

The idea behind this condition is to exclude purpose built blocks because the occupiers will be self-contained and there is no reason to privilege a landlord merely living under the same roof as others without more enforced cohabitation. The original drafting of the exception was too sweeping as it excluded the situation where the occupation of an individual flat in a purpose built block was divided between the landlord and a tenant, who then proved immovable.

The statutory definition of purpose built block of flats is one which as constructed contains two or more flats.

(3) Did the landlord occupy another dwelling forming part of the building at the time of the grant of the tenancy?

The lack of a statutory definition of building has led to a number of borderline cases where unconventional conversions and extensions have been achieved. What is or is not part of a building is a question of fact that the appellate courts are happy to delegate to lower courts.

(4) Has the landlord or successor ever since occupied as his residence another dwelling-house which formed part of the building?

The ideal here is complete continuity of occupation, but the criteria have had to be relaxed because of the stipulation in Sched 2, para 5 of the 1977 Act that the test is the same as occupation by a statutory tenant. Occupation of several homes is, therefore, possible. In *Wolff v Waddington* (1989) 22 HLR 72, the Court of Appeal were satisfied that occupation of just over a year by the landlord was sufficient, even though she was from America and intended to go back there to live. In *Jackson v Pekic* (1989) 22 HLR 9, leaving furniture in a flat for several years was deemed to be insufficient.

An awkward fact situation was assessed in *O'Sullivan v Barnett* [1994] 1 WLR 1667, since the tenant had a good *prima facie* claim to a protected tenancy rather than a restricted contract. The difficulties were caused by the fact that both tenant and resident landlord migrated to new premises on conversion of the existing house, but the tenant moved over several weeks before the landlord. The exclusion from protected status in s 12 only operates if 'the tenancy was granted by a person who, *at the time that he granted it*, occupied as his residence another dwelling-house which also forms part of that building'. The Court of Appeal caused no surprise by rejecting a literal interpretation and claiming that it was really a concerted move of both households and that it would be wholly artificial to subdivide the transaction into stages.

Crown property: s 13

As amended by s 73 of the Housing Act 1980, this provides that a tenancy is excluded from protection at any time when the interest of the landlord belongs to the Crown, or to a government department, or is held in trust for the Crown for the purposes of a government department, unless the interest is managed by the Crown Estate Commissioners. The only thing to be said about this exclusion is that, by definition, tenancies can flit in and out of protection depending on property transfers. This volatility can also arise with fluctuating valuations.

Local authorities, etc: s 14

Again, this is an obvious exclusion to indicate for the avoidance of doubt that statutory schemes are mutually exclusive. Sometimes, lack of clear stipulation can allow interlopers from other tenures to try to gain rights under another code. See *Lambeth LBC v Udechuku* (1981) 41 P & CR 200, where the attempt was to achieve 'restricted contract' status. London Borough Councils are one of the specific exceptions here along with county councils. district councils and housing action trusts.

Housing associations: s 15

The relevant landlords in this category are registered or co-operative housing associations, the Housing Corporation, Housing for Wales or a charitable housing trust. Housing association tenancies have enjoyed a chequered legal existence and have been regarded by many as suitable for their own distinct tenancy with special legal criteria. Instead, they have been lumped in first with local authority tenants so far as security of tenure is concerned and then made uneasy bedfellows of assured tenants under the Housing Act 1988. The Rent Act 1977 has not always been totally denied to them, as pre-1988 Act tenancies traditionally enjoyed a fair rent.

Housing co-operative: s 16

A tenancy is not protected when the landlord's interest belongs to a housing co-operative, but could have secure status under the Housing Act 1985.

Business tenancies: s 24

A tenancy cannot be a regulated tenancy if it is governed by Pt II of the Landlord and Tenant Act 1954. The definition of a business tenancy is:

> ... any tenancy where the property comprised in the tenancy is or includes premises which are occupied by the tenant and are so occupied for the purpose of a business carried on by him or for those or other purposes.

Company lets

At this point, it is appropriate to consider some agreements not specifically excluded from regulated status in the Rent Acts, but operating in the shadow of the Acts. The tortuous legal position under the Rent Acts is that a company let can be a protected tenancy, but on expiry of that contractual tenancy no statutory tenancy can spring up because a statutory tenancy exists only so long as a tenant occupies as a residence and a company cannot reside. However, there is no problem about the protected tenancy because, ironically, the protected tenant need not satisfy any residence qualification.

The consequence is that company lets have no security after the contractual term. How precisely do the legal mechanics operate? *Hilton v Plustitle* [1988] 1 WLR 149 is a good example and was decided when the robust approach to shams and artificial transactions in *Street v Mountford* should have cast a longer shadow than it did on the Court of Appeal. The facts were that the prospective tenant saw an advertisement for company lets and understood that it would be the company that would be the tenant and would nominate her as the occupier of the flat. Accordingly, she bought a company, Plustitle Limited, off the shelf for £150 and became a shareholder and director. She then entered into an occupation agreement via the company.

When landlord and tenant, or rather occupier, fell out, she maintained that the company let was a sham. Lord Justice Croom-Johnson repeated the classic definition of a sham in *Snook v London and West Riding Investments Ltd* [1967] 2 QB 786, p 802:

> ... if it has any meaning in law, it means acts done or documents executed by the parties to the 'sham' which are intended by them to give to third parties or to the court the appearance of creating between the parties legal rights and obligations different from the actual legal rights and obligations (if any) which the parties intend to create. [For] acts or documents to be a 'sham', with whatever legal consequences follow from this, all the parties thereto must have a common intention that the acts or documents are not to create the legal rights and obligations which they give the appearance of creating.

The reasoning from this point is not difficult to predict. This was no sham on those criteria, since it was a genuine company let and the transaction did represent the true position. This blinkered approach is linked to a basic attitude towards avoidance/evasion found in Lord Justice Buckley's remarks in *Shell-Mex and BP Ltd v Manchester Garages Ltd* [1971] 1 WLR 612, where he said: 'One has first to find out what is the true nature of the transaction and then see how the Act operates on that state of affairs if it bites at all.' According to Martin (in *Residential Security*, 1989, p 78), to regard such a letting as a sham 'would be to rewrite the company law doctrine of corporate personality'. It is surely not necessary to redefine established law, only rule out its effectiveness in a housing context where the notion of corporate personality is hardly at home.

So, although to the detached observer the company let is as artificial and suspect an agreement as the most vociferous non-exclusive occupation agreement, it is judicially sanctioned as an avoidance device. The terminology of the Housing Act 1988 perpetuates their status outside legislation by stipulating that assured tenants have to be individuals occupying as their only or principal home. How far they are still used is uncertain, but, as with holiday lets, there may be some continuity through sentimental attachment, if for no other reason, and it is clear that assured shortholds have not had a trouble free existence, since there are moves in the Housing Act 1996 to facilitate their creation.

STATUTORY TENANCIES

Introduction

In *Marcroft Wagons v Smith,* the Master of the Rolls let off some invective, in the decent obscurity of Latin, at the statutory tenancy:

> But it is now clear that, to use the formula which I think has been applied, a new '*monstrum horrendum, informe, ingens*' [vast fearsome deformed monster] has come into our ken – the conception of a statutory tenancy – the conception that a person may have such a right of exclusive possession of property as will entitle him to bring an action for trespass against that property but which confers no interest whatever in the land: it is, as has been said, a statutory right of irremovability.

Because of its special nature as a legislative encroachment on common law principles, the statutory tenancy will never satisfy the purists. Here, an outline of the main legal principles will be given without too much emphasis on the jurisprudential problems created.

Certain elements are non-controversial. By virtue of s 2(1)(a) of the 1977 Act, a protected contractual tenant becomes a statutory tenancy on termination of the contract 'if and so long as he occupies the dwelling-house as his residence'. As already indicated in the discussion of company lets, there is a residential condition for statutory tenancies which is absent from protected tenancies. A classic illustration of the residential test and supporting justification is contained in *Skinner v Geary* [1931] 2 KB 546. Geary had been a weekly tenant for many years, but had not actually lived in the property since 1919. When notice to quit was served on him in 1930, the house was occupied by his sister in law. From county court through to the Court of Appeal, there was unanimity that Geary did not satisfy the statutory requirements and could not use occupation by relatives as his own. Lord Justice Scrutton (p 564) produced a typically perceptive purposive argument:

> One object of the Acts was to provide as many houses as possible at a moderate rent. A man who does not live in a house and never intends to do so, is, if I may use the expression, withdrawing from circulation that house which was intended for occupation by other people. To treat a man in the position of the appellant as a person entitled to be protected is completely to misunderstand and misapply the policy of the Acts.

What counts as occupation as a residence?

As this is essentially a question of fact and degree, some sample cases can be given, but no unshakeable principles. In *Brown v Brash & Ambrose* [1948] 2 KB 247, the tenant was unavoidably detained for two years in prison. His wife and children remained in occupation for a while, but then departed with most of the furniture. It was held that the tenant was not residing and that absence of this type could be so protracted as to constitute an end of occupation. However, if the tenant had the intention to return, he could assist himself by installing a caretaker or leaving sufficient furniture as a symbol of continuity. In the inevitable Latin, possession for the purposes of claiming a statutory tenancy involved demonstration of an *animus possidendi* (intention to return/possess) and of a *corpus possessionis* (physical evidence of possession). So, in this case, the physical evidence was lacking with the removal of most of the furniture, whatever the status of the will to possess.

The opposite obtained in *Colin Smith Music v Ridge* [1975] 1 WLR 463, where a statutory tenant left his mistress and children and surrendered his tenancy to the landlord. In that instance, the physical signs of continued occupation were there, but the intention to possess was not. If she had been wife, instead of mistress, her position would have been stronger as she could have acquired the statutory tenancy.

It is possible, though, perhaps, surprising, in view of the original purpose of the Rent Acts, that statutory tenancies can be sometimes claimed of two residences. Someone dividing his or her time between residences for work reasons could qualify. In *Hampstead Way Investments v Lewis-Weare* [1985] 1 All ER 564, the House of Lords assessed a situation where a tenant slept five nights a week after work in a flat, but spent the rest of the time with his wife and step daughter in a house nearby. It was held that the limited use of the flat was not enough to sustain a claim of a statutory tenancy of it.

The terms of the statutory tenancy

According to s 3(1) of the 1977 Act, so long as he stays in possession, a statutory tenant is obliged to observe and is entitled in turn to benefit from all the terms and conditions of the prior protected tenancy, so far as consistent with the provisions of the Act. This section is the obvious mechanism for spelling out the continuity of basic elements, such as rent obligations, covenants to repair and the covenant for quiet enjoyment. There are certain terms which would, however, be inconsistent with the Acts provisions and would not be carried over, such as the (redundant) term to give up possession at the end of the contractual tenancy.

Some further terms are imported into statutory tenancies by the Rent Act itself. By s 3(2), the tenant is obliged to give the landlord access to the dwelling-house and all reasonable facilities for carrying out repairs. Section 3(3) stipulates that the statutory tenant must give notice to quit as required under the original contract or, if no notice was required, not less than three months.

Statutory succession

As has already been indicated, the prolonging of security by means of statutory succession is as contentious as interference with rent. The first succession was instituted in 1920 and the possibility of two in 1965, so that it would be perfectly feasible for a family asset to last for generations and decades, and for the asset to be derived from an oral agreement. Unsurprisingly, the deregulatory purposes in the 1988 Act extended to phasing,out succession rights, so that, in many instances, successors can now only inherit an assured tenancy. When the Bill was going through Parliament, there was concern about the plight of many carers looking after elderly relatives in the community with an expectation of succeeding to a valuable asset: a statutory tenancy with a fair rent. The reassurances that the rights of existing tenants were not affected was, therefore, potentially misleading, although strictly accurate, since carers were not existing tenants, but had legitimate expectations of succeeding to the same rights as existing tenants. Economy with the truth is not uncommon in such circumstances.

The rules for succession have become phenomenally complex and much turns on the date of death of relevant persons in relation to the commencement date of the 1988 Act. The case law also affords the opportunity to see the courts attempting over decades to come to grips with the concept of 'family' in determining rights of succession. With recent family rather than spouse successions derived from pre-1988 occupation being often to assured tenancies and market rents, the rights have become less significant.

Successions governed by pre-Housing Act 1988 rules

Where the tenant in question died before the commencement date of the Housing Act 1988, 15 January 1989, the traditional and more generous rules apply. Two successions are possible and in each case priority goes to a surviving spouse and failing that a member of the deceased's family. Spouses must be resident in the dwelling-house immediately prior to the death of the tenant or first successor, whereas family members must have been resident for six months prior to the relevant death, not necessarily in the house claimed by way of succession. It is likely that the same latitude in the case of family members would be extended to private tenants as was bestowed on a brother in the public sector case of *Waltham Forest LBC v Thomas* [1992] 2 AC 198. There, two brothers had been living together for over two years, but had moved just before the death of the tenant; it was held that the surviving brother acquired a secure tenancy of the new abode.

Successions when the death happens on or after 15 January 1989

At this point, the Housing Act 1988 adds in different criteria into the Rent Act 1977 to restrict succession entitlements for family members in particular. The rules in outline are as follows.

(a) Where the original tenant dies

In such circumstances, a surviving spouse can succeed to a statutory tenancy if resident immediately prior to the death. Cohabitees, defined as persons living with the tenant as husband or wife, are also entitled to succeed. This concession comes after years of judicial agonising over whether a childless cohabiting couple could conceivably constitute a family.

Family members are next in the queue in the absence of a surviving spouse. However, two years rather than six months residence up to the point of the death is required. Significantly, in keeping with the programme already described, such family members only obtain assured tenancies, with the obvious implications for rent rights.

(b) When the first successor dies

Where the first successor was a statutory tenant, only succession to an assured tenancy is possible. The preconditions are that any claimant must have been both a member of the original tenant's family and of the first successor's family and resident in the dwelling-house for two years up to and including the first successor's death.

What is a family?

Although, as just demonstrated, the 1988 reforms have taken away much of the incentive for family members other than spouses in particular to claim succession rights, it is interesting to consider the approach taken by the courts to the gap in the Rent Acts where the definition of family might have been expected. The public sector criteria are more specific, but the private sector criteria have always suffered from indeterminacy. It is clear that 'family' cannot on an ordinary language interpretation be equated with a more colourless and neutral term like 'household'.

What sort of relationship will satisfy the criteria? It is not helpful to begin with the classic statement from *Ross v Collins* [1964] 1 WLR 425, p 432: 'it still requires, it seems to me, at least a broadly recognisable de facto familial nexus' because it begs the question.

The history of judicial attitudes to suitable relationships is worth exploring briefly, even if the 1988 Act has diminished the practical value of such claims. In the earlier years, in *Gammans v Ekins* [1950] 2 KB 328, it was held that 20 years of close, but unmarried association did not make the survivor a member of the late tenant's family. Lord Justice Asquith was censorious in stating 'To say of two people masquerading, as these two were, as husband and wife – there being no children to complicate the picture – that they were members of the same family, seems to me an abuse of the English language'.

In *Dyson Holdings v Fox* [1975] 3 All ER 1030, Lord Denning displayed a less hostile face than usual to the Rent Acts. It was a classic 'fireside equities' case involving an unmarried woman of 73 years threatened with eviction after the landlords discovered, 12 years after the death of her partner, that she was not his widow. They had lived together as husband and wife for 21 years until his death in 1961. Lord Denning was typically prepared to take the bull by the horns and assert that the Court of Appeal was not bound to follow *Gammans v Ekins*, but also argued that on principles of ordinary language interpretation she was a member of his family. The Court accepted the rather risky proposition that, since language could change with social attitudes, the meaning of family in a statute could alter over the decades. One difficulty is that it is doubtful that social attitudes had changed that dramatically by the relevant date of 1961, when the cohabitee died.

Long term heterosexual cohabitation can, therefore, be rewarded, even if there are no children of the liaison. Elements of permanence and stability are required. A case on the wrong side of the line was *Helby v Rafferty* [1978] 3 All ER 1016, where the relationship was as close as could be imagined and Mr Rafferty nursed his dying partner for several years. Contra-indications were that she believed in independence and there was no evidence that either contemplated marriage. Other excluded categories are close platonic friendships.

The issue of the admissibility of stable and permanent homosexual relationships has become more pressing in the emergent national and international climate of elimination of discrimination on the grounds of sexual orientation. *Fitzpatrick v Sterling Association Ltd* [1998] Ch 304, is the recent focus for such a debate and the Court of Appeal were divided on the issue as to whether the survivor of such a relationship qualified to succeed as either a member of the tenant's 'family', or someone who had been living with him as 'wife or husband'. In practice, there was some difference between the findings, as membership of the family merely conferred on a claimant an assured tenancy, whereas the other finding secured a statutory tenancy. However, it is important not to exaggerate the differences between assured and statutory tenants, given that roughly comparable security of tenure provisions do not tell the whole story. More significant, surely, is the fact that assured tenancies are basically subject to market rents, while, as demonstrated elsewhere in this book, 'fair rents' have had a tendency, in recent years, to converge with market rents, despite some recent governmental intervention to curb the more excessive increases.

An obvious obstacle in the way of a favourable outcome for Mr Fitzpatrick was the clear decision to the contrary on comparable language in the 1980 Housing Act for secure tenants in *Harrogate Borough Council v Simpson* (1984) 17 HLR 205. There, the Court of Appeal refused to accept the survivor of a lesbian relationship as one of a couple living together as husband and wife and counsel for Mr Fitzpatrick argued unsuccessfully that social attitudes to homosexuality had changed radically over the intervening 12 years.

One of the majority, Lord Justice Waite, reached his conclusion with some regret and conceded that, 'if endurance, stability, interdependence and devotion were the sole hallmarks of family membership', the case would be decided very differently. Mr Fitzpatrick had been living with his partner for nearly 20 years and had nursed him following a stroke from 1986 until his death in 1994. The Lord Justice acknowledged the discriminatory nature of the present law 'rooted in the concept of the family as an entity bound together by ties of kinship or marriage'. He pinpointed another arbitrary feature, that friends fell outside the statutory definition, absent of any sexual element in their relationship, despite possibly the same closeness and permanence. Nevertheless, he thought, along with Lord Justice Roch, that parliamentary reform, rather than judicial intervention through some 'new linguistic twist', was the way ahead.

The dissenting judgment of Lord Justice Ward merits attention, even if, or, perhaps, because, when the House of Lords eventually pronounces on the matter on appeal, the result is likely to be the same as the Court of Appeal because of the constitutional propriety and perceived tidiness of specific legislative intervention as opposed to incremental judicial reform in a morally contentious area. His judgment ranged widely across decisions in other jurisdictions which would have allowed for succession, in such a case; it cited jurisprudential work on legal reasoning; and resulted in the view that, in the face of such apparently discriminatory legislation, it was incumbent on him to resolve any ambiguities in the statute in favour of the claimant and that he should be bold enough to 'err on the side of preventing that discrimination'.

Accordingly, he was prepared to hold that the appellant had lived with the late tenant as husband or wife, thereby securing a statutory tenancy under the Rent Acts. So far as the lesser claim to an assured tenancy as a family member was concerned, he took a functional view of the matter, stating that 'The question is more what a family does, rather than what a family is'. In this case, the relationship was based on many different functions: sexual; social; economic; and emotional, admittedly lacking any procreative function, but still to be considered de facto familial, as in the already quoted celebrated dictum from *Ross v Collins* [1964] 1 WLR 425: 'It still requires, it seems to me, at least a broadly recognisable de facto familial nexus.'

The Lord Justice ended by saying that he would rather be criticised for being ahead of the times than for being behind them. Such criticism, muted by the recognition that the statutory language of entitlement to succession is increasingly archaic, in all probability awaits him in the House of Lords. In the meantime, Mr Fitzgerald has claimed a moral victory, irrespective of the ultimate result.

GROUNDS FOR POSSESSION

Introduction

Section 98 of the Rent Act 1977 spells out the structure of security of tenure:

(1) Subject to this part of the Act, a court shall not make an order for possession of a dwelling-house which is for the time being let on a protected tenancy or subject to a statutory tenancy unless the court considers it reasonable to make such an order and either:

(a) the court is satisfied that suitable alternative accommodation is available for the tenant or will be available for him when the order in question takes effect; or

(b) the circumstances are as specified in any of the Cases in Pt II of Sched 15 to this Act.

(2) If apart from sub-s (1) above, the landlord would be entitled to recover possession of a dwelling-house which is for the time being let on or subject to a regulated tenancy, the court shall make an order for possession if the circumstances of the case are specified in any of the Cases in Pt II of Sched 15.

Despite liberality in other areas of contracting out of the Rent Acts, traditionally the courts guard their own jurisdiction jealously and are opposed to consensual repossession. In *Appleton v Aspin* [1988] 1 WLR 410, a protected tenant agreed with the purchaser to vacate when the property was sold with vacant possession but then declined to go. It was held that only a recognised Rent Act ground could avail the purchaser. Reasonableness involves consideration of a wide range of matters, including the needs and behaviour of the parties.

Suitable alternative accommodation

Just as there is a wide range of types of landlord, so there are variations in grounds for possession. The option of recovering possession on provision of suitable alternative accommodation is obviously more suited to larger institutional landlords than the small landlord. The statutory criteria in s 98 of the Act and Sched 15, paras 3–8 are an attempt at compromising between the desire to facilitate decanting tenants where appropriate and respecting their wishes not to be uprooted. The public sector criteria are subtly different.

One remote possibility in the age of municipal asset stripping is that a local authority will provide a certificate stating that it will provide suitable alternative accommodation (Sched 15, Pt IV, para 3). Otherwise, the basic requirements for the exercise of the court's discretion are that the proposed alternative is suitable in terms of security and also in respect of the tenant's circumstances. In relation to security of tenure, therefore, the expectation would be a public sector 'secure' tenancy or a long fixed term tenancy. Even after the phasing out of protection under the 1977 Act, it is still open to the court to order the creation of a protected and not an assured tenancy.

The most significant criteria for displacement are that the alternative accommodation must be reasonably suitable to the needs of the tenant and his family with regard to proximity to work, to the tenant's means and to their needs as regards extent and character. This raises difficult questions of interpretation. Does 'needs' include spiritual and other intangible needs? What if a particular locale is related to a certain life-style which would have to be forfeited in the other accommodation? How broad an interpretation should be put on the 'character' of a dwelling?

In the early case of *Redspring v Francis* [1973] 1 WLR 134, it was established that environmental factors had to be taken into account and that people could not be transplanted from quiet to noisy neighbourhoods. Smells could also be a factor and the proposed new abode was in a busy street near a chip shop. Lord Justice Buckley, incidentally, preferred to call it a fried fish shop and noted with the common touch that it 'emits smells of a kind which one would expect to be emitted from an establishment of that sort'.

In *Siddiqui v Rashid* [1980] 1 WLR 1018, there was some retrenchment on apparently generous references in *Redspring* to the importance of individual lifestyle and it was stated that the notion of character did not extend to access to a circle of friends or cultural interests. A similarly restricted view was taken in *Hill v Rochard* [1983] 1 WLR 478, where a whole idiosyncratic lifestyle, complete with ponies and Krishnamurti weekends, derived from occupation of a country house with acres of land, was obliterated by transfer to a modern house on an estate on the fringes of a village. Presumably, the pragmatic consideration underlying these cases is that excessive emphasis on subjective factors such as lifestyle would confer irremovability on some occupants without regard to the point of the legal criteria. If the accommodation offered is physically comparable or, indeed, superior and the obvious objective environmental factors are taken into account, then some decanting is justified. It is, perhaps, more contentious and reminiscent of Edgar Allan Poe that the alternative accommodation can be part of the existing dwelling, but it is settled law and, for instance, in *Mykolyshyn v Noah* [1970] 1 WLR 1271, the tenant lost a sitting room because it had only been used to store furniture. Even if on the face of it, the alternative accommodation is suitable, there is still the overriding discretion over the reasonableness of making an order to be exercised. In *Battlespring v Gates* (1983) 11 HLR 6, a lady who had lived in a flat for 35 years was protected against a predatory property company.

Discretionary grounds

Here, by definition, the court has to be satisfied that it is reasonable to make an order. The unfettered nature of the discretion is shown in the judicial guidance usually cited, from Lord Greene MR in *Cumming v Danson* [1942] 2 All ER 653, p 655:

> The duty of the judge is to take into account all relevant circumstances as they exist at the date of the hearing. That he must do in what I venture to call a broad, common sense way as a man of the world, and come to the conclusion giving such weight as he thinks right to the various factors in the situation. Some factors may have little or no weight, others may be decisive, but it is quite wrong for him to exclude from his consideration matters which he ought to take into account.

Lord Greene carefully avoids stipulating anything, particularly in the last sentence.

Case 1: rent/other obligations

> Where any rent lawfully due from the tenant has not been paid, or any obligation of the protected or statutory tenancy which arises under this Act has been broken or not performed.

The unfettered discretion announced above has been narrowed down to a reluctance to order possession on the grounds of rent arrears and nothing else if there is some chance of arrears being paid off. Sometimes, however, if the tenant has a bad record, even payment into court of the full amount outstanding will not save him from repossession (*Dellenty v Pellow* [1951] 2 KB 858). If the reason for withholding rent is disrepair occasioned by landlord's breach of covenant, then it may not be reasonable to order possession (*Televantos v McCulloch* [1991] 1 EGLR 123). Examples of non-trivial breaches of covenant which have led to an order being granted are unauthorised business user and subletting without the consent of the landlord.

Case 2: nuisance/annoyance and immoral/illegal user

> Where the tenant or any person residing or lodging with him or any subtenant of his has been guilty of conduct which is a nuisance or annoyance to adjoining occupiers, or has been convicted of using the dwelling-house or allowing the dwelling-house to be used for immoral or illegal purposes.

The scope of cases of this nature is currently under review in relation to public sector tenancies and there are measures in the 1996 Housing Act to combat antisocial behaviour by secure tenants and assured housing association tenants. In fact, it is one of the criticisms of the Act that it does nothing to combat abuses by private tenants and indeed owner-occupiers. The nature of illegal acts in relation to premises has been extensively discussed in *Schneider & Sons v Abrahams* [1925] 1 KB 301 and *Abrahams v Wilson* [1971] 2 QB 88. In the earlier case, it was held that where the tenant had been convicted of receiving stolen property at the premises he was 'using' the dwelling-house for illegal purposes. Lord Justice Bankes said that the section of the statute in question, the Rent and Mortgage Interest Restrictions Act 1923, did not only include offences where use of the premises was an essential part, but it was necessary to demonstrate that the tenant had taken advantage of his tenancy and of the opportunity to commit the offence. In the later case, the conviction was for possession of a small amount of cannabis found on the premises. The Court of Appeal rejected the claim that possession should be granted for one isolated incident.

So far as the nuisance or annoyance grounds are concerned, it was established in *Cobstone Investments v Maxim* [1985] QB 140 that 'adjoining occupiers' should have a generous interpretation to mean more than just adjacent and include those likely to be affected. Those travelling far afield to engage in behaviour, such as racial harassment, are, therefore, not in breach of this ground. Nuisance is not to be construed in the technical sense, sometimes to be found in tort cases, but has a common sense meaning. 'Annoyance' has been quaintly defined as something which 'reasonably troubles the mind and pleasure not of a fanciful person, but of the ordinary sensible English inhabitant of a house' (*Tod-Heatley v Benham* (1888) 40 Ch D 80, p 98). 'Immoral' purposes may seem too vague and moralistic in a pluralistic society, but, clearly, covers such behaviour as keeping a brothel. Heterosexual living in sin has been held not to be immoral in *Heglibiston Establishment v Hayman* (1977) 36 P & CR 351. The back to basics campaign may have changed that perception.

Case 3: deterioration of dwelling-house

> Where the condition of the dwelling-house has, in the opinion of the court, deteriorated owing to acts of waste by, or the neglect or default of, the tenant or any person residing or lodging with him or any subtenant of his and, in the case of any act of waste by, or the neglect or default of, a person lodging with the tenant or a subtenant of his, where the court is satisfied that the tenant has not, before the making of the order in question, taken such steps as he ought reasonably to have taken for the removal of the lodger or subtenant, as the case may be.

It is unfortunate that the doctrine of waste, an esoteric part of land law, is used in this context. The latest Law Commission report (No 238) on repairs recommends its abolition with regard to tenancies. Technically, it refers to any act which alters the nature of the property let and can, in theory, include improvements. Ironically, the only case in this connection to reach appellate level involved the neglect of a garden rather than a house and the possession order was suspended for a year to give the tenant a chance to tidy up (*Holloway v Povey* (1984) 15 HLR 104).

Case 4: deterioration of furniture

> Where the condition of any furniture provided for use under the tenancy has, in the opinion of the court, deteriorated owing to ill treatment by the tenant or any person residing or lodging with him or any subtenant of his and, in the case of any ill treatment by a person lodging with the tenant or a subtenant of his, where the court is satisfied that the tenant has not, before the making of the order in question, taken such steps as he ought reasonably to have taken for the removal of the lodger or subtenant, as the case may be.

This case is clearly modelled on its predecessor and dates from 1974, when furnished tenancies were upgraded. Depending on the state of the furniture, it may be difficult to distinguish between fair wear and tear and deterioration caused by the tenant or others.

Case 5: tenant's notice to quit

> Where the tenant has given notice to quit and, in consequence of that notice, the landlord has contracted to sell or let the dwelling-house or has taken any other steps as the result of which he would, in the opinion of the court, be seriously prejudiced if he could not obtain possession.

Informal agreement to depart will not activate this section. If notice to quit has been duly served, a mere intention on the part of the landlord to sell or let is insufficient. The landlord must be contractually committed or in some other respect seriously prejudiced.

Case 6: assignment/subletting

> Where without the consent of the landlord, the tenant has assigned or sublet the whole of the dwelling-house, the remainder being already sublet.

This is another instance of protecting landlords from strangers. The prohibition is on the total parting with possession either through assignment or subletting, and the criteria by definition only affect protected tenants as a statutory tenancy is generally unassignable and parting with possession on a subletting would mean that occupation of the premises, one of the statutory tenancy preconditions, could not be met.

Case 7: controlled tenancies

This case concerned 'controlled' tenancies under earlier Rent Acts and was repealed in 1980 by the Housing Act of that year. 'Controlled' has to be distinguished from 'regulated' in respect of interference with market rents. The 'control' mechanism was to freeze rents until further notice, whereas 'regulated' rents are more flexible and responsive to changing conditions, perhaps too responsive.

Case 8: ex-employees

> Where the dwelling-house is reasonably required by the landlord for occupation as a residence for some person engaged in his whole time employment, or in the whole time employment of some tenant from him or with whom, conditional on housing being provided, a contract for such employment has been entered into, and the tenant was in the employment of the landlord or a former landlord, and the dwelling-house was let to him in consequence of that employment and he has ceased to be in that employment.

Although the language is cumbersome, the purpose is relatively clear: to enable landlords to replace disgruntled ex-employees with new employees. If the occupation is to enable the occupier the better to perform duties in employment, then, on the traditional rules, it will be a licence and fall outside this framework anyway. This case has been shortened and simplified in the 1988 Act.

Case 9: landlord reasonably requires possession

> Where the dwelling-house is reasonably required by the landlord for occupation as a residence for:
>
> (a) himself; or
> (b) any son or daughter of his over 18 years of age; or
> (c) his father or mother; or
> (d) the father or mother of his wife or husband,
>
> and the landlord did not become landlord by purchasing the dwelling-house or any interest therein after [certain specified dates].

Further guidance on this important criterion, which exposes as mythology some preconceptions that possession is irrecoverable and landlords forced to endure security of tenure, is to be found in Sched 15, Pt III, para 1 of the 1977 Act:

> A court shall not make an order for possession of a dwelling-house by reason only that the circumstances of the case fall within Case 9 in Pt 1 of this Schedule if the court is satisfied that, having regard to all the circumstances of the case, including the question whether other accommodation is available for the landlord or tenant, greater hardship would be caused by granting the order than by refusing to grant it.

The courts are, therefore, involved in delicate balancing acts. Unsurprisingly, the onus of establishing greater hardship is on the tenant. The exclusion of purchasers is designed to stop entrepreneurial tactics of taking over freeholds and moving the sitting tenants out. An illustrative case in an area where generalisations are difficult, because each case will depend on its particular facts, is *Thomas v Fryer* [1970] 1 WLR 845. The plaintiff had been left a quarter share in a house and bought out the other interests in it. On a common sense, ordinary language approach, it was thought that such a family arrangement did not constitute a 'purchase'. On the point of greater hardship, there was evidence of the likely deleterious effect on the plaintiff's health of being denied possession. The tenant and her family had lived in the property in dispute for over 30 years. The lower court granted possession and the Court of Appeal upheld the decision. This is typical, as the higher court will only intervene if there has been some error of law or a fallacious finding of fact.

There have been difficulties of interpretation in the case of joint landlords. Is it necessary for both landlords or only one to need to occupy? The requirement of two would go against recent trends in the law to accept that one joint tenant can act for both. The point was left open in *Tilling v Whiteman* [1980] AC 1, where, in litigation on Case 11, it was held that one actor was sufficient.

There have also been difficulties occasioned by the drafting of the various family members eligible under the case. In *Potsos and Potsos v Theodotou* (1991) 23 HLR 356, the landlords were relying on category (b), but the son in question was the child of Mrs Potsos' previous marriage. On a pragmatic approach, mindful of the absurdity of a too literal construction of these categories, the Court of Appeal allowed the claim for possession.

Case 10: overcharging a subtenant

> Where the court is satisfied that the rent charged by the tenant:
>
> (a) for any sublet part of the dwelling-house which is a dwelling-house let on a protected tenancy or subject to a statutory is or was in excess of the maximum rent for the time being recoverable for that part, having regard to Pt III of this Act; or
>
> (b) for any sublet part of the dwelling-house which is subject to a restricted contract is or was in excess of the maximum (if any) which is lawful for the lessor, within the meaning of Pt V of this Act to require or receive having regard to the provisions of that Part.

This is another ground which has never been much used, perhaps because profiteering by subtenants in this fashion was not widespread and which is increasingly unlikely to be used with the gradual demise of regulated tenancies and restricted contracts.

Mandatory grounds for possession

By definition, the court has no discretion, if any of the aftermentioned grounds are made out, to adjourn proceedings or postpone the date for possession for a substantial length of time. Under the Housing Act 1980, s 89(1), there is limited scope for postponing for 14 days or up to six weeks if earlier possession would cause exceptional hardship.

Case 11: returning owner-occupier

> Where a person (in this Case referred to as 'the owner-occupier') who let the dwelling-house on a regulated tenancy had, at any time before the letting, occupied it as his residence and:
>
> (a) not later than the relevant date the landlord gave notice in writing to the tenant that possession might be recovered under this Case; and
>
> (b) the dwelling-house has not [since certain specified dates] been let by the owner occupier on a protected tenancy with respect to which the condition mentioned in paragraph (a) above was not satisfied; and
>
> (c) the court is of the opinion that of the conditions set out in Pt V of this Schedule one of those in paras (a) and (c) to (f) is satisfied.
>
> Those conditions are:
>
> (a) that the dwelling-house is required as a residence for the owner or any member of his family who resided with him when he last occupied it as a residence; or
>
> (c) that the owner has died and the dwelling-house is required as a residence for a member of his family who was residing with him at the time of his death; or
>
> (d) that the owner has died and the dwelling-house is required by a successor in title as his residence or for the purpose of sale with vacant possession; or
>
> (e) the dwelling-house is subject to a mortgage, made by deed and granted before the tenancy, and the mortgagee:
>
> (i) is entitled to exercise a power of sale conferred on him by s 101 of the Law of Property Act 1925; and
>
> (ii) requires the dwelling-house for the purpose of disposing of it with vacant possession in exercise of that power; or
>
> (f) the dwelling-house is not reasonably suitable to the needs of the owner, having regard to his place of work, and he requires it for the purpose of disposing of it with vacant possession and of using the proceeds of that disposal in acquiring, as his residence, a dwelling-house which is more suitable to those needs.

This is another important case in practice, where, as with other mandatory grounds, the emphasis is on prior warning to the tenant of the likely recovery of possession. However, the court has the power to ignore the relevant dates and the requirement of prior notice if it is deemed just and equitable for possession to be granted. An indicative case on this point is *Jones v White* (1993) EGCS 178. The owners had not lived in the property since 1964 and the tenants had moved in in 1972 without any Case 11 notice, but on the understanding that the plaintiffs might want to recover possession at some stage. Of course, in 1972, as furnished tenants, they could not have protected status, but were upgraded by the 1974 Rent Act. At first instance, it was held that it was just and equitable to dispense with the notice requirement and grant possession. On appeal, a different approach was taken, discounting the informal notice in 1972 before security of tenure had been achieved. After a typical balancing exercise, it was held that possession should not be granted because of the lengthy occupation enjoyed by the defendants and the attendant trauma of eviction as against the relatively modest residential requirements of the plaintiffs.

There is a clear difference between this case and Case 9 in respect of reasonableness. As was stated in *Megarry*, The Rent Acts, quoted in *Kennealy v Dunne* [1977] 1 QB 837 by Lord Justice Stephenson:

> It appears that all the landlord need establish is that he genuinely (and not merely colourably) seeks possession in order to use the dwelling-house for the stated purpose; and if he does this it seems to be immaterial that other and more reasonable courses of action are open to him. In short, the issue is merely whether the requirement is genuine, not whether it is reasonable; and sometimes the genuine may be far from reasonable.

In this case, the tenants were arguing that because the owners had other property available for occupation, the word 'reasonable' should be interpolated; not surprisingly, in a mandatory case, the court ruled out such an interpretation.

If possession is granted and there is a quick sale by the returning owner, there is the possibility of appealing against the order and invoking the now familiar idea of a sham. However, in *Whitworth v Lupton* (1993) EGCS 172, the Court of Appeal took the view that occupation, albeit for a short time with a view to selling, was not inconsistent with residence for the purposes of the Act.

The history of this case has not been trouble free and, in 1985, in *Pocock v Steel* [1985] 1 WLR 229, the Court of Appeal rattled many owners by excluding the operation of the case unless the landlord had been in occupation immediately before the letting. For those working abroad for long periods, one of the obvious class of beneficiaries of this case, this would have involved many special journeys to maintain control and the decision was speedily reversed in the Rent (Amendment) Act 1985, demonstrating that legislative change can sometimes be swift where important vested interests are concerned. It is significant, as will be seen later, that the Housing Act 1988 in many respects makes repossession easier.

Case 12: retirement homes

> Where the landlord intends to occupy the dwelling-house as his residence at such times as he might retire from regular employment and has let it on a regulated tenancy before he has so retired and:
>
> (a) not later than the relevant date the landlord gave notice in writing to the tenant that possession might be recovered under this Case; and
>
> (b) the dwelling-house has not, since 14 August 1974, been let by the owner on a protected tenancy to which the condition mentioned in para (a) above was not satisfied; and

(c) the court is of the opinion that of the conditions set out in Part V of this Schedule one of those in paras (b) to (e) is satisfied.

Paragraph (b) stipulates that the owner has retired from regular employment and requires the dwelling-house as a residence.

The elaborate mechanics of this are largely derived from Case 11 and it might have been kinder to amalgamate the cases. There is a difference between them in that, for Case 12, there is no requirement of prior occupation at any time. In practice, it has proved unproblematical and there is no authority on its interpretation; a likely pressure point is the meaning of 'regular' in 'regular employment'. It has no specific counterpart under the Housing Act 1988, but is probably covered by the owner-occupier Ground 1.

Case 13: out of season lettings

Where the dwelling-house is let under a tenancy for a term of years certain not exceeding 8 months and:

(a) not later than the relevant date the landlord gave notice in writing to the tenant that possession might be recovered under this Case; and

(b) the dwelling-house was, at some time within the period of 12 months ending on the relevant date, occupied under a right to occupy it for a holiday.

The purpose of this is relatively clear – to allow for occupation out of season – but the drafting has produced some elaborate speculation. What exactly is meant by 'occupied under a right to occupy for a holiday'? The formula suggests that certain exclusive occupation licences could qualify and it has also been suggested (Yates and Hawkins, *Landlord and Tenant Law*, 2nd edn, 1986, p 461) that holiday occupation by the landlord himself would satisfy condition (ii). The terminology does not readily support this view, as a landlord would occupy in his/her own right.

These out of season lets could also spell trouble for occupants after eviction. Some local authorities have taken the view that people in such circumstances are intentionally homeless.

Case 14: vacation lets

Where the dwelling-house is let under a tenancy for a term of years certain not exceeding 12 months and:

(a) not later than the relevant date the landlord gave notice in writing to the tenant that possession might be recovered under this Case; and

(b) at some time within the period of 12 months ending on the relevant date, the dwelling-house was subject to such a tenancy as is referred to in s 8(1) of this Act.

This case assists the flourishing practice of vacation lettings by universities and other institutions of higher education. The wording is such that it covers a private landlord who lets his properties to universities for student lets in term time. It also, mysteriously, could cover the situation where university property is sold to a private landlord. The drafting style in many of these cases is opaque.

Case 15: ministers of religion

This can be summarised as safeguarding houses normally used by ministers of religion if a tenant is given written notice that possession might be recovered by virtue of this case and the dwelling is required by a minister. There have apparently been no problems articulated with Case 15, but it is not difficult to imagine acrimonious debate about the claims of some esoteric cult to be a 'religion'.

Cases 16–18 deal with various agricultural tenancies and will not be analysed here.

Case 19: protected shorthold tenancies

> Where the dwelling-house was let under a protected shorthold tenancy (or is treated under s 55 of the Housing Act 1980 as having been so let) and:
>
> (a) there either has been no grant of a further tenancy of the dwelling-house since the end of the protected shorthold tenancy or, if there was such a grant, it was to a person who immediately before the grant was in possession of the dwelling-house as a protected or statutory tenant; and
>
> (b) the proceedings for possession were commenced after appropriate notice by the landlord to the tenant and not later than three months after the expiry of the notice.
>
> A notice is appropriate for this Case if:
>
> (i) it is in writing and states that proceedings for possession under this Case may be brought after its expiry; and
>
> (ii) it expires not earlier than three months after it is served nor, if, when it is served, the tenancy is a periodic tenancy, before that periodic tenancy could be brought to an end by a notice to quit served by the landlord on the same day;
>
> (iii) it is served:
>
> (a) in the period of three months immediately preceding the date on which the protected shorthold tenancy comes to an end; or
>
> (b) if that date has passed, in the period of three months immediately preceding any anniversary of that date; and
>
> (iv) in a case where a previous notice has been served by the landlord on the tenant in respect of the dwelling-house, and that notice was an appropriate notice, it is served not earlier than three months after the expiry of the previous notice.

There is also provision for certain tenancies to qualify as shorthold if the court thinks it just and equitable to condone departure from some of the formalities.

The Byzantine complexity of these provisions must have been of itself quite enough to discourage landlords from adopting shortholds. They were introduced in the Housing Act 1980 (along with prototype 'assured' tenancies) supposedly to stimulate the market, but embodied a great British compromise. Security was limited by the stipulation of fixed terms of one to five years, but originally a fair rent was also mandatory, a requirement which enabled a precise record to be kept of the take up of shortholds (save, presumably, the rare ones smuggled in by the courts under the 'just and equitable' criteria). So few were granted in the early years that the requirement of a 'fair rent' was relaxed, first outside and then in London, by courtesy of the Secretary of State. By August 1981, there were only 3,500 shortholds known to the Department of the Environment. The Labour party had also announced that it would repeal the provisions when it came to power and impose full security on shortholders (see Martin, *Residential Security*, 1989, p 52). With the luxury of hindsight, it seems bizarre to contemplate introducing this hybrid – regulated rent without security – in the heyday of licences in the early 1980s.

It is unclear how many protected shortholds survive; in theory, some could still be subsisting. If for some reason there were an agreement to create such a shorthold earlier than 15 January 1989, then, in principle, a tenancy of this type existing after that date will be susceptible to a Case 19 action after the fixed term has expired. On the other hand, if there is a protected shorthold in existence after the relevant date and a new tenancy is granted, the new tenancy will be an assured shorthold governed by the 1988 Act.

In view of their almost total disappearance, there is no reason to savour the procedural complexities that caused many possession actions to founder and necessitated a much more streamlined approach in the new improved assured shortholds. However, in summary, the procedures were so inflexible that landlords missing their window of opportunity to evict might have had to wait months to serve another notice. Admittedly, there was, in the rules, provision for notice by the tenant, something sadly lacking from the assured shorthold equivalent.

One interesting facet of all shorthold agreements is the concern that they should not be imposed on protected or statutory tenants, who may well be unaware of their rights and prepared to sign another agreement. Section 52(2) of the Housing Act 1980 attempted to tackle this problem by stating that 'A tenancy of a dwelling-house is not a protected shorthold tenancy if it is granted to a person who immediately before it was granted, was a protected or statutory tenant of that dwelling-house'. In *Dibbs v Campbell* (1988) 20 HLR 374, the landlord, as frequently happens, had failed to observe the procedural formalities for a valid protected shorthold under which the tenant surrendered the original tenancy and agreed to the imposition of a shorthold, but engineered a new agreement. When the landlord then sought possession and the tenant invoked s 52(2), the Court of Appeal held that a protected tenancy can be terminated by surrender and so the tenant was not protected immediately before the grant of the shorthold.

Case 20: armed forces

Along the lines of Cases 11 and 12, this case enables members of the regular armed forces of the Crown to recover possession of dwelling-houses acquired by them when they served notice if the court is satisfied that they require the house as a residence. Leaving the armed forces is not a precondition.

INTERMEDIATE PROTECTION: RESTRICTED CONTRACTS

These agreements have already been mentioned in passing, and part of their definition is the notion of 'exclusive occupation' as expounded by Lord Denning in the *Luganda* case. As an intermediate level of protection, characteristically offering some rent regulation, but virtually no security, they have had a shadowy existence, partly because talk of Rent Act protection is ambiguous. The maximum rights belong to 'protected' and statutory tenants, but the restricted contract level was enough of an inconvenience to generate all the perverse ingenuity surrounding non-exclusive occupation agreements, designed by definition to overshoot the intermediate level, as well as top security.

The origins of the phrase 'exclusive occupation' can, incidentally, be traced back to the Furnished Houses (Rent Control) Act 1946, yet more emergency legislation with a supposedly short life expectancy, aimed this time at preventing a 'ramp' in furnished lettings. Whether any specialised sense was intended by the phrase or whether it was chosen as equivalent to exclusive possession, is impossible to determine. Certainly, the definitions of lessor and lessee perpetuated from the 1946 Act are generous enough to invite some flirtation with licences. A lessee is defined as someone who has the right to occupy the dwelling as a residence. Subsequently, the constituency of the category has been altered, with furnished lettings being upgraded in 1974 and the new resident landlord exception generating most of the qualifying occupants. Following the *Luganda* case, certain contractual licensees paying for furniture or services also satisfy the definition.

Although the evidence from the latest OPCS survey is that around 8% of agreements are restricted contracts and other agreements with limited security, they should be disappearing fairly rapidly, for the following reasons. As with protected tenancies, they are being phased out by the Housing Act 1988. Section 36 of that Act declares that a tenancy or other contract entered into after the commencement of the Act cannot be a restricted contract unless entered into via a pre-commencement contract. Such pre-commencement contracts must have been rare indeed. Those restricted contracts predating the commencement date, 15 January 1989, will struggle along, but, even the limited security traditionally enjoyed, of six months stay of execution, was removed by the Housing Act 1980. Surviving agreements can, again, under s 36, lose their restricted contract status after the commencement date if there is a change in the rent agreed other than by reference to the rent tribunal. The powers of rent tribunals (rent assessment committees by another name) are the capacity to approve, increase or reduce the rent to the amount deemed reasonable. Registrations of rent last for two years.

For the sake of formal completeness, the current membership of this vanishing category can be identified as follows:

(1) under s 19(2), the precondition is that 'one person grants to another person, in consideration of a rent which includes payment for the use of furniture or services, the right to occupy as a residence'. Certain furnished licensees are, thus, included, as are those getting less than substantial board. Unfurnished contractual licensees, therefore, lose out, but they must be thin on the ground anyway;

(2) by virtue of s 20, resident landlord agreements within the exception are to be treated as restricted contracts, notwithstanding that the rent does not include payment for furniture or services;

(3) under s 21, where a tenant has exclusive occupation of any accommodation but is sharing other accommodation with his landlord or with the landlord and others, again, a restricted contract arises irrespective of provision of furniture or services. Just when arrangements of this type have been pronounced virtually extinct, one surfaced in the case of *The Mortgage Corporation v Ubah* (1997) 29 HLR 489. The facts also raised the question of the existence of a separate dwelling and the possibility of full protection, as they involved the use of shared kitchen facilities. In addition, it concerned the activities of a limited company that replaced the individual landlord. Was the use of a kitchen relevant to a company 'without appetite or culinary capability'?

The Court of Appeal held that the original sharing arrangements did create a restricted contract and the fact that a company could not readily use a kitchen did not enhance the occupant's rights. The sharing rights had not been forfeited, but were in abeyance and could be revived on a change of landlord. What mattered was not whether the rights were currently being exercised, but whether they were capable of being exercised as and when the landlord was capable of doing so. By the same token, the landlord's continuing rights prevented the premises from qualifying for maximum protection as 'premises let as a separate dwelling' under s 1 of the 1977 Act. This decision is in line with established doctrine, which, in the absence of sham arrangements, attaches more importance to the terms of agreements, rather than to de facto user.

RENT RIGHTS: FAIR RENTS

As has been just demonstrated, there are vestiges of restricted contracts in existence with virtually no rent rights. What of the position of regulated tenants? It would be ironic, given the intentions of those who initiated the system of rent regulation in 1965, if their rent rights were so reduced as to devalue the security of tenure still enjoyed, but that is what has happened. In recent years, following the introduction of assured tenancies under the 1988 Act operating at market rents, there has been pressure on the 'fair rent' system that supposedly was a counterpart to security of tenure. It has been argued that changed market conditions have transformed the basis of calculation of a fair rent and that, in particular, the conditions of scarcity inseparable from intervention in the market have been superseded in many areas by the operation of market forces. It will be necessary to give an outline of the traditional approach to the determination of a fair rent and then to show how it has been eroded by recent decisions. The most significant case is the Court of Appeal decision in *Spath Holme Ltd v Greater Manchester and Lancashire Rent Assessment Committee* (1996) 28 HLR 107. Leave to appeal to the House of Lords was refused.

How to get a fair rent registered

Perhaps, surprisingly, the system, with limited exceptions such as the protected shorthold experiment already outlined, is an opt in system rather than a mandatory one. Either party to a regulated tenancy can apply to a rent officer for a fair rent to be registered for the property. In fact, in the early years of the system, the majority of applications were from landlords anxious to elevate historically and, indeed, hysterically low 'controlled' rents. Local authorities can also apply where housing benefit is at stake.

The fair rent then registered is the fair rent for the dwelling in question and binds not just the parties themselves, but future tenancies. If the registered rent is lower than that contractually agreed, then the excess cannot be recovered from the tenant after registration. If it is higher, then the landlord can raise the rent by following procedures which differ for protected and statutory tenants.

Once a rent has been registered, there is an embargo on new applications unless two years have elapsed, there is a joint application by landlord and tenant or there has been a change in the condition of the premises, the terms of the tenancy, the furniture provided or in any other relevant circumstances.

The legal criteria for determining a fair rent

Section 70 of the Rent Act provides:

(1) In determining, for the purposes of this Part of this Act, what rent is or would be a fair rent under a regulated tenancy of a dwelling-house, regard shall be had to all the circumstances (other than personal circumstances) and in particular to:

  (a) the age, character, locality and state of repair of the dwelling-house;

  (b) if any furniture is provided for use under the tenancy, the quantity, quality, and condition of the furniture; and

  (c) any premium, or sum in the nature of a premium, which has been or may be lawfully required or received on the grant, renewal, continuance or assignment of a tenancy.

(2) For the purposes of the determination it shall be assumed that the number of persons seeking to become tenants of similar dwelling-houses in the locality on the terms (other than those relating to rent) of the regulated tenancy is not substantially greater than the number of such dwelling-houses in the locality which are available for letting on such terms.

The traditional picture of legal regulation of the determination of fair rent is of a non-interventionist approach, leaving it to the officer or assessment committee to choose their preferred method of calculation, the popular ones being reference to comparables and assessment of a fair rate of return on capital value. One sticking point would, however, be where the calculations have not observed the statutory criteria as by not taking account of scarcity where it exists.

The *Spath Holme* case has virtually eradicated the difference between fair rents and assured market rents and will have to be analysed in some depth. The House of Lords has refused leave to appeal against the Court of Appeal decision, so it represents the law for the foreseeable future. It is estimated that hundreds of thousands of private tenants and housing association tenants will be affected and the housing benefit bill could, therefore, rise dramatically.

The dwellings in question were flats in Manchester let on regulated tenancies. In the aftermath of the 1988 Act, when vacancies arose in the same block the flats were re-let on assured tenancies. The landlord was naturally anxious to narrow the gap between the higher rents for the new lettings and the old registered fair rents and made a series of applications. The immediate cause of the present litigation was the fact that the Committee decided to use registered fair rent comparables rather than assured tenancy comparables. The justifications put forward for this preference for the old were: the security of tenure available under an assured tenancy; the continued existence of scarcity; and the fact that the registered rent comparables had not been shown to be flawed. The landlord then appealed these lower than market rent determinations and, at first instance, Mr Justice Harrison quashed them and remitted them for determination by a differently constituted committee. The Rent Assessment Committee appealed to the Court of Appeal because there was concern that in future they would not be entitled to choose registered rent comparables from other blocks in preference to assured tenancy comparables in the same block, but would have to work through the assured comparables first.

Lord Justice Morritt emphasised that the starting point for calculation had to be the market rent. The precedents were clear on this as when, in *Tormes Ltd v Landau* [1971] 1 QB 261, Lord Chief Justice Parker referred to 'fair rent which will be market rent less scarcity'. The Lord Justice explored the justifications advanced by the committee for their calculation of what was fair. He detected an error of law in the assertion that, even if the landlord's arguments about scarcity were accepted, it would not be fair three years on to increase the rent by over 100%. This presupposition that fair and reasonable rents were identical could not stand with the decision in *BTE Ltd v Merseyside and Cheshire Rent Assessment Committee* (1991) 24 HLR 514, where Hutchinson J had argued that rent cannot be reduced on these grounds to what the committee thinks reasonable. If there is no scarcity in an altered market then there can be no discounting for it under s 70(2).

Further reasons involved comparison of the security of tenure enjoyed under the two Acts and the significance of the supposed disregard of personal circumstances. The Committee had argued that, for the purpose of comparing like with like, the rents under assured tenancies would have to be discounted because the security of tenure enjoyed by a regulated tenant had to be disregarded as a personal circumstance (see s 70(1)). The landlords, however, came up with the argument that the security of tenure attached to a regulated tenancy was substantially the same as that enjoyed under an assured tenancy,and was not a personal circumstance to be disregarded.

Lord Justice Morritt then had to examine the origins of the rule that a regulated tenant's security of tenure had to be disregarded as a personal circumstance. It dated from *Mason v Skilling* [1974] 1 WLR 1437, where the issue was whether the presence of a sitting tenant, which would obviously affect valuation, was such a circumstance. Lord Reid said:

> In my view, the tenant's right to remain in possession is a personal circumstance. A right to possess a house (or anything else) appears to me to pertain to the person who has the right, whether the right is statutory or contractual. The house itself remains the same whoever is entitled to possess it. Moreover, under the Act, the tenant's right to possess lasts so long, but only so long, as he complies with certain obligations.

The Lord Justice favoured a flexible approach to personal circumstances and did not think that a circumstance which was personal in one context, such as the capital value test, was applicable when the chosen method was comparables under assured tenancies. In the case of rent comparables, the personal attributes of the tenant had no relevance to the assessment of a fair rent for a property. The Committee thought that tenancies with security of tenure command a higher rent than others. If they were correct in that assumption, they were wrong in law to hold that rents for assured tenancies would have to be discounted for that reason, since similar security was enjoyed by regulated tenants and was a circumstance to be taken into account.

The reasoning here is obscure and the underlying assumption that there is little to choose between the 1977 and 1988 security of tenure packages is surely mistaken. See, for example, this comment in Smith, *The Law of Landlord and Tenant*, 4th edn, p 231:

> Although the landlord of an assured tenant is not entitled to evict the tenant without an order of court, the grounds on which he may do so are in general wider than those which govern Rent Act tenants.

It could be that the Committee had the wrong idea of the significance of scarcity, but the landlords and the Court of Appeal had the wrong idea about the comparability of the two codes.

The Court of Appeal were satisfied that previous judicial statements about the primacy of existing registered fair rents were only applicable in the previous market conditions, where the evidence of tenancies at open market rents was in short supply. In the altered post-1988 Act circumstances, the proper approach was as follows:

> In this case, there are a number of flats in the same block let on assured tenancies at, by definition, open market rents which are virtually identical to those for which a fair rent is to be determined. In my judgment, if, in those circumstances, a Rent Assessment Committee wishes to exercise its discretion to adopt some other comparable or method of assessment it will be failing in its duty to give reasons if it does not explain why.
>
> In this case, the third reason given by the Rent Assessment Committee as recorded by the judge was that the registered comparables had not been demonstrated to be unsound. That is not, of course, a reason for rejecting the assured tenancy comparables. It is not for the court to say in advance what would be a good reason for doing so, but if such a reason involves 'working through' such comparables so be it: that consequence is no ground for rejecting the validity of its cause. But, it should also be noted that the registered rent comparables are not in their nature any more or less sound than the open market rent with or without discount.
>
> Any registered rent has built into it at least two variables, namely the open market rent and the discount for scarcity. Each should have been considered at the time of the original determination. The assessment of the soundness of the registered rent for use as a comparable would require each of these variables to be reconsidered at the time of their possible use as a comparable.

As can be seen from the analysis reviewed here, the difficulties of ascertaining a fair rent are considerable. From a literal approach to the statute, it is clear that the rather artificial assumptions about scarcity relate only to supply and demand of regulated tenancies. With the phasing out of the Rent Acts, there is naturally a progressive decline in the number of regulated tenancies, and market forces are more operative with assured tenancies, but does that in turn mean that the whole apparatus of rent regulation should be swept away? What is the point of perpetuating security of tenure for those qualifying for regulated tenancies and then denying them one of the major components of the protection, the right to a fair rent? The mutually exclusive nature of the 1977 and 1988 Act provisions might encourage the assumption that the one market approach taken in *Spath Holme*, requiring rent officers and assessment committees to consider assured comparables first, is misguided. There are, of course, valuation difficulties when no new fair rents can be created and direct comparables are necessarily of the same age or older when it comes to re-registration, but it does seem that here, as elsewhere, the judiciary is helping along a process of deregulation and being much more interventionist than ever before.

The trend towards compelling rent officers and assessment committees to be heavily influenced by market rents has continued and, in *Curtis v The Chairman of the London Rent Assessment Committee* (1996) 28 HLR 841, a Committee was castigated and its determination quashed because it declined to consider the market rent for an identical flat as the appropriate basis for calculation, instead, preferring to apply an 'uplift' to the previous registered rent.

Concern about this continued convergence of fair and market rents prompted the incoming Labour government to issue a consultation paper 'Limiting fair rent increases', in May 1998. In 1999, it was announced that a form of capping of increases was to be introduced. Increases are to be limited to the change in the Retail Prices Index since the last registration of a fair rent, plus 7.5% for the first application after 1 February 1999 and to the change in the RPI plus 5% for subsequent registrations. These limits have no application to approximately half of the private sector regulated tenants who have no fair rent registered. They also come far too late to be of substantial assistance to those who have already seen their fair rent triple or quadruple in line with the logic of the *Spath Holme* directive.

The proper approach to a different, but, nonetheless, significant issue in relation to s 70 of the 1977 Act surfaced in *Queensway Housing Association Ltd v Chiltern Thames and Eastern Rent Assessment Committee* (1999) 96(5) LSG 36. The basic problem is the relationship between scarcity and amenity and the proper interpretation of the formula 'in the locality' within s 70(2). How broadly or narrowly is the locality to be defined? If, say, the whole of the South East of England has common enhanced amenity characteristics, attracting incomers and, thereby, creating scarcity, is that vast area 'the locality'? Certainly, at the other end of the scale, it has been established, in *Metropolitan Property Services v Finegold* [1975] 1 WLR 349, that localised distortion, such as the presence of an American school creating a local scarcity, was not the kind of factor to be assessed under 70(2), which required, rather, 'a broad, overall, general scarcity affecting a really substantial area', rather than just a few streets near a school.

Mr Justice Richards' solution to the interpretational problems was as follows. The proper approach was to consider the alternatives reasonably available to potential tenants of the property in question. If an area of high amenity produced scarcity, but there was a wider area not so affected by scarcity in which the tenant might reasonably settle, then there was no reason to make any deduction under s 70(2). Conversely, if the shortage and scarcity were widespread, encompassing the whole area where a tenant could reasonably be expected to live, then a deduction was appropriate, even if that shortage was caused by high amenity. Such a distinction may not seem to provide instant illumination or a touchstone for all difficulties, but it is designed for use in marginal cases only.

Premiums

By virtue of s 119 of the 1977 Act, it is an offence for any person to require the payment of any premium in addition to the rent, as a condition of the grant, renewal or continuance of a protected tenancy. However, returnable deposits which are reasonable in the circumstances and less than one-sixth of the annual rent are outside the definitions.

CHAPTER 2

ASSURED TENANCIES AND THE HOUSING ACT 1988

ASSURED TENANCIES

Introduction

As has already been discussed, the ambition behind the 1988 Act and the introduction of new assured and assured shorthold tenancies was to revitalise the private sector. The grandiose claims made by proponents of the 1988 Act have not been fulfilled, although there has been a slight increase in the number of lettings. There is grave danger of the '*post hoc, propter hoc*' fallacy operating and any increases being ascribed to the 1988 deregulation.

Although there is some security of tenure for assured tenants, assured shortholders, by definition, have none and neither tenancy has anything of substance by way of rent rights, despite elaborate statutory machinery for rent assessment committee jurisdiction in certain circumstances. Assured shortholds have predictably become popular and much more numerous than assured tenancies (hitherto referred to only as 'assured') *per se* and there is no evidence that assured rents are higher because of greater security of tenure. However, the latest initiative in the Housing Act 1996 for future lettings intends, among other measures, was to extend the scope of shortholds and make assured less prevalent still, partly because landlords have been failing to meet the formal requirements for creating shortholds and have created simple assured by mistake.

This reform of the 1988 framework criteria is linked to plans to attract investment in both existing assured and assured shorthold and property intended for such lettings through Housing Investment Trusts. The relatively modest take-up of a previous comparable initiative, the Business Expansion Scheme, which was, however, unavailable for assured shortholds, does not inspire confidence in new investment initiatives. An additional destabilising factor is that 'new' Labour has no quarrel with assured shortholds, but could seek to change the extreme insecurity associated with six month shortholds.

It could be asked, at this point, whether it would not have been easier just to phase out the Rent Acts without any retroactive legislation and then to allow the market to operate without the elaborate statutory machinery in place in the 1988 Act. As has been seen, provision of security for assured shortholds has resulted in inconvenience for many landlords with failed shortholds. Why re-regulate to such an extent when supposedly deregulating? Perhaps, part of the answer lies in the psychological, as well as financial effects of *Street v Mountford* [1985] AC 809 and landlords' need for reassurance that they will be shielded from the vagaries of judicial interpretation. Certainly, the clear message from the government when publicising the 1988 provisions was that it was safe to be a landlord again and rely on statutorily guaranteed criteria. It also obviously affects the psychology of investment.

Where did the jargon and apparatus of 'assured' come from? After so many years, the draftsman must have combed Roget's *Thesaurus* for synonyms and virtually run out, as the best – 'protected' and 'secure' – have already been appropriated. The solution was to pick up on another unsuccessful experiment conducted in the Housing Act 1980,under which new tenancies of purpose built and approved housing were to be governed mainly by the business tenancy code – basically, a right to renewal on paying the going market rent, so conferring some security but no rent rights. 'Assured' of this type did not capture the investor's imagination and, again, as with protected shortholds, precise figures could be given for the derisory take up, since landlords had to be approved by the Secretary of State and records of completions kept. What little investment there was was mainly in sheltered housing. Even the alteration of the preconditions in the Housing and Planning Act 1986 to include renovated empty property, rather than just new buildings failed to stimulate investment. The 1988 version is, therefore, not a direct descendant in that the criteria have been changed to exclude reference to approved properties and approved landlords and become more universal; the label has been appropriated and, for the sake of neatness and convenience, 'old' assured have been converted into 'new' assured. Housing association tenants have also been lumped in with the private sector and assured tenancies for agreements after the commencement date of the 1988 Act. Assured shortholds are intended to be used only exceptionally by housing associations, although they can perform the useful function of offering an equivalent to local authority 'introductory' tenancies.

There is a strong argument that 'assured shorthold' is an oxymoron and contravenes the Trade Descriptions Act, since the occupant is merely assured of a short market rates occupancy and is hardly the beneficiary of the legislation. Its predecessor, the protected shorthold, was, at least, initially worthy of the name as it carried a fair rent obligation with it. The rags to riches story of assured, from humble beginnings in the 1980 Act, to dominance of the private sector following the 1988 Act, is well expressed in the *Book of Common Prayer*: 'The same stone which the builders refused; is become the head stone in the corner' (Psalm 118, verse 22).

The legal framework of assured under the 1988 Act will now be explored. It is apparent that some of the criteria have been cobbled together from the Rent Act 1977, especially the security of tenure grounds for possession. Some important definitional aspects have been derived from the Housing Act 1985 version of 'secure' tenancies. Other criteria are new minted, so there are no precedents to fall back on when interpretation, as often, becomes difficult.

The meaning of an assured tenancy

Section 1 of the 1988 Act provides:

(1) A tenancy under which a dwelling-house is let as a separate dwelling is for the purposes of this Act an assured tenancy if and so long as:

(a) the tenant or, as the case may be, each of the joint tenants is an individual; and

(b) the tenant or, as the case may be, at least one of the joint tenants occupies the dwelling-house as his only or principal home.

Some continuity and some change are immediately apparent from this formulation. The insistence on a tenancy let as a separate dwelling presumably replicates the doctrine laboriously built up under the Rent Acts. However, the stipulation of individuals and continued occupation as only or principal home is new to the private sector, although established for council tenants.

One obvious consequence of this definition is that company lets, which as already demonstrated could be protected tenancies, cannot be assured. Certain sharing arrangements, as discussed in relation to protected tenancies, could also fall outside the definition as they are less than a separate dwelling. The solution put forward in the Housing Act is to be found in s 3 and along the lines of s 22 of the 1977 Act. Where there is exclusive occupation of any accommodation and sharing of other accommodation with other tenants and that is the only reason why the tenancy would not be assured, then there is deemed to be an assured tenancy of the separate accommodation and similar court supervision of the shared accommodation under s 10 of the 1988 Act.

A useful reaffirmation of this principle is found in the Court of Appeal's decision in *Miller v Lovina Eyo* (1998) NPC 95. It concerned the not uncommon phenomenon of the landlord and family moving into occupation with a tenant who had previously been sharing common facilities with another (departed) tenant. There were no express terms in the initial agreement to govern the multiple occupancy. The court concluded that the plaintiff had an assured tenancy from which she had been unlawfully evicted through intimidation. The following proposition from *Isaacs v Titus* [1954] 1 All ER 470 was invoked:

> Where a tenant shared accommodation with a person other than the landlord and that person vacated the premises, the landlord did not automatically step into the shoes of that person so that the tenant now shared the accommodation with the landlord.

Apparently, unlike the *Vaughan* case previously discussed, there were no problems in ascribing tenancies to the original occupants in their circumstances of partial sharing. Perhaps, the smaller scale of the multiple occupation and the presumed lack of mobility between bedrooms allowed the assumption of a tenancy to crystallise, unlike the 'musical bedrooms' scenario in *Vaughan*.

If there is a resident landlord, irrespective of sharing that will exclude a tenant from assured status and, unlike the 1977 Act, there is no intermediate safety net in the shape of a restricted contract equivalent to catch such agreements. In these situations of sharing, careful attention has to be paid to the terms of the Protection from Eviction Act 1977, if all else fails, to see if occupants are, at least, entitled to a day in court, even if they can mount no realistic challenge to an action for possession.

Another innovation in the definitional section is the recognition that there may be joint tenants. As has been noted, in the Rent Acts, there is no acknowledgment of the existence of such a phenomenon. As Lord Justice Scrutton put it in *Skinner v Geary* [1931] 2 KB 546 at p 558: '... there is no evidence that Parliament or the draftsman ever thought out what rights they were giving to the tenant of a house to which the Acts applied.'

The wording 'occupies the dwelling-house as his only or principal home' is subtly different to the Rent Act formulation of 'if and so long as he occupies the dwelling-house as his residence' in s 2 for statutory tenants. As stated, the 1988 wording is derived from the Housing Act 1985 and there is authority in the shape of *Crawley Borough Council v Sawyer* (1987) 20 HLR 98 for the proposition that a tenant can maintain a home through keeping furniture there, even if not in occupation of the premises for over a year and even if the services have been disconnected. Clearly, if there is complete abandonment of the premises, there is no difficulty in saying the assured tenancy has disappeared, but what of the typical two homes case where the tenant divides his time between two properties without necessarily thinking of either as his principal home? It is arguable that the same laxity will not be extended to two homes persons claiming to have passed the threshold of assured tenancies as has been afforded to statutory tenants in the past.

Tenancies excluded from protection

These are to be found in Sched 1 to the Housing Act 1988 and contain some familiar items. As previously indicated, board and attendance no longer figure in the list, but otherwise there is close correspondence with the list in the 1977 Rent Act.

Tenancies entered into before commencement

This exempts a tenancy which is entered into before, or pursuant to a contract made before, the commencement of the Act, 15 January 1989. It expresses the proposition that the rights of existing tenants are not to be adversely affected.

Tenancies of dwelling-houses with high rateable values

If a tenancy has a rateable value of over £1,500 in Greater London or £750 elsewhere, it cannot be assured if it predated 1 April 1990. For tenancies entered into after 1 April 1990, generally speaking, if the rent payable is over £25,000 a year the same holds. In other words, only the luxury end of the market is again excluded.

Tenancies at a low rent

A tenancy where no rent is payable cannot be assured. Equally, it will not be assured if entered into before 1 April 1990 (or in pursuance of an earlier agreement) and the rent is less than two-thirds of the rateable value of the dwelling-house on 31 March 1990. For tenancies after 1 April 1990, there can be no assured status if the rent payable per annum is less than £1,000 a year in Greater London or £250 elsewhere. These last figures will clearly not exclude many tenancies.

Business tenancies

A tenancy to which Pt II of the Landlord and Tenant Act 1954 applies cannot be assured. The intersection between residential and business user has already been explored; the test is fundamentally whether the business user is a significant purpose of the tenant's occupation or more ancillary and unconnected.

Licensed premises

This exclusion mirrors that in the Rent Act 1977.

Tenancies of agricultural land

The schedule excludes a tenancy under which agricultural land, exceeding two acres, is let together with the dwelling-house. This has to be read in conjunction with s 2(1) of the 1988 Act which says, in relation to dwelling-houses let with other land, that, if and so long as the main purpose of the letting is to provide a home for the tenant(s), the other land shall be treated as part of the dwelling-house. Failing that, if the main purpose is different, then there can be no letting as a separate dwelling and, hence, no tenancy.

Tenancies of agricultural holdings

Excluded, here, is a tenancy under which the dwelling-house is comprised in an agricultural holding within the meaning of the Agricultural Holdings Act 1986 and the house is occupied by the person responsible for the control of the farming, whether as tenant or as servant or agent of the tenant. This is the same as the exclusion in the Rent Act.

Lettings to students

This covers the identical ground to the Rent Act 1977 and specifies a person who is intending or intending to pursue a course of study provided by a specified educational institution.

Holiday lettings

Despite concern about this exclusion as an avoidance device, it has been re-enacted without change from the 1977 version and says 'a tenancy the purpose of which is to confer on the tenant the right to occupy the dwelling-house for a holiday'. Tenancies of this type are, by virtue of s 31(7) of the 1988 Act, also excluded along with licences from s 3 of the Protection from Eviction Act 1977 if they involve the right to occupy premises for a holiday only. To that extent, if the relative merits of avoidance devices are being weighed up, the holiday letting, if unchallenged, also offers a way around day in court and notice to quit requirements and is therefore easier for landlords to operate than company lets. It also would provide an incentive to avoid meddling with assured or assured shorthold.

Resident landlords

This substantially reproduces the conditions set out in s 12 of the 1977 Act. The emphasis on living in the same building and occupying at all times afterwards is duplicated, along with the exception of a purpose built block of flats. However, in tune with the philosophy of the 1988 Act, it is stipulated that the resident landlord must be an individual and occupy the premises in question as his 'only or principal home'. Therefore, unlike the 1977 Act, where the generosity of the occupational requirements for statutory tenancies was extended to resident landlord occupation, the two homes landlord is going to have difficulty relying on more casual or intermittent occupation for the purposes of the 1988 Act.

It is also significant that there is no intermediate safety net like a restricted contract for tenants of resident landlords under the 1988 Act. Another factor to be borne in mind is that the 1988 Act also excludes certain categories of occupancy from the court order and notice to quit provisions of the Protection from Eviction Act 1977. Tenancies or licences are excluded if there is any sharing of accommodation with the landlord or licensor or a member of the family of the landlord or licensor and the only or principal home requirements are satisfied. Accommodation is extensively defined to exclude only storage areas and staircases, passages, corridors and other means of access. Clearly, some tenants of resident landlords do not share any accommodation and will, therefore, have the bedrock protection of the Protection from Eviction Act 1977, ss 3 and 5. Those who do share, even minimally, with the persons identified will lose their rights under the Act, even if they are not sharing living accommodation, such as kitchens, but just bathrooms or lavatories.

Crown tenancies

As under the 1977 Act, tenancies where the interest of the landlord belongs to the Crown or to a government department or is held on trust for the crown cannot be assured. The exception to this is where the interest is under the management of the Crown Estate Commissioners.

Local authority tenancies, etc

There is a list of excluded tenancies where the landlord is: a local authority; the Commission for the New Towns; the Development Board for Rural Wales; an urban development corporation; a development corporation; waste disposal authorities; a residuary body; a fully mutual housing association; and a housing action trust.

Transitional cases

For the avoidance of doubt, the concluding case in the schedule is of tenancies covered by different codes of protection. So protected tenancies, housing association tenancies within the meaning of Pt VI of the 1977 Act, secure tenancies and Rent (Agriculture) Act 1976 protected occupancies are incapable of being assured. This case was necessary, since not all the private sector tenancies mentioned will necessarily predate 15 January 1989 and, thus, be excluded by the first paragraph in the schedule, pre-commencement tenancies.

Temporary housing duties for the homeless

An additional exclusion from assured status arises from s 1(6) of the 1988 Act, the purpose of which is to provide equivalent safeguards to those already enjoyed by local authorities.

Where various temporary housing duties are created while the status of applicants are being investigated or they have been found to be intentionally homeless and they remain in occupation, there is a safety net for local authorities in Sched 1, para 4 of the Housing Act 1985 guaranteeing that no secure tenancy can arise until a year has elapsed from notification of any decision on status. Since housing associations are increasingly assisting authorities in discharge of these Housing Act duties, s 1(6) establishes that there can equally be no assured tenancy until a year has passed. The sub-section talks in general terms of a local authority making arrangements with 'another person' to provide accommodation, so the ambit is, in principle, wider than just housing associations.

SECURITY OF TENURE

There are some significant differences between the 1988 procedures for assured tenancies and the operation of the 1977 Act. The apparatus in the Rent Acts for the creation and perpetuation of statutory tenancies following contractual tenancies is superseded and the model is more the methods used in the Housing Act 1985 for secure tenancies. In addition, it is easier for a tenant to extricate himself from an agreement by surrender or other action or by the requisite notice to quit under the 1988 Act. Another salient feature of the 1988 Act already mentioned is that, substantively, the emphasis in the grounds for possession is more landlord friendly, with more stringent mandatory grounds in operation than under the 1977 Act.

The machinery deployed in the 1988 Act to facilitate possession is unnecessarily cumbersome, though some find it easier than the 1977 Act machinery, and involves distinguishing between periodic assured tenancies and fixed term assured tenancies. In the case of periodic tenancies, s 5 spells out that service by a landlord of a due notice to quit shall be ineffective in relation to a periodic assured tenancy and repossession is not possible without a court order. So, the initial contractual arrangement merely continues without blossoming into a statutory tenancy.

Fixed term agreements, by contrast, do by definition have a definite end through the passing of time and, therefore, continuity has to be artificially arranged by the specification in s 5(2). This states that if a fixed term assured tenancy comes to an end otherwise than by virtue of a court order or a surrender or other tenant action, then the tenant is entitled to remain in the dwelling house. This wording implicitly takes in the two common situations of expiry by the passing of time and expiry by invocation of a 'break clause'. A break clause is a provision in a lease permitting either party to terminate the tenancy by service of notice to quit at specified intervals during the fixed term. So, somewhat obliquely, a periodic tenancy springs up here also. The elements of this periodic tenancy are set out in s 5(3) as the same terms as those of the fixed term tenancy.

One of the elaborate features of the new law is the attitude taken to forfeiture as a means of determining a tenancy. One very common clause in any tenancy agreement would be to specify the right to exercise a power of re-entry or forfeiture for breach of a term or condition of a tenancy. At first sight, where s 5(1) talks of 'power for the landlord to determine the tenancy in certain circumstances', it would include the exercise of the reserved right of re-entry as a prelude to forfeiture. However, under s 45(4), in connection with Pt I of the Act, for the avoidance of doubt, 'a power for a landlord to determine a tenancy does not include a reference to a power of re-entry or forfeiture for breach of any term or condition of the tenancy'. Therefore, by implication, in s 5(1) the only preserved power is the exercise of options contained in break clauses.

Thus, in the case of forfeiture, the emphasis is thrown back on ending the assured tenancy through a court order. The starting point is s 7(1) which makes it plain that a pre-requisite for making a possession order is satisfaction of one or more of the grounds set out in Sched 2 to the Act. Specifically, in relation to the fixed term assured, s 7(6) makes it clear that possession will not be granted unless:

> (a) the ground for possession is Ground 2 or Ground 8 in Pt 1 of Sched 2 to this Act or any of the grounds in Pt II of that schedule, other than Ground 9 or Ground 16; and
>
> (b) the terms of the tenancy make provision for it to be brought to an end on the ground in question (whether that provision takes the form of a provision for re-entry, for forfeiture, for determination by notice or otherwise).

Therefore, not all the grounds for possession are available to landlords during the fixed term. The meaning of (b) is elusive. Characteristically, clauses concerned with forfeiture would not specify detailed grounds in a fashion perhaps required by 'making provision' in sub-s (a). The typical Parthian shot from landlords in a tenancy agreement is:

> Provided that if the rent or any instalment or part thereof shall be in arrear for at least 14 days after the same shall have become due (whether legally demanded or not) or if there shall be a breach of any of the agreements by the tenant the landlord may re-enter on the property (subject always to any statutory restrictions on his power so to do) and immediately thereupon the tenancy shall determine without prejudice to the other rights and remedies of the landlord.

On a restrictive reading, such standard forfeiture clauses only single out the grounds of non-payment of rent and breach of covenant and leave other grounds untouched. It would, however, be asking a lot to expect all the available grounds to be specifically incorporated in a re-entry clause.

Whatever the complexities of recovery of possession in fixed term tenancies, at least the picture for periodic assured is relatively clear cut, whether for the original or continuation tenancy. All the grounds for possession contained in Sched 2 are available in these circumstances, provided the procedural formalities for recovery of possession are observed.

Notice of proceedings for possession

For all assured, there are stipulations in s 8 of the 1988 Act, amplified by statutory instrument dictating the prescribed form notice must take. The general instruction in sub-s (3) is that the notice must inform the tenant that:

> (a) the landlord intends to begin proceedings for possession of the dwelling-house on one or more of the grounds specified in the notice; and

(b) those proceedings will not begin earlier than a date specified in the notice; and

(c) those proceedings will not begin later than 12 months from the date of service of the notice.

Because of its practical importance, this section has come under close judicial scrutiny. In *Mountain v Hastings* (1993) 25 HLR 427, the Court of Appeal held that the notice was inadequate when the landlord merely said 'at least three months rent is unpaid' in response to the requirement to give the full text of the ground relied on. This was not enough to be allowed to proceed under Ground 8.

The Housing Act measures proposals on domestic violence and anti-social behaviour have necessitated some addition to the requirements in s 8 and these will be covered when Grounds 14 and 14A are analysed.

GROUNDS FOR POSSESSION

The pattern of mandatory and discretionary grounds familiar from the 1977 Act is continued, although, in the 1988 Act, the mandatory grounds come first. Many of the grounds are identical to those in 1977 and will not be further explored. The focus will naturally be on variations, such as the owner-occupier ground and innovations, such as possession for demolition and construction work, and a profusion of rent arrears grounds. The Housing Act 1996 has also changed the nuisance/annoyance ground and introduced a new ground to combat domestic violence.

Mandatory grounds

Ground 1: landlord's prior or future occupation

Not later than the beginning of the tenancy the landlord gave notice in writing to the tenant that possession might be recovered on this ground or the court is of the opinion that it is just and equitable to dispense with the requirement of notice and (in either case):

(a) at some time before the beginning of the tenancy, the landlord who is seeking possession or, in the case of joint landlords seeking possession, at least one of them occupied the dwelling-house as his only or principal home, or

(b) the landlord who is seeking possession or, in the case of joint landlords seeking possession, at least one of them requires the dwelling-house as his or his spouse's only or principal home and neither the landlord (or in the case of joint landlords, any one of them) nor any other person who, as landlord, derived title under the landlord who gave the notice mentioned above acquired the reversion on the tenancy for money or money's worth.

This is a compilation in some ways of three 1977 Act Cases: 9, 11 and 12. Does it not also meet the predicament of ex-servicemen in Case 20?

It is significant that any prior occupation as only or principal home 'at some time' suffices, so there is no danger of an equivalent to *Pocock v Steel*. Also, unlike Case 11, the landlord does not have to explain why possession is required. There is no requirement of occupation as a residence after repossession and therefore using the ground with a view to sale is legitimate.

Paragraph (b) has been likened to Case 9, but is much more facilitative of possession by landlords, assuming they have not bought themselves into the position. There is no hint of a reasonableness requirement and the ground is, after all, mandatory. There is not even any condition that the landlord should have occupied at any time in the past. On the other hand, it is true that the constituency of those family members in a position to recover possession has been narrowed in the 1988 provisions and the specification of requirement as only or principal home again is stricter than requiring as a residence.

Ground 2: dwelling-house subject to mortgage

The dwelling-house is subject to a mortgage granted before the beginning of the tenancy and:

(a) the mortgagee is entitled to exercise a power of sale conferred on him by the mortgage or by s 101 of the Law of Property Act 1925; and

(b) the mortgagee requires possession of the dwelling-house for the purpose of disposing of it with vacant possession in exercise of that power; and

(c) either notice was given as mentioned in Ground 1 above or the court is satisfied that it is just and equitable to dispense with the requirement of notice.

Something comparable to this is to be found in Case 11 of the 1977 Act. In the unfortunate event of default on mortgage payments, this ground allows a landlord to recover possession so that the mortgagee can sell with vacant possession. The mortgage must have been granted before the beginning of the tenancy. Banks and building societies and other lenders will be anxious to ensure that the appropriate notice is served on tenants, but usually there is a prohibition against letting. In that latter case, the tenancy does not usually bind the mortgagee.

Ground 3: out of season lets

The tenancy is a fixed term tenancy for a term not exceeding eight months and:

(a) not later than the beginning of the tenancy the landlord gave notice in writing to the tenant that possession might be recovered on this ground; and

(b) at some time within the period of 12 months ending with the beginning of the tenancy, the dwelling-house was occupied under a right to occupy it for a holiday.

Because of the possibility of unlikely holiday lets in strange places, this ground, designed to help the genuine landlord, could assist the avoidance device by offering the prospect of out of season lets to vary the monotony of a string of holiday lets. Obviously, it enables the genuine holiday landlord to be sure of recovering possession at both high and low season. It is a close descendant of Case 13 in the 1977 Act.

Ground 4: vacation lets of student accommodation

The tenancy is a fixed term tenancy for a term not exceeding 12 months and:

(a) not later than the beginning of the tenancy the landlord gave notice in writing to the tenant that possession might be recovered on this ground; and

(b) at some time within the period of 12 months ending with the beginning of the tenancy, the dwelling-house was let on a tenancy falling within para 8 of Sched 1 to this Act.

This is the 1988 counterpart to Case 14 of the 1977 Act and guarantees repossession at the end of the vacation letting. Term time lettings to students by specified educational institutions are of course specifically excluded from assured status.

Ground 5: ministers of religion

The dwelling-house is held for the purpose of being available for occupation by a minister of religion as a residence from which to perform the duties of his office and:

(a) not later than the beginning of the tenancy the landlord gave notice in writing to the tenant that possession might be recovered on this ground; and

(b) the court is satisfied that the dwelling-house is required for occupation by a minister of religion as such a residence.

This is the same ground as Case 15 under the 1977 Act and is self-explanatory. How commonly it is used is another matter.

Ground 6: intention to demolish/reconstruct/carry out substantial works

The landlord who is seeking possession or, if that landlord is a registered housing association or charitable housing trust, a superior landlord intends to demolish or reconstruct the whole or a substantial part of the dwelling-house or to carry out substantial works on the dwelling-house or any part thereof or any building of which it forms part and the following conditions are fulfilled:

(a) the intended work cannot reasonably be carried out without the tenant giving up possession of the dwelling-house because:

(i) the tenant is not willing to agree to such a variation of the terms of the tenancy as would give such access and other facilities as would permit the intended work to be carried out; or

(ii) the nature of the intended work is such that no such variation is practicable; or

(iii) the tenant is not willing to accept an assured tenancy of such part only of the dwelling-house (in this subparagraph referred to as 'the reduced part') as would leave in the possession of his landlord so much of the dwelling-house as would be reasonable to enable the intended work to be carried out and, where appropriate, as would give such access and other facilities over the reduced part as would permit the intended work to be carried out; or

(iv) the nature of the intended work is such that such a tenancy is not practicable; and

(b) either the landlord seeking possession acquired his interest in the dwelling-house before the grant of the tenancy or that interest was in existence at the time of that grant and neither that landlord (or in the case of joint landlords, any of them) nor any other person who, alone or jointly with others, has acquired that interest since that time acquired it for money or money's worth.

This is a novelty for mainstream private sector tenancies, although 'old' assured had such a provision. The equivalent is to be found in the public sector in Ground 10 of Sched 2 to the Housing Act 1985 and it has performed a useful function there on occasions as a means of recovering possession where other grounds are lacking or difficult, as well as a means of getting works done. A similar provision is to found in s 30(1)(f) of the business tenancy code in the Landlord and Tenant Act 1954.

As with other sectors of housing, it is possible that private sector landlords will manufacture an intention to demolish or reconstruct as a means of getting possession; therefore, the case law from the business sector will be applicable to ensure that only genuine intentions are respected. Objective evidence, such as planning permission, building plans and financial capability, is likely to be influential. In the end, according to Lord Denning in *Fisher v Taylors Furnishing Stores Ltd* [1956] 2 QB 78, p 84:

> ... the court must be satisfied that the intention to reconstruct is genuine and not colourable; that it is a firm and settled intention, not likely to be changed, that the reconstruction is of a substantial part of the premises, indeed so substantial that it cannot be thought a device to get possession; that the work is so extensive that it is necessary to get possession of the holding in order to do it; and that it is intended to do the work at once and not after a time.

Other points to note in this ground are that it is not applicable where a protected or statutory tenancy has been converted to an assured on succession by a family member. In addition, as an antidote to speculative development, it is not possible to use the ground if the landlord purchased the freehold after the tenancy was created. If the ground is successfully invoked, the tenant is entitled to reasonable moving expenses under s 11 of the 1988 Act.

Ground 7: death of periodic tenant

> The tenancy is a periodic tenancy (including a statutory periodic tenancy) which has devolved under the will or intestacy of the former tenant and the proceedings for the recovery of possession are begun not later than 12 months after the death of the former tenant or, if the court so directs, after the date on which, in the opinion of the court, the landlord or, in the case of joint landlords, any one of them became aware of the former tenant's death.
>
> For the purposes of this ground, the acceptance by the landlord of rent from a new tenant after the death of the former tenant shall not be regarded as creating a new periodic tenancy, unless the landlord agrees in writing to a change (as compared with the tenancy before the death) in the amount of the rent, the period of the tenancy, the premises which are let or any other term of the tenancy.

Unlike the 1977 Act, there is a presumption against continuity of tenancies and, in the case of assured periodic tenancies, there is a risk, in some instances, that the person who inherits under the general law of inheritance will not be acceptable to the landlord. This situation is entirely separate from the circumstances covered by s 17 of the Act under which, on the death of a sole periodic tenant, the assured tenancy will vest in a resident spouse or cohabitee and, therefore, does not devolve under a will or intestacy.

Thus, the purpose of this ground is to give the landlord long enough to vet the suitability of the person who has inherited the tenancy and be sure that eviction is inevitable if proceedings for possession are initiated. The provision about acceptance of rent institutionalises the position adopted in *Marcroft Wagons v Smith* [1951] 2 KB 496 of reluctance to infer the existence of a new tenancy, which, in this case, would defeat the object of the exercise. However, an ill advised landlord might agree in writing to a change in the rent or some other relatively minor term and find himself lumbered with a new periodic assured tenancy.

Ground 8: non-payment of rent

> Both at the date of service of the notice under s 8 of this Act relating to the proceedings for possession and at the date of the hearing:
>
> (a) if rent is payable weekly or fortnightly, at least 13 weeks' rent is unpaid;
>
> (b) if rent is payable monthly, at least three months' rent is unpaid;
>
> (c) if rent is payable quarterly, at least one quarter's rent is more than three months in arrears; and
>
> (d) if rent is payable yearly, at least three months' rent is more than three months in arrears;
>
> and for the purpose of this ground 'rent' means rent lawfully due from the tenant.

This ground is unprecedented in its specification of precise arrears periods and in being mandatory. There is no prospect of suspended possession orders and a more flexible approach. In fact, s 101 of the Housing Act reduces the relevant periods still further than in (b), from three to two months and make the weekly and fortnightly tenancy limit eight weeks, rather than 13. This last is not a long time if it also remembered that the non-appearance of housing benefit is no defence to an action for rent.

Because there are two other, discretionary rent grounds, Grounds 10 and 11, there is scope for manoeuvring by both tenant and landlord. Since there is a dual requirement in Ground 8 that rent be unpaid both at the time of the initial notice and the date of the hearing, a tenant only has to produce something towards the arrears to ward off the fate in Ground 8, although the prospects under the discretionary grounds can be uncertain, particularly for persistent arrears. Landlords would be well advised to invoke the various rent grounds in the alternative when appropriate when serving notice, as between them they appear to cover most fact situations where there is default.

The last part of this ground is also significant, as it gives a tenant the opportunity to defend a rent action by counterclaiming that the landlord is in breach of a repairing covenant.

Discretionary grounds

Ground 9: suitable alternative accommodation

> Suitable alternative accommodation is available for the tenant or will be available for him when the order for possession takes effect.

Proponents of the 1988 Act were anxious for this to be a mandatory ground, to facilitate transfers of tenants, but the proposal was amended to discretionary status as with the 1977 Act. This ground closely resembles the previous criteria, save for alterations necessitated by the different nature of the assured tenancy. There is still optimistic scope for the local authority certificate, but the comparables identified are assured tenancies not subject to the notice of intended repossession in Grounds 1–5, or an unspecified tenancy which will offer reasonably equivalent security of tenure. Assured shortholds are naturally not deemed suitable. Again, under s 11, the landlord is obliged to pay the tenant's reasonable removal expenses.

Ground 10: rent lawfully due

> Some rent lawfully due from the tenant:
>
> (a) is unpaid on the date on which the proceedings for possession are begun; and
>
> (b) except where sub-s (1)(b) of s 8 of this Act applies, was in arrears at the date of the service of the notice under that section relating to those proceedings.

Clumsy cross-referencing makes the purpose of (b) not immediately apparent, but all it means is that, sometimes, the court has discretion to dispense with the service of a s 8 notice if it considers it just and equitable so to do. If there is such a dispensation, then rent arrears at the commencement of proceedings are enough. Case 1 under the Rent Acts is very similar to this and both are likely to lead to suspended possession orders.

Ground 11: persistent delay in paying the rent

> Whether or not any rent is in arrears on the date on which proceedings for possession are begun, the tenant has persistently delayed paying rent which has lawfully become due.

This was also originally intended to be a mandatory ground, to act as a more powerful deterrent to those who escape the toils of Ground 8 by paying off some or all arrears after the notice warning of imminent proceedings for possession. Section 8 of the 1988 Act as seen gives the defaulting tenant a window of opportunity between the service of the notice of proceedings for possession and the court proceedings proper.

Ground 12: breach of obligation other than rent

> Any obligation of the tenancy (other than one related to the payment of rent) has been broken or not performed.

The mushrooming of rent arrears grounds in the 1988 Act has caused this general purpose criterion to split from its partner under the Rent Acts and stand alone. It gives the court the widest possible scope to determine the gravity of breaches and must often subsume some of the more specific grounds.

Ground 13: deteriorating dwelling-house

> The condition of the dwelling-house or any of the common parts has deteriorated owing to acts of waste by, or the neglect or default of, the tenant or any other person residing in the dwelling-house and, in the case of an act of waste by, or the neglect or default of, a person lodging with the tenant or a subtenant of his, the tenant has not taken such steps as he ought reasonably to have taken for the removal of the lodger or subtenant.

For the purposes of this ground, 'common parts' means any part of a building comprising the dwelling-house and any other premises which the tenant is entitled under the terms of the tenancy to use in common with the occupiers of other dwelling-houses in which the landlord has an estate or interest.

This tortuously drafted ground has become more complicated than its predecessor in the Rent Act 1977, Case 3, through its inclusion of the common parts. These parts are carefully not defined in this ground, but can be taken to mean stairways, corridors and passages in blocks of flats and, presumably, communal gardens and other facilities shared as of right rather than de facto.

Ground 14: nuisance/annoyance and illegal/immoral user

The tenant or any other person residing in the dwelling-house has been guilty of conduct which is a nuisance or annoyance to adjoining occupiers, or has been convicted of using the dwelling-house or allowing the dwelling-house to be used for immoral or illegal purposes.

This is virtually identical to Case 2 of the 1977 Act, save that, in this ground, the guilty parties have merely to reside in the dwelling-house, whereas, under the earlier Act, such persons must be residing with the tenant. In keeping with the general onslaught on anti-social behaviour, there is provision in the Housing Act 1996, s 148, to give landlords, particularly housing associations, more extended grounds for possession.

The new Ground 14 to be substituted reads as follows:

The tenant or a person residing in or visiting the dwelling-house:

(a) has been guilty of conduct causing, or likely to cause a nuisance or annoyance to a person residing, visiting or otherwise engaging in a lawful activity in the locality; or

(b) has been convicted of:
  (i) using the dwelling-house or allowing it to be used for immoral or illegal purposes; or
  (ii) an arrestable offence committed in, or in the locality of, the dwelling-house.

As with the identical ground for 'secure' tenants, the aim is to amplify the law against nuisance and annoyance by extending its ambit to visitors and allowing for eviction where antisocial behaviour is likely to have an adverse effect even if there are no victims. (b)(ii) was added to the original formulation in the Bill to widen the ambit of the grounds still further.

New Ground 14A: domestic violence – assured tenancies

Section 149 of the 1996 Act inserts the following new ground:

The dwelling-house was occupied (whether alone or with others) by a married couple or a couple living together as husband and wife and:

(a) one or both of the partners is a tenant of the dwelling-house;

(b) the landlord who is seeking possession is a registered social landlord or a charitable housing trust;

(c) one partner has left the dwelling-house because:

(i) of violence or threats of violence by the other towards that partner; or

(ii) a member of the family of that partner who was residing with that partner immediately before the partner left; and

(d) the court is satisfied that the partner who has left is unlikely to return.

As a response to the problem of domestic violence, this provision has been criticised for excessively narrow definition; what of couples other than heterosexual? The original formulation of this new ground contained no reference to the threat of violence and also included the quaint additional stipulation that the accommodation afforded by the dwelling-house is more extensive than is reasonably required by the remaining partner. The arbitrariness of evicting only in the event of under occupation was recognised during the passage of the Bill and the threatening violence was understandably included.

Additions to s 8 of the Housing Act

By virtue of s 150 of the Act, where domestic violence is the ground of the notice, some additional requirements are imposed. Where such notice is served on the tenant and the partner who has left the dwelling-house is not the tenant or party to the proceedings, the court has to be satisfied that a copy of the notice has been served on the partner who has departed or that reasonable steps have been taken to trace that person. If Ground 14A is added to a notice with leave of the court, the court cannot entertain the proceedings unless similar steps are taken.

Section 151 enables a landlord to start possession proceedings at an earlier stage than usual in the case of anti-social behaviour under Ground 14, thereby making eviction quicker. The court can entertain proceedings for possession as soon as the notice of intention to seek possession has been served, but possession is not possible before the expiry of that notice.

Ground 15: furniture deterioration

> The condition of any furniture provided for use under the tenancy has, in the opinion of the court, deteriorated owing to ill treatment by the tenant or any other person residing in the dwelling-house and, in the case of ill treatment by a person lodging with the tenant or by a subtenant of his, the tenant has not taken such steps as he ought reasonably have taken for the removal of the lodger or subtenant.

As with the previous ground there is marginal variation, this time to Case 4 of the 1977 Act.

Ground 16: ex-employees

> The dwelling-house was let to the tenant in consequence of his employment by the landlord seeking possession or a previous landlord under the tenancy and the tenant has ceased to be in that employment.

We have here a streamlined version of Case 8 from 1977 and, in principle, the discretion can be exercised in favour of the landlord even if there is no intention to move in a new employee.

New Ground 17: grant induced by false statement

> The tenant is the person, or one of the persons, to whom the tenancy was granted and the landlord was induced to grant the tenancy by a false statement made knowingly or recklessly by:
>
> (a) the tenant; or
>
> (b) a person acting at the tenant's instigation.

This addition to the grounds is put forward in s 102 of the Act. It is derived from Ground 5 in Sched 2 to the Housing Act 1985, which has a clear ambition to evict those who have jumped a queue by misrepresenting their circumstances and have obtained public sector housing. Housing associations are the most likely assured landlords to make use of this for similar reasons if it is enacted. In the freer market conditions of the private sector, such an aim is not apposite, but the very generality of the ground makes it in principle available if such factors as, for example, employment circumstances or welfare benefit dependency or childlessness are wrongly represented.

Summary

It is apparent from this list that some Rent Act grounds have not been reincarnated in the 1988 Act. There is no need for a case like Case 5 involving notice to quit because of the easier termination of an assured tenancy by the tenant. Equally, Case 6 does not apply. The overall impression in keeping with the underpinning ideology is that the 1988 grounds are more landlord friendly than the 1977, particularly, with the triad of rent arrears grounds tailored for every eventuality. The owner-occupier ground is easier to satisfy in the later Act and there is not the same commitment to balancing of interests as under the greater hardship test. If and when assured shortholds become even more pervasive following the alterations in the Housing Act 1996, the grounds for assured will assume less importance.

The new proposals to combat violence and antisocial behaviour have been generally welcomed as an addition to the existing armoury. The Housing Act 1996 introduces a power of arrest for breach of injunctions against anti-social behaviour (s 153).

Succession to assured tenancies

As was seen with the succession provisions under the 1977 Rent Act, in the past, more than one succession has been allowed and the prize has been security of tenure at a fair rent. However, the advent of assured has removed both the political will to perpetuate succession and the advantages traditionally enjoyed. Under the 1988 Act, there can be only one succession to assured tenancies and this applies only to periodic tenancies. On the death of a fixed term tenant, the tenancy devolves according to the will of the tenant or the intestacy rules. The same procedure applies to periodic assured tenancies, unless s 17 of the 1988 Act supervenes. Under it, where a sole periodic assured tenant dies and immediately before the death the tenant's spouse was occupying the dwelling-house as his or her only or principal home and the tenant was not a successor, then the tenancy vests in the spouse. Heterosexual cohabitation is also rewarded by sub-s (4), which states that a person living with the tenant as husband or wife will also qualify.

The section carefully restricts the ambit of the succession provisions by defining various circumstances where a deceased tenant is deemed to be a successor and, hence, the last possible beneficiary of s 17. Such successions are where the tenant became sole tenant by right of survivorship on the death of a joint tenant or where an assured tenancy was acquired from a Rent Act tenant who died after the commencement date of the 1988 Act. Also counted as successors are, naturally, those who have acquired the tenancy by virtue of s 17 or under the will or intestacy of a previous tenant. Even if a new tenancy is granted to a successor, it does not reactivate succession rights if the tenancy has throughout been of the same or a substantially similar dwelling-house.

Assignment and subletting of assured tenancies

Yet again, the distinction between fixed term and periodic assured is of significance here. There is no statutory prohibition of assignment or subletting in respect of fixed term agreements and terms are therefore a matter of negotiation in the original agreement. In the case of periodic tenancies, including those consequent on a fixed term, s 15 of the 1988 Act enunciates the general principle that it is an implied term that, except with the landlord's consent, the tenant shall not wholly or partially assign the tenancy or sublet or part with possession of whole or part. Sub-section (2) provides that the concession in s 19 of the 1927 Landlord and Tenant Act that consent must not be unreasonably withheld, is not applicable to such an implied term and, therefore, landlords have the option not to accept the most reasonable of substitutes and press ahead with eviction under Ground 12 for breach of covenant if the tenant defies the prohibition. This is all part of the process of tilting the balance back towards landlords.

Sub-section (3) creates an exception to the general implication of the implied term in the case of contractual assured periodic tenancies where the terms have already been settled, whether generously or restrictively by the parties or a premium is required on the grant or renewal of a tenancy.

ASSURED RENT RIGHTS

There is elaborate machinery in the 1988 Act which, however, does not have significant impact on contractually agreed rents. The watchword of the 1988 Act is 'deregulation', and, as already seen, regulated rents under the 1977 Act are approaching ever closer to the broadly market based assured rents. However, the 1988 Act does allow a role for the Rent Assessment Committee, in certain limited circumstances, and distinguishes between types of tenancy in this regard, so some detailed exposition is unavoidable, even if, in practical terms, the 'invisible hand' of the market is controlling all.

One starting point is that, where there is a fixed term tenancy, there is no statutory intervention at all, but the parties are left to their own devices and can, for example, include a regular rent review clause for the benefit of the landlord. If there is no rent review clause in an agreement, the landlord will have to wait until the expiry of the fixed term and the ensuing statutory periodic tenancy. The assumption built into s 5(3) of the Act is that the rent will be as before. This assumption is easily displaced by the landlord serving a notice under s 13(2) in prescribed form proposing a new rent. The amount of notice to which a tenant is entitled varies with the type of tenancy; yearly tenants are entitled to six months and short term (less than monthly), one month. The next step is either that the notice acts as a stimulus for another agreement to be reached, in which case that will be operative, or the tenant refers the notice to the rent assessment committee.

The criteria for the committee's determination of a rent are a far cry from s 70 of the 1977 Act with its assumptions about scarcity and the operation of the market. In s 14 of the 1988 Act, it is stated that, given certain criteria to be examined, the idea is that the committee decide the rent at which 'the dwelling-house concerned might reasonably be expected to be let in the open market by a willing landlord' under an assured tenancy with comparable terms. The committee has to disregard any effect on the rent ascribable to the granting of a tenancy to a sitting tenant, any increase in the value of the dwelling-house attributable to certain improvements and any reduction in value of the dwelling-house occasioned by the tenant's failure to comply with any terms of the tenancy. Once the rent has been determined, it will take effect at the date proposed in the notice unless otherwise agreed. It is not the same as a Rent Act registered rent, binding on future occupation. Instead, the statute carefully stipulates that there is nothing in either ss 13 or 14 to prevent landlord and tenant varying the terms of their agreement, including rent, as they see fit.

Periodic tenancies

The same machinery under s 14 is available to the landlord who must, however, bide his time if there is some rent review clause in the original contract. There is special provision that no notice of increase can require an increase to take effect before a year after the start of the first period of the tenancy.

Other terms of assured tenancies: access for repairs

Under s 16, 'it shall be an implied term of every assured tenancy that the tenant shall afford to the landlord access to the dwelling-house let on the tenancy and all reasonable facilities for executing therein any repairs which the landlord is entitled to execute'.

Varying terms of an assured tenancy apart from rent

On the expiry of a contractual assured tenancy, a statutory periodic tenancy will arise on the same terms. If either party wishes to alter any terms, they may serve a notice under s 6 of the 1988 Act within a year of the ending of the contractual term. If no action is then taken, the proposed variation will take effect after three months. Otherwise, to oppose a change, there must be an application to the rent assessment committee, which can then decide if the terms proposed are what might reasonably be expected in such a tenancy.

ASSURED SHORTHOLD TENANCIES

These have often been characterised as the landlord's dream tenancy, with guaranteed insecurity of tenure and negligible if not non-existent rent rights. They are, therefore, understandably the most prevalent form of tenancy in the private rented sector at over a third of all lettings. Many of the lessons of the failure of protected shortholds have been absorbed and reflected in usually less convoluted drafting and procedures. However, with a subspecies of assured, there is always the danger that some procedural mistake or miscalculation of status could lead to the creation of an assured tenancy and security of tenure by mistake. Therefore, partly to counteract such mistakes and partly to make the market more attractive to investors, the Housing Act 1996 proposes to make assured shorthold the rule, unless specifically provided otherwise, the 'default' tenancy.

The definition of an assured shorthold tenancy

The salient characteristics are spelt out in s 20 of the 1988 Act. The first precondition is that it is an assured tenancy and so, for instance, resident landlords within para 10 of Sched 1 to the 1988 Act cannot grant shortholds. The other basic conditions are that it must be a fixed term tenancy granted for a term certain of not less than six months, with no power for the landlord to determine the tenancy at any earlier time. Therefore, the minimum time is shorter than for protected shortholds, but there is no upper limit. The appropriate notice in prescribed form must also be served before the tenancy is entered into and must state that the tenancy is to be a shorthold. There is no discretion as elsewhere to dispense with the requirement of notice if it appears just and equitable.

Because of the constriction of tenants' rights with shortholds, various technical challenges have been mounted. In *Bedding v McCarthy* (1994) 41 EG 141, the claim was that the full six months minimum had not been granted because the assured shorthold agreement was signed on the morning of the day of commencement of the tenancy shortly after the requisite notice had been served and, thus, a few hours of the tenancy had been lost. The Court of Appeal were unimpressed and reiterated the doctrine that fractions of a day are immaterial in such circumstances. The ingenious further argument for the tenant that backdating the start of the tenancy to the beginning of the day would invalidate the subsequent notice was also rejected and it was held that the tenancy is entered into at the moment of signature.

Sometimes, however, the courts will intervene to maintain basic procedural standards, as in *Symons v Warren* (1995) (unreported) CL, 15 September, where the landlord's name had been incorrectly entered as 'Simmons' on the s 20 notice and the notice had not been signed by the landlord or the agent. The defendant was, therefore, an assured tenant.

In relation to determination, we have to return to the complexities introduced by the interaction of s 45(4) of the 1988 Act and these provisions. Since 'a power to determine the tenancy' does not include a power of re-entry or forfeiture for breach of terms or conditions of the tenancy, it is possible and, indeed, advisable for the landlord to include a re-entry clause so as, for example, to guarantee repossession under the normal grounds for arrears of rent even before the six months have elapsed. By contrast, there is no power for the tenant in the 1988 Act to determine the shorthold prematurely, although there was such a power with protected shortholds. The lack of provision for tenants in the 1988 Act creates problems if shortholders do leave early without finding substitutes or successors and are thrown back on arguments about the landlord having a duty to mitigate his losses by attempting to fill the vacancy.

Another practical problem which the Act does tackle is the attempt by a landlord to impose an assured shorthold on an existing assured tenant. Section 20(3) states that the new tenancy cannot be an assured shorthold, provided it was granted to someone who 'immediately before' was an assured tenant. As with *Dibbs v Campbell* (1988) 30 EG 49, in the case of protected shortholds, if the tenant is held to have surrendered the previous tenancy and there is some interval, however short, the new tenancy may be a shorthold.

Sub-section (4) of s 20 also covers the situation where an assured shorthold ends and a new tenancy of the same or substantially similar premises comes into being with the same parties involved. The new tenancy will be a shorthold, despite bypassing the formal requirements, such as notice already outlined, unless the landlord has a rush of blood to the head and notifies the tenant that it is not to be a shorthold.

Protected shortholders, very much a minority, are not given the protection extended to other protected tenants on the grant of a new tenancy. By virtue of s 34(3), if a landlord grants a new tenancy on or after 15 January 1989 to a protected shortholder, this will result in an assured shorthold.

The Housing Act 1996 and assured shortholds

As already outlined, the plan is to make shortholds automatic and operative without prior notice, to avoid the awkwardness of failed shortholds conferring security of tenure. To cushion the blow, there is provision in s 97 of the 1996 Act imposing a duty on the landlord in post-Act tenancies to provide a statement of the terms of the tenancy. It must also be born in mind that tenancies which cannot be assured, such as resident landlord lettings, are unaffected. The exceptions to the proposition that assured tenancies entered into after the commencement date of the Housing Act 1996 will be shorthold are very tightly drawn and may produce the opposite of previous experience, unintended shortholds, which are, however, ideologically and pragmatically easier for the proponents of the Act to accept.

The exceptions are listed in Sched 7 to the Act and will be inserted as Sched 2A to the 1988 Act. They are as follows:

(1) Tenancy excluded by notice

Here, a landlord must serve notice in advance of granting the assured tenancy that it is not to be an assured shorthold. Housing associations will presumably be alerted to this.

(2) Tenancy excluded by notice

In this instance, the requisite notice is served after the assured tenancy has been entered into, and states that the tenancy is no longer an assured shorthold. This would appear to be a way of rectifying mistakes.

(3) Tenancies containing exclusionary provision

The disclaimer of shorthold status is built into the tenancy agreement.

(4) Statutory tenancies

Various forms of succession under the Rent Acts as amended by the 1988 Act are excluded, save for protected shortholds (see s 39(7) of the 1988 Act).

(5) Former secure tenancies

This covers the circumstances where secure tenancies become assured as with voluntary transfer.

(6) Tenancies under Sched 10 to the Local Government and Housing Act 1989

This affects certain long residential tenancies which otherwise might be in danger of missing assured status following alteration under the 1989 Act.

(7) Tenancy replacing non-shorthold

This substantially reproduces the thinking in s 20(3) as already outlined.

(8) Tenancy replacing assured following secure

This is the follow up to (5) above and applies to the tenancy following the end of the assured.

(9) Assured agricultural occupancies

This relates to the 1988 Act scheme for agricultural workers, under which shortholds are inappropriate.

The logic of the 1996 reforms is, therefore, to obviate the need for any formalities for creation of assured shortholds. However, in the case of pre-1996 Act shortholds, there is still room for analytical manoeuvre about the content of the crucial s 20 prior notification. The picture is complicated by the judicial need to incorporate the more relaxed and flexible approach to formalities taken by the majority in the House of Lords in the important case of *Mannai Investment Co Ltd v Eagle Star Life Assurance Co Ltd* [1997] 3 All ER 352. *York v Casey* (1999) 31 HLR 209 shows the Court of Appeal getting the message from the superior court, although the latter did not dwell on the resemblances and differences between contractual and statutory notices and any consequential policy implications. The House of Lords took comfort from the fact that mistakes in contractual notices are mercifully rare, but the same cannot be said of statutory notices.

The details of the case show how easily things can go awry. In September 1996, surveyors employed by the plaintiff landlords wrote to the defendants offering them an assured shorthold of the premises in question for six months from 28 September. They enclosed a notice, supposedly in satisfaction of s 20(1)(c) of the 1988 Housing Act. However, the names of the landlords were given as Mr York and Ms Ross, with the commencement date set at 28 September, but the term date involved a black hole or similar scope for time travel in appearing as 6 September 1996. The defendants duly signed this somewhat confused notice and returned it. A tenancy agreement was then drawn up with the correct commencement date, but neither party signed it and the landlord was just given as Mr York.

The defendants went into possession, but resisted the claim that they should depart on 27 March 1997, arguing that the s 20 notice was invalid. The Court of Appeal, therefore, had to apply the logic of the *Mannai* decision, the validity test being whether a reasonably minded recipient would apprehend how the notice was supposed to operate, despite some minor mistake. As already stated, *Mannai* itself dealt with contractual notices in the commercial sphere, but it was apparent from *Germax v Spiegel (*1978) P & CR 204 that the same objective criterion was applicable to statutory notices. Was the termination date sufficiently clear, despite the obvious error? No reasonable recipient could properly be in reasonable doubt that the termination date had been mutually fixed at 27 March 1997. In addition, the variation in nomenclature for the landlord in the uncompleted tenancy agreement did not adversely affect the validity of the s 20 notice.

RENT RIGHTS

It may seem paradoxical that those with extreme insecurity of tenure should have any rent rights at all conferred on them, since they may not enjoy any good fortune for very long. However, on close examination, the provisions in s 22 are more of a facade, aiming only at 'excessive' rents. In any event, not all shortholders can apply. Those holding over after expiry of the fixed term are excluded from s 22, but can use s 14 after a s 13 notice by a landlord. The minimal rights under s 22 are to be further reduced by s 100 of the Act, which will, for new shortholds, prohibit any application to the rent assessment committee after the first six months of the tenancy.

The criteria for determination

The purpose of any reference is for the committee to determine the rent 'the landlord might reasonably be expected to obtain' under the assured shorthold. The committee must not make a determination unless they consider that there is a sufficient number of houses in the locality let on assured tenancies, shorthold or otherwise, and that the rent in question is 'significantly higher' than that reasonably obtainable having regard to comparables. In the nature of things, it is unlikely that tenants will think of applying and, even if they do, it is unlikely to avail them unless a rent is conspicuously excessive. That level is unlikely to be reached by any remotely worldly wise landlord.

Overall, the criteria, unlike fair rents, appear to have nothing to do with scarcity; all that has to be established is that the assured and assured shorthold market is sufficiently buoyant in the locality to allow for comparisons. In the unlikely event of a determination of excess, that excess is irrecoverable from the tenant from such date as the committee may direct and there can then be no increase by the landlord for a year. Once a shortholder departs, a new rent for the newcomer can be agreed as the determination, unlike a fair rent, does not bind the premises.

Security of tenure

As with ordinary assured, the landlord would be well advised to reserve a right of re-entry in the agreement. By this expedient, so long as it is explicit enough to satisfy s 7(6), there should be no problem in recovering possession on Grounds 2, 8 and 10–15 at any stage in the tenancy, including the first six months.

The basic mechanism for recovery of possession is designed to be much simpler than the game of cat and mouse that afflicted protected shortholds. The fundamental proposition is that two months notice is sufficient for termination. On the minimum length of shorthold, a notice after four months, but no later, will suffice. In s 21(1), it is stated that the court shall make an order for possession if satisfied that the shorthold has ended and no new assured is in existence, other than an assured shorthold periodic tenancy, and the requisite two months notice has been given. The implication of this is that notice can be given at any appropriate moment for the landlord, either towards the end of the fixed term or at any point thereafter. The only exception to a two month notice is suggested by s 20(4), where it is stipulated that, if the period of the tenancy agreed on expiry of the fixed term is longer, such as quarterly, then the common law rules about requisite period of notice are activated and the tenant could expect three months warning. It is unlikely that many landlords will agree to a variation of this sort from standard practice, even with good tenants.

On the face of it, a landlord seeking to recover possession has to satisfy both the requirement in s 21(1) of not less than two month's notice and the stipulation in s 21(4) that the date specified in the notice is not earlier than the earliest day on which the tenancy could be brought to an end by notice to quit. In *Ujima Housing Association v Richardson* (1995) (unreported) CL, 15 December, the notice was not less than two months, but the timing of the notice was awry. The tenancy ran from Tuesday to Monday in the assured periodic shorthold following the expiry of the fixed term, and the date set in the notice was, however, a Thursday. The judge, perhaps surprisingly, read the two requirements disjunctively and concluded that a notice complying with either s 21(4) or 21(1) would be valid.

CHAPTER 3

HOMELESSNESS

INTRODUCTION

There has, for some time, been consensus among political parties and pressure groups that the pervasive problem of homelessness is an indictment of any ostensibly civilised society. However, there is perennial dispute about the causes of homelessness and the degree to which homeless individuals and households should be screened to assess whether the lack of accommodation is their own fault, necessitating a different response from housing agencies to that given to the 'unintentionally' homeless. In recent years, much of the focus has been on the most obvious manifestations of homelessness, 'rough sleeping' in London and other cities and the new Social Exclusion Unit has targeted homelessness along with other aspects of its remit from the Labour government to 'develop integrated and sustainable approaches to the problems of the worst housing estates, including crime, drugs, unemployment, community breakdown and bad schools'. The strategy of the new Labour administration is to formulate and execute a strategy for neighbourhood renewal and concentration of resources on the most deprived areas, thereby indirectly alleviating and preventing the problems of homelessness. Indeed, strategies for the prevention of homelessness loom much larger in the latest draft Code of Guidance (March 1999) than ever before.

So far as legal mechanisms are concerned, the long standing provisions of the Housing (Homeless Persons) Act 1977 were altered significantly by the Housing Act 1996 and the law's delays mean that issues predating the inception of the reforms in 1996 still filter through the courts. It will, therefore, still be necessary to focus on both 'old' and 'new' law and this double vision also makes sense because there is a large measure of continuity between the substance of the 1985 Act, which replaced the 1977 legislation, and the changes made in 1996. The incoming Labour administration in 1997 made some marginal changes to improve the legal rights of the homeless, without resurrecting anything major, such as an eventual right to a permanent home.

It is worth focusing on the original content of and justification for the pioneering legislation in 1977, which stemmed from a Private Member's Bill. The background was the perception that existing rights, such as those found in the National Assistance Act of 1948, were inadequate, containing only emergency obligations. Media coverage and dramatisations, such as 'Cathy Come Home', led to the pressure for legislation, spearheaded by groups such as Shelter. The underlying aim of the 1977 Act which, as will later be seen, was weakened by various amendments in its progress through Parliament was succinctly stated by the sponsor of the legislation, Stephen Ross:

> In 1948, it was believed that a short stay in some kind of temporary accommodation would be adequate to tide people over until they could make arrangements for somewhere permanent to live. That may have been so then, but the nature of homelessness today is certainly not like that. Fires and floods still happen, certainly, but

> we are not now dealing with a situation in which people can sort out their own housing problems after a short stay in what is known as temporary accommodation. The need of most homeless people is a permanent solution to their problem which they have been unable to arrange themselves [Hansard, Vol 926, Col 898].

It is significant that the contrast between temporary and permanent solutions was the core of the justification for the new legislation. As will be demonstrated in this chapter, until only a few years ago, the judiciary, the Code of Guidance on the law, local authorities and policy analysts were uniformly disposed to read permanent obligations on housing authorities into the legislation, despite the lack of any specific reference to anything like 'settled' or 'permanent' accommodation in the statutory language. However, in the last decade or so there has been increasing pressure on local authority housing resources, compelling the judiciary to acknowledge that permanent accommodation is a matter of aspiration, rather than entitlement, if it is physically impossible, at any rate in the short term, properly to house the full duty unintentionally homeless. Alongside this pragmatic judicial erosion of a putative permanent duty, there was a long campaign from the Conservative administration to denigrate the legislation as productive of queue jumping and social injustice, culminating in the 1996 Act, which stipulated that the full duty was only temporary. It should be added that the landmark decision, in *R v Brent London Borough Council ex p Awua* [1995] 3 All ER 495, showed the House of Lords anticipating the 1996 legislation and capitalising on the absence of the terminology of permanence to produce their own restrictive interpretation of the law. The modifications to the law made by the Labour administration fall well short of the ideal of permanence already described.

The causes of homelessness

Levels of officially acknowledged homelessness are still much higher than those in the late 70s, when the pioneering Act was introduced. Approximately 50,000 households were accepted as homeless in the earlier days, as opposed to 140,000, in 1993, and 120,000, in 1995. It does not require the services of a demographic genius to assert that the most obvious cause of homelessness is the physical factor of the lack of available affordable accommodation in the vicinity. So far as public sector provision is concerned, the sharp decline in council house building since the 1970s and the lack of any countervailing contribution from other sectors, coupled with the erosion of the sector through the success of the 'right to buy', have provided one *prima facie* plausible explanation for the difficulties increasingly experienced by households and individuals struggling in the housing market. Structural factors, such as changes in the housing market and demographic trends towards more diffuse household formation, should figure very early in any attempted explanation of a phenomenon which must be multifactorial. Studies, such as that of Greve, *Homelessness in Britain* (1990), provide the rationale that factors, such as low income, unemployment and relationship breakdown, are some of the contributory causes and that it is only in exceptional pathological cases that individuals set out to exploit and abuse the legislation. Recent research also suggests that domestic violence is a very powerful contributory factor to the creation of homelessness among women.

This modest multifactorial and non-judgmental approach to the causation of homelessness is in sharp contrast to the approach taken by the Conservative administration from 1993 onwards, an approach dominated by moralistic assumptions, supposedly backed by empirical evidence, that homelessness was more a matter of individual choice to jump housing queues. Since this punitive approach is still embedded in the present law, even as amended by subsequent administrations of a different persuasion, some historical background is inevitable, even if (fortunately) space prohibits a full description of the bizarre progress of the 'back to basics' campaign which underlay the reforms of homelessness law.

The context of the present law

According to Goodlad and Gibb, in *Housing and Social Justice* (1994) p 7, 'The immense growth in homelessness over the past decade is the most visible symptom of social injustice in the housing system'. The years since that statement was made have seen a certain flattening out of the homelessness statistics, but they are still at alarmingly high levels, especially for officially determined criteria. Again, in 1994, research conducted by Shelter (*Homelessness in England – Local Authority Practice*) demonstrated that most local housing authorities were perfectly content with the current legislative framework, if anything, believing that it was too restrictive and miserly in failing adequately to prioritise single persons and childless couples. Until 1993, successive Conservative administrations were also content to leave the homelessness legislation largely alone. This strategy of non-intervention also had the support of most local authorities, who believed that the system was working effectively.

However, the arrival of the 'back to basics' campaign in that year signalled a concern dramatically to reduce the rights enjoyed by the statutorily homeless and to place more emphasis on competition for housing, being channelled through general allocation criteria, rather than specific homeless rules. The immediate stimuli were Conference pronouncements, such as the following by Peter Lilley:

> I've got a little list, I've got a little list.
>
> Of young ladies who get pregnant to jump the housing queue.

This snatch from a supposedly comic operetta, castigating those who were abusing the Welfare State, was given high seriousness in a 1994 consultative document, *Access to Local Authority and Housing Association Tenancies*. This document expressed, in weightier tones, general dissatisfaction beyond anxieties about single mothers:

> By giving the local authority a greater responsibility towards those who can demonstrate 'homelessness' than towards anyone else in housing need, the current legislation creates a perverse incentive for people to have themselves accepted as homeless within the meaning of Pt III of the Housing Act 1985.

The argument was, therefore, a general and potentially devastating one that the legislation itself was inherently productive of injustice as it encouraged and enabled the undeserving to queue jump and attain quality permanent housing at the expense of more dutiful citizens languishing patiently on local authority waiting lists. Advocates of reform cited the initial misgivings of opponents of the 1977 Act and dark forebodings about a charter for scroungers and scrim shankers. The argument in the 1994 document was underpinned by research conducted by Prescott-Clarke and others, 'Routes into local authority housing; a study of local authority waiting lists and new tenancies'. However, the evidence emerging from that research does not afford convincing proof of worrying levels of exploitation or superior accommodation gained by use of the homelessness law 'fast track'. There is evidence to support the contrary conclusion that, typically, homeless individuals and households received fewer and inferior offers of accommodation than those qualifying by the long term route of general allocation under s 22 of the Housing Act 1985. So far as the diabolisation of single mothers is concerned, there is particular research, such as that of Ermisch (*Household Formation and Housing Tenure Decisions of Young People*, 1996, ESRC), to suggest that Peter Lilley's accusations were unwarranted. Further evidence that teenage mothers do not have the grand design of jumping housing queues is to be found in *Teenage Mothers*, a 1998 study by the Policy Studies Institute. Although approximately a third of such mothers were council tenants, they were exonerated as a class from any 'malice aforethought', knowing little about housing law and policy.

The basic mechanism adopted in the 1996 Act to create 'lesser eligibility' for the homelessness rules is contained in s 193 of the Act, which reduces obligations owed by housing authorities to full duty applicants to, at best, the provision of temporary accommodation for two years with the possibility of renewal in certain circumstances. The original time limit in the Bill was only one year, reflecting the assumption in the White Paper, *Our Future Homes, Opportunity, Choice, Responsibility,* 1995, that 'Being without a home is a searing experience, but it is usually a short term crisis'. At the Committee stage in the House of Commons, the Conservative government accepted that a two year minimum would be more appropriate. However, s 197 of the Act contained an escape clause for authorities disinclined, for whatever reason, to offer even that degree of security to a full duty individual or household. Under the terms of that section, any duty dwindled to the point of a mere obligation to provide appropriate advice and assistance if the authority were satisfied that other suitable accommodation was available for the applicant in the district. The possibility of some short term arrangement in the private sector would be a cardinal example of this alternative suitability.

The Labour manifesto commitment to restore hope to the homeless was ostensibly fulfilled not by offering any guarantees of permanence, but by rewriting the terms of s 197 to indicate that other accommodation is not to be considered suitable unless the local authority is satisfied that it will be available for occupation by the applicant for at least two years. This, then, dovetails with the two year specification in s 193 to create a somewhat flimsy floor of rights for the full duty homeless, a guarantee that two years' worth of accommodation of some description will be available. The contrast is with the old s 197, under which an assured shorthold of six months duration could trigger the alternative duty of advice and assistance. Under the modifications made by the Homelessness (Suitability of Accommodation) (Amendment) Order 1997 SI 1997/1741, it is envisaged either that, say, a private landlord will offer a tenancy of a fixed term of two years or, more realistically, a shorter term offer with a commitment to two years dependent on good behaviour.

Another aspect of the 1996 Act reforms which must be mentioned at this stage is the decision in s 167 as originally formulated to exclude the statutory homeless from the reasonable preference categories enshrined in the predecessor section: s 22 of the Housing Act 1985. In keeping with the diminution of the full duty owed to the homeless under the separate homelessness rules, the intention was to stress that homelessness *per se* in the absence of other qualifying characteristics, such as family size or medical problems, was not a factor to enhance an applicant's chances of getting housed under the reasonable preference criteria. In other respects, the criteria for attracting reasonable preference were made broader and more specialised in terms of various disadvantages in the housing market, so the exclusion of the homeless from reasonable preference status was all the more striking. Certainly, any element of 'perverse incentive' allegedly present in the statutory framework in the 1985 Act was ruthlessly expunged by the provisions of the 1996 Act just described, although there were bound to be problems in ensuring that unsympathetic authorities refrained from privileging the homeless within the broadly discretionary framework of s 167, the general allocation criteria.

In any event, the incoming Labour government took steps, in the Allocation of Housing (Reasonable and Additional Preference) Regulations 1997 SI No 1902, to restore the statutorily homeless of various types to 'reasonable preference' status. This reform could speedily be engineered by statutory instrument and in itself cost nothing. The Code of Guidance issued in August 1997, however, revealed some strong ambitions for the amendment.

The idea was:

> ... to ensure that local authorities are able to address the problems that homelessness can give rise to by providing long term accommodation; the provision of such accommodation would, in effect, end any duties under Pt VII of the 1996 Act. In devising their allocations schemes, authorities will need to balance the needs of households to whom they owe a homelessness duty with those of households attracting reasonable preference on other grounds. Authorities will be aware, however, that homeless households often manifest various characteristics of underlying need that fall within the other reasonable preference categories. It would be legitimate to give greater preference in such cases.

The overall picture is, therefore, a move away from the moralistic prioritisation of certain forms of responsible family life to a more undifferentiated, but, nevertheless, half hearted promotion of the rights of the homeless of whatever description. The balancing act that is inevitable and invidious when setting the claims of the homeless against the non-homeless is bound to be affected by the view taken by local authority functionaries of the extent and value of the full duty owed to the homeless under 'their' part of the legislation, the relatively miserly two years. There are, apparently, no immediate plans to change the basic outline of the law or the relationship between the homelessness and general allocation criteria. It has been suggested by pressure groups that some return should be made to a greater commitment than two years to the statutorily homeless. The difficulty with any such expansion would be, as already suggested, that the realities of economic constraints and shortage of stock would prevent local authorities from fulfilling any more substantial duty, at any rate, expeditiously. Duties would then degenerate on closer judicial analysis to obligations simply to do the best available, with the provision of short term or staging post accommodation being inevitable components of any duty. A strong sense of *déjà vu* would then be inescapable.

Although the value of pursuing a claim under the homelessness provisions has, as already demonstrated, been undermined by the 1996 Act and not significantly enhanced by the 1997 piecemeal alterations, it is still advisable to give an outline of the old and new criteria in this sphere. A quick glance at both the 1985 and 1996 Acts would confirm that there is a very large measure of continuity between the two. Indeed, it is, perhaps, surprising that the full panoply of existing definitions and gradations of rights and the differentiation of the intentional and unintentional are largely preserved in the 1996 Act, in view of the convergence in the expectations of the various categories of applicant. Another important aspect of the operation of the homelessness rules is the impact of the Code of Guidance, which is periodically updated – the latest version is in the pipeline – and, frequently, goes into great detail in elucidating the content of the various statutory duties. However, although authorities are required to have regard to the precepts in the Code, they are not directly binding on them and, in recent years, some of the exhortations in the Code have been superseded by judicial fiat. The *Awua* case, shortly to be analysed, is a classic instance of this fragility, since Lord Hoffmann roundly rejected any idea such as 'authorities should not require homeless people to spend a specified period in temporary accommodation or in different types and classes of such accommodation'.

The definition of homelessness

The traditional and unhelpful definition of homelessness is to be found in s 58 of the 1985 Act and the main thrust of it is that 'a person is homeless if he has no accommodation'. The legal definition of homelessness and its relationship to rooflessness is naturally a contentious matter. If homelessness were broadly defined to reflect the inadequacies of substandard accommodation rather than rooflessness *per se*, that, in turn, would put housing authorities under immense pressure. The unquantifiable 'dark figure' of the hidden homeless, people in inadequate accommodation with friends or relatives or elsewhere, is always lurking behind attempts at definition and behind figures of official acceptances as homeless. Conversely, a narrow and restrictive definition would render an elaborate legislative framework superfluous.

Over the years, the upper echelons of the judiciary have certainly acted as zealous social gatekeepers restricting the ambit of the law. A classic earlier example is the case of *R v Hillingdon LBC ex p Puhlhofer* [1986] AC 484, where an ordinary language approach to the unqualified use of the word accommodation meant that a family living with some difficulty with inadequate facilities in one room were, nonetheless, held to have accommodation. The family, with two small children, were living in one room in a guest house and there were no washing or cooking facilities in the room. However, the House of Lords made it clear that not all habitations would count as accommodation; the obvious example of Diogenes in his barrel or a shed in a field with no services would not qualify.

Disquiet about the draconian nature of the *Puhlhofer* decision led to some amendments inserted by s 14(1) of the Housing and Planning Act 1986. Under the amendments, accommodation does not count unless it is 'reasonable' for the applicant to continue to occupy it and reasonableness has a local reference point in terms of general housing circumstances in the district. The current Code of Guidance goes into some detail about the relevant criteria. They include physical conditions, overcrowding, the type of accommodation and violence or the threat of violence from outside the home, such as racial harassment. Interestingly, the criteria also encompass affordability and 'consideration should be given to whether the applicant can no longer pay the housing costs without being deprived of basic essentials, such as food, clothing, heating, transport and other essentials'. In practice, however, the 'reasonableness' requirement is not necessarily much of an encroachment on the discretion of authorities or a significant departure from previous criteria. A typical instance of its recent operation is to be found in *R v Kensington and Chelsea Royal London Borough Council ex p Ben-El-Mabrouk* (1995) 27 HLR 564, where the Court of Appeal, not unmindful of the fact that there were 4,500 houses in multiple occupation in the authority's area, concluded that it was reasonable for the applicant to remain in a property where there were no satisfactory means of escape from, and a real risk of, fire.

Section 58 as amended by the 1986 Act reads as follows:

(1) A person is homeless if he has no accommodation in England, Wales or Scotland.

(2) A person shall be treated as having no accommodation if there is no accommodation which he, together with any person who normally resides with him as a member of his family or in circumstances in which it is reasonable for that person to reside with him;

(a) is entitled to occupy by virtue of an interest in it or by virtue of an order of a court; or

(b) has an express or implied licence to occupy, or in Scotland has a right or permission or an implied right or permission to occupy; or

(c) occupies as a residence by virtue of any enactment or rule of law giving him the right to remain in occupation or restricting the right of another person to recover possession.

(2A) A person shall not be treated as having accommodation unless it is accommodation which it would be reasonable for him to continue to occupy.

(2B) Regard may be had, in determining whether it would be reasonable for a person to continue to occupy accommodation, to the general circumstances prevailing in relation to housing in the district of the local housing authority to whom he has applied for accommodation or for assistance in obtaining accommodation.

In addition, by virtue of s 3, a person is homeless if he has accommodation but cannot secure entry to it, or it is probable that occupation will lead to violence or the threat of it from some other occupier, or it is a question of a moveable structure, vehicle or vessel 'designed or adapted for human habitation and there is no place where he is entitled or permitted both to place it and to reside in it'. Gypsies are clearly included in this last category, and homelessness is likely to be on the increase for them in the wake of the provisions in the Criminal Justice and Public Order Act 1994 to facilitate eviction of unauthorised occupants of private land.

The traditional interpretation of s 58(2) in the Code of Guidance conveys a broad approach to those to be treated as having no accommodation. For instance, it would include those occupying under a licence when the licence has been terminated. Persons asked to leave by friends or relatives would qualify, as would those required to leave hostels or refuges. Those no longer entitled to occupy their dwelling because their landlord has defaulted on mortgage payments on it would also be included.

The recent decision in *Awua* has, along the lines of the *Puhlhofer* decision, created acute controversy as it redefines statutory rights and duties drastically and affects the definition and implications of homelessness as well as the doctrine of intentionality.

The facts were that the applicant had children and was accepted as unintentionally priority need homeless by Tower Hamlets and was given a private sector two bedroom flat as a temporary measure. She was subsequently offered more permanent accommodation, but refused it and was then evicted from the temporary accommodation. She approached Brent for housing because of a previous connection with them and Brent determined that she was intentionally homeless because she had turned down the offer of suitable accommodation from Tower Hamlets. At first instance, the judge granted her judicial review of Brent's decision on the assumption that the temporary accommodation could not constitute settled accommodation – she had not ceased to be homeless and was, therefore, not intentionally homeless.

The Court of Appeal reversed this decision and relied on the established proposition that temporary staging post accommodation could count as settled when it came to assessing intentionality. However, the House of Lords thought that the issue of whether accommodation was or was not settled was only relevant in assessing a chain of causation after 'departure from accommodation which it would have been reasonable to continue to occupy and homelessness separated from that departure by a period or periods of accommodation elsewhere' (Lord Hoffman, p 461).

The House of Lords also determined that it was not only the loss of settled accommodation that could justify a finding of intentional homelessness. The issue in terms of s 58 was whether the accommodation in question was available to her and reasonable for her to continue to occupy. On these facts, although it was temporary accommodation, it satisfied the criteria and she was intentionally homeless. The temporary accommodation enjoyed by Mrs Awua certainly lasted for longer than the stay of those accommodated in refuges and night shelters, so where does the sweeping House of Lords judgment leave those in that predicament? There is authority from *Din v Wandsworth LBC* [1983] 1 AC 657 and *R v Ealing LBC ex p Sidhu* (1983) 2 HLR 45 to the effect that certain short term occupants are still homeless or, as it was expressed in Din:

> I consider that to be homeless and to have found some temporary accommodation are not mutually inconsistent concepts. Nor does a person cease to be homeless merely by having a roof over his head or a lodging, however precarious [p 677].

The *Awua* verdict does not preclude the acceptance of some categories other than the literally roofless as homeless, so it is possible that they satisfy s 58; however, if the accommodation offered to successful full duty applicants is also to be temporary, as sanctioned by *Awua*, there may be little point in establishing a full duty. As will be seen later, the content of the full duty in the Housing Act may be more generous. The further ramifications of the decision will be explored in due course.

THE IMPACT OF THE 1996 ACT

There are no dramatic changes to the definitional aspect of homelessness. Section 175 modifies the wording slightly to state that lack of accommodation 'in the United Kingdom or elsewhere' constitutes the test, rather than accommodation in England Wales or Scotland. Otherwise, the crucial features of homelessness and the threat of homelessness are retained. The apparent generosity of spirit in enlarging the scope of territory should be assessed in the light of the provisions in ss 185 and 186, which contain provision for restricting access to the homelessness rules by persons from abroad deemed ineligible for assistance and by asylum seekers. If asylum seekers and dependents have any accommodation, however temporary, available for their occupation, under s 186 they are disqualified from all help save advice and information.

As in other contexts, the judiciary have anticipated the spirit of these reforms. In *R v Westminster City Council ex p Castelli*; and *R v Same ex p Tristan Garcia* (1996) 28 HLR 125, the rights of HIV positive EU immigrants in relation to Pt II of the 1985 Act were assessed. It was held, against a background of hostility, to 'benefit tourism' that the applicants, with no reasonable prospect of employment in the UK, could not invoke the homelessness legislation and should go home, although no active steps were being taken to repatriate them. They had received letters from the Home Office Immigration and Nationality Department saying that it was not satisfied that they were legally resident in the UK. The judge dismissed their application for judicial review and considered that the duties owed by local authorities, in these circumstances, were substantially the same as if they had been illegal immigrants who had failed to find employment. In his estimation, Parliament, in formulating the homelessness legislation, could not have intended to impose obligations on authorities to persons who were not economically self-sufficient.

The Court of Appeal, however, reversed that decision in February 1996 ((1996) 28 HLR 616) and held that Westminster acted unlawfully in refusing to find accommodation. They stated that the applicants could be described as 'lawfully here'. As Lord Justice Evans put it:

> ... it was sufficient for present purposes to hold that a European national who had, or might have, ceased to be a qualifying person in fact, but who had not been given and overstayed a limited leave to remain and had not been informed that the secretary of state had decided that he should be removed, did not belong to the category of persons 'not lawfully here' who were not to be regarded as 'persons for the purposes of ss 62 and 63'.

As part of the increased focus, in the 1996 Act, on responses to the problem of domestic violence, there is amplification of the criteria on unreasonableness of continued occupation. Whereas the original formulation in s 58(3) of the 1985 Act declares that a person is homeless, albeit with accommodation, if it is probable 'that occupation of it will lead to violence from some other person residing in it or to threats of violence from some other person residing in it and likely to carry out the threats', ss 177 and 178 of the 1996 Act go in for more elaborate and explicit exposition.

Section 177(1) states:

> It is not reasonable for a person to continue to occupy accommodation if it is probable that this will lead to domestic violence against him, or against (a) a person who normally resides with him as a member of his family, or (b) any other person who might reasonably be expected to reside with him. For this purpose 'domestic violence', in relation to a person, means violence from a person with whom he is associated, or threats of violence from such a person which are likely to be carried out.

The meaning of associated person is then elaborately defined in s 178(1). There is always a danger that attempts at exhaustive definition misfire, since the judiciary are capable of regarding any omission as deliberate, but, here, the draftsman does seem to have covered all the bases. A person is associated with another person if:

> ... they are or have been married to each other, they are cohabitants or former cohabitants, they live or have lived in the same household, they are relatives, they have agreed to marry one another (whether or not that agreement has been terminated), in relation to a child, each of them is a parent of the child or has, or has had, parental responsibility for the child.

Threatened with homelessness

It is not just actual, but potential homelessness that is contemplated. Under s 58(4) of the 1985 Act, a person is so threatened if it is 'likely that he will become homeless within 28 days'. Various forms of impending eviction are naturally covered by this and the Code of Guidance has consistently urged local authorities not to demand actual possession orders before agreeing to act. With the introduction of the reasonableness requirement following *Puhlhofer,* there is some danger of confusion between homelessness and the threat of it in view of the fact that it may not be reasonable to stay in occupation that is about to be repossessed. The definition of threatened homelessness is retained in the 1996 Act in s 175(4).

Applications on behalf of minors and persons suffering from mental impairment

Difficult questions have arisen in respect of the rights of the very young and those so incapacitated that they may not be able to understand an offer of accommodation that is made. Is it feasible that, for example, four year old children can make applications in their own right, claiming that they are 'vulnerable' in terms of the legislation? Perhaps, more difficult to assess is the quandary as to whether disabled persons who cannot comprehend proceedings under the legislation are, nonetheless, entitled to benefit from it. It could be asserted that the disabled are catered for under different legislation, but the Housing Act is quite general in its terms. So far as dependent children are concerned, there is the apprehension that their 'vulnerability' and innocence of any intentional homelessness caused by their parents could be used to circumvent the provisions designed to penalise where homelessness is deliberate.

The House of Lords, in *R v Oldham Metropolitan Borough Council ex p Garlick*; *R v Bexley London Borough Council ex p Bentum*; and *R v Tower Hamlets London Borough Council ex p Ferdous Begum* [1993] AC 509, came down solidly behind the view that, in such circumstances, local authorities had no duty to process the applications further. The Bentums had been found by Bexley to be intentionally homeless because they had deliberately omitted to make their mortgage payments. Mr Bentum then applied in the name of his four year old son for accommodation. Similarly, Mrs Garlick had been found to be intentionally homeless after eviction for rent arrears and then applied through her four year old son. According to Lord Griffiths, dependent children of this type did not qualify for priority need consideration in their own right:

> Such a child is, in my opinion, owed no duty under this Act, for it is the intention of the Act that the child's accommodation will be provided by the parents or those looking after him and it is to those people that the offer of accommodation must be made, not to the dependent child.

The further justification for excluding children, who, *prima facie,* might qualify under the 'other special reason' of the vulnerability category of priority need, was the salient point that any more generous view would negate sections of the statute and 'would mean that the disqualification of intentional homelessness had no application to families with dependent children'. This means that the sins of the parents do have to be visited on the children, so far as the homelessness legislation is concerned, unless, as will be discussed later, some innocent spouse or partner can bail out the family.

However, the judge naturally also drew attention to the obligations of local authorities under the Children Act 1989, especially s 20(1)(c), which requires accommodation to be provided for children in the event of 'the person who has been caring for him being prevented (whether or not permanently and for whatever reason) from providing him with suitable accommodation or care'. This means that accommodation of some description must be forthcoming.

What, however, of the predicament of vulnerable and mentally incapacitated adults who, by definition, cannot look elsewhere for accommodation so easily if disentitled to use the homelessness legislation? The House of Lords was unanimous in disallowing the claims by children, but there was a dissenting voice when it came to Ferdous Begum, a 24 year old Bangladeshi woman who could not speak or hear, but could communicate by sign language within the family. In her case, her father had been held to be intentionally homeless, having left accommodation in Bangladesh which the family could reasonably have continued to occupy. It was open to her to argue that her incapacitation prevented her colluding in the damaging decision to leave Bangladesh. Tower Hamlets were not impressed by this argument and turned it against the family by stating that any lack of acquiescence or involvement must also extend to any application on her part for housing. This argument prevailed at first instance, but lost in the Court of Appeal.

Lord Griffiths again came down on the side of the local authority, arguing that 'the Act is primarily to do with the provision of bricks and mortar and not with care and attention for the gravely disabled which is provided for in other legislation'. This seems an attenuated view of the intended scope of the vulnerability section of priority need. The further justification offered boils down to assertion rather than argument:

> But, I can see no purpose in making an offer of accommodation to a person so disabled that he is unable to comprehend or evaluate the offer. In my view, it is implicit in the provisions of the Act that the duty to make an offer is only owed to those who have the capacity to understand and respond to such an offer and, if they accept it, to undertake the responsibilities that will be involved. If a person is so disabled that he cannot do this, he is not left destitute, but is protected by the National Assistance Act.

Bearing in mind that the homelessness legislation privileges those 'vulnerable as a result of old age, mental illness or handicap or physical disability or other special reason', imposing some rationalist filter of cognitive competence goes against the grain of the provisions requiring, for example, method in madness. The only dissenting judge, Lord Slynn, refused to 'read into the statute a requirement of capacity which is not spelled out there, but would give the provisions their ordinary meaning', thereby making much more sense of the law. Undeniably, the pragmatic justification for taking a hard line in cases of apparent circumvention of penalties for intentionality is forceful and could contribute to fairness overall, but it is hard to see how the particular justifications offered by the House of Lords, in this instance, are anything other than meagre and, indeed, at some points, self-contradictory in terms of the obvious purposes underlying the legislation.

PRIORITY NEED

Introduction

The categories of priority need predate the initial legislation in 1977 and have survived intact ever since. Various pressure groups, have at various times, attempted to enlarge the scope of the categories or specifically include groups, such as the HIV positive, but no changes have ever been made. The current Code of Guidance suggests that those suffering from domestic violence should also be included and stresses that authorities should not fetter their discretion by presupposing that, for example, the young single homeless can never be considered vulnerable. A range of suggestions was made while the Housing Bill was proceeding, but none was accepted. There is a power built into the 1985 Act and retained in the 1996 Act for the categories to be altered, if necessary, by the Secretary of State via statutory instrument.

The definition of priority need is to be found in the Housing Act s 59(1):

> The following have a priority need for accommodations:
>
> (a) a pregnant woman or a person with whom a pregnant woman resides or might reasonably be expected to reside;
>
> (b) a person with whom dependent children reside or might reasonably be expected to reside;

(c) a person who is vulnerable as a result of old age, mental illness or handicap or physical disability or other special reason, or with whom such a person resides or might reasonably be expected to reside;

(d) a person who is homeless or threatened with homelessness as a result of an emergency such as flood, fire, or other disaster.

This definition has been reproduced: s 189 of the 1996 Act, with the exception of the redundant second reference to a pregnant woman in category (a). The various categories will be reviewed in turn.

(a) Pregnancy

This is one category under which single mothers are believed, under existing rules, to gain a fast track to permanent housing; presumably, they can also qualify under category (b). Clearly, the sub-section anticipates that the father of the child or some other cohabitee can also qualify; indeed, the father could apply to the authority in his own right. The existing Code of Guidance emphasises that the duration of the pregnancy is immaterial and urges sympathetic consideration of cases where the pregnancy ends before housing has been allocated.

(b) Dependent children

The wording and purpose of this is relatively straightforward. Single parent families currently qualify along with the conventional nuclear family. According to the Code of Guidance, children under 16 years of age qualify as dependents along with those under 19 years in full time education or training or otherwise unable to support themselves. The Code also emphasises that authorities should do their utmost to avoid splitting families, unless such action is necessitated by factors such as child abuse. Where a family is split, it is not open to an authority to apply some test of whether a child is wholly and exclusively dependent on one parent as a means of disclaiming responsibility.

(c) Vulnerability

The vagueness of the definition has put this category under much pressure as the other categories are relatively well defined. The residual 'or other special reason', particularly, invites claims denied elsewhere. The pressure of the 'vulnerability' criteria could intensify after the implementation of Pt VII of the 1996 Act early in 1997. The current Code of Guidance goes into great detail. A 'flexible and pragmatic approach' is advocated towards the elderly and a sensitive and sympathetic attitude to those discharged from psychiatric and other hospitals where mental illness or handicap are involved. Young people have to be subjected to some sort of risk assessment, in view of the various dangers to which they could be exposed, including sexual and financial exploitation.

The case law on vulnerability is also instructive. The established proposition is that vulnerability is not to be taken at large, but to be construed in terms of the housing market or in access to housing, rather than other factors. In an early case, it was stated that 'vulnerability, in the context of the legislation means less able to fend for oneself, so that injury or detriment will result when a less vulnerable man will be able to cope without harmful effects' (*R v Waveney Council ex p Bowers* [1983] 1 QB 238, pp 244–45, *per* Lord Waller). Such formulations are extremely vague and give authorities great leeway for interpretation without falling fall of *Wednesbury* absurdity or perversity criteria.

Subsequent cases on vulnerability have demonstrated great reluctance, on the part of the courts, to entertain judicial review in an area traditionally regarded as one of factual determination and administrative discretion. In *R v Lambeth LBC ex p Carroll* (1988) 20 HLR 142, the court set out the typical approach to judicial review in such instances. First, 'vulnerable' meant less able to fend for oneself when homeless or in finding and keeping accommodation. Secondly, when an applicant claimed to be vulnerable for medical reasons, it was appropriate and necessary for the authority to take account of medical opinion, unless the condition of the applicant was so obvious as to obviate further analysis. Thirdly, medical opinion could, in some circumstances, be conclusive if it covered the question of self-sufficiency in the housing market and clearly related vulnerability to one or more of the criteria set out in s 59. If, however, the vulnerability fell outside the specific conditions itemised and within the residual 'other special reason', then it was up to the local authority to determine if the reason was a special one for the purposes of the section.

That last concession to local authority discretion obviously makes it very difficult to challenge any rejection of a reason as less than special. In conclusion, the court stated that authorities could reasonably make enquiries beyond the medical in assessing vulnerability, as by consultation with social services. On the facts of *Carroll,* the application for judicial review was granted, since the local authority had not explored the question as to whether the applicant was vulnerable for any other special reason, but had seized on an opinion that he was not. This reinforces the point that proper observance of procedure will protect authorities, as questions of medical fact and degree are not justiciable.

Other recent cases have amplified this non-interventionist approach. In *R v Sheffield City Council ex p Leek* (1994) 26 HLR 669, the medical condition at issue (as often, in these appealed cases) was epilepsy, but there was a significant variation of the facts involving a claim by the mother of an 18 year old epileptic to be in priority need; the mother was not vulnerable herself, but was residing with a child claiming that status. The evidence submitted suggested that, although the epilepsy was fairly well controlled by medication, the 18 year old had an immature personality and would encounter emotional, medical and social problems trying to fend for himself outside sheltered accommodation.

The Court of Appeal were happy to endorse statements in the House of Lords encouraging care in the community, as when, in *Garlick* [1993] AC 509, Lord Griffiths said that 'many vulnerable people are cared for in the community by their relatives or other good hearted people'. Lord Justice Neill was happy to accept that carers for the vulnerable could qualify for priority need. On the facts of the case, the council had acted unlawfully in failing to reconsider the case after the initial rejection of priority need status and subsequent submission of evidence from the GP. However, the court declined to give declaratory relief and settle the true status of the applicant, preferring to remit the matter to the council to decide on full consideration of the evidence whether statutory vulnerability had been established.

Another case, *Ortiz v City of Westminster* (1995) 27 HLR 364, is no departure from the trend, but rather adds to the pressure on applicants by homing in on the practical aspects of demonstrating vulnerability in a housing context. The applicant was a woman of 24 with a history of drug addiction and alcoholism who lost accommodation when admitted to a detoxification unit. On leaving the unit, she applied to Westminster for housing, armed with two medical certificates testifying to the problems discharge would cause her in the absence of suitable accommodation. Westminster argued that she was not vulnerable, since there were places available in the private sector or the possibility of bed and breakfast or supervised hostel accommodation. Her application for judicial review of the rejection was unsuccessful and she appealed against the decision.

The Court of Appeal gave her short shrift and argued that she had failed to satisfy the first evidential hurdle in the test for vulnerability, that to some material extent she was less able to obtain suitable accommodation than the ordinary person. The second hurdle, which she had not even reached, was the demonstration that failure to obtain suitable alternative accommodation would make her suffer more than most. The Court rejected her argument that, once she had established that she had a particular need for suitable accommodation and would suffer more than most if she failed to secure it, she was, *ipso facto*, within the statutory definition of vulnerability. There was, in her case, no indication that she would have difficulty in finding accommodation or of her having a need for special accommodation.

The interpretation of vulnerability and 'other special reason', in particular, came under close scrutiny in a recent Court of Appeal decision concerned with the rights of asylum seekers. Any decision favourable to the applicants has received a death blow from the provisions in the 1996 Act, ruling out assistance for asylum seekers through the homelessness legislation, in keeping with the general deprivation of welfare benefits. However, the decision in *R v Kensington and Chelsea Royal London Borough Council ex p Kihara; R v Hammersmith and Fulham London Borough Council ex p Ilunga-Ilunga; R v Westminster City Council ex p Pavlov;* and *R v Islington London Borough Council ex p Araya* (1997) 29 HLR 147 is memorable not just for its citation length, but because any general pronouncements on the vulnerability criterion will still be operative in the post-1996 Act world, given that the whole priority need category has survived intact.

This was another judicial review action, brought by asylum seekers who had not claimed at the point of entry into the UK, but 'in country' and were, therefore, according to the relevant regulations, not entitled to income support and housing benefit. Incidentally, an identically constituted Court of Appeal had, four days earlier, reached the conclusion that the benefit regulations excluding asylum seekers were themselves unlawful in *R v Secretary of State for Social Security ex p Joint Council for the Welfare of Immigrants*; and *R v Secretary of State for Social Security ex p B* [1997] 1 WLR 275. The Home Secretary is determined to reverse that decision through primary legislation.

The basic issue, in the homelessness context, was whether the local authorities in question were correct in holding that ineligibility for State benefit did not constitute a special reason and, therefore, priority need through vulnerability within s 59 of the 1985 Act. At first instance, in April 1996, Mr Justice Popplewell dismissed the applications and held that the applicants were not in priority need because he considered that the vulnerability criterion should be interpreted according to the *eiusdem generis* rule and, hence, 'other special reason' had to be read in the light of the foregoing genus 'old age, mental illness or handicap or physical disability'. Lack of money, or 'financial impecuniosity', as he preferred to call it (is there any other sort of impecuniosity?), was not of the same genus as the preceding factors.

In the Court of Appeal, a very different view was taken of the operation of the vulnerability criteria. Lord Justice Neill expressed dissatisfaction with the approach, suggested as far back as *Bowers*, that there was properly a two stage inquiry: the first stage being to consider whether there was or was not vulnerability; and the second to assess whether such vulnerability arose from any of the factors itemised. He regarded this approach as potentially confusing and stated a preference for treating the whole issue as a composite question. In his view, otherwise, one could look at all the factors pointing to vulnerability in general terms and overlook the fact that such factors might be relevant to establishing some 'special reason' for vulnerability.

The Lord Justice's account of the correct approach, likely to be put under the judicial microscope in the near future, is as follows:

> (1) 'Vulnerable' means vulnerable in the context of a need for housing accommodation.
>
> (2) The *eiusdem generis* rule has no application for the purpose of construing 'other special reason'. In my judgment, this is a free standing category which, though it has to be construed in its context, is not restricted by any notion of physical or mental weakness other than that which is inherent in the word 'vulnerable' itself. Though the word 'reason' is in the singular, I am satisfied that the housing authority would be entitled to look at a combination of circumstances.
>
> (3) The word 'special' indicates that the difficulties faced by the applicant are of an unusual degree of gravity, and are such as to differentiate the applicant from other homeless persons. On the other hand, it is to be remembered that there is a special provision in s 59(1)(d) to cater for persons who are homeless 'as a result of an emergency such as flood, fire or other disaster'.
>
> (4) Though I appreciate the enormous burden placed on housing authorities by the problem of homelessness, the words 'special reason' seem to me to require, as no doubt in fact takes place, a careful examination of the circumstances of the individual applicant.
>
> I turn therefore to the issues which arise in this case. I am satisfied that financial impecuniosity *by itself* is not a special reason within the meaning of s 59(1)(c). To my mind, an absence of means alone does not mark out the applicant's case from the generality of cases to a sufficient degree to constitute a 'special reason'.

Lord Justice Neill continued by arguing that it would be unrealistic to decide the appeal on the basis that the applicant's vulnerability could be attributed to vulnerability viewed in isolation. 'Other special reason' allowed an examination of all the personal circumstances of an applicant, circumstances to include, but not be limited to, physical or mental characteristics or disabilities. Accordingly, he rejected the view of the first instance judge that the preceding words in the section constituted a genus into which 'other special reason 'had to be fitted as a species. On the facts, the applicants were in priority need, because of, *inter alia*, their 'utter poverty and resourcelessness' (Lord Justice Simon Brown).

The picture is, therefore, following this decision that any mechanical two stage test for assessing vulnerability is disapproved and the *eiusdem generis* rule is irrelevant. For what it is worth, although its status is merely advisory, the current Code of Guidance pinpoints factors, such as young people susceptible to financial and sexual exploitation, as likely constituents of 'other special reason' and no one could pretend that such vulnerability is of the same genus as the earlier specific items, if, indeed, they are sufficiently homogeneous to form such a genus. Although it is commonplace that the canons of statutory interpretation are highly flexible, there does not seem to be a recognisable genus in the particular words preceding the crucial phrase, unlike other contexts where there is obviously a general principle to be extracted from particular items. The clichéd illustration of this is that 'guinea pigs, gerbils, hamsters and other animals' can, in context, be taken to exclude wild animals from the concluding general phrase. The approach favoured by the Court of Appeal, in this instance, certainly enables authorities and judges to take a more rounded and realistic view of the individual circumstances of applicants, without being hidebound by artificial rules or technicalities.

In *R v London Borough of Camden ex p Pereira* (1999) 31 HLR 317, there was an endorsement of the composite approach rather than the two stage test derived from *Ortiz*. Mr Pereira was a single person in his 40s with a history of drug addiction, but had been 'clean' for two years. He was unemployed and on income support. Reports on his condition suggested that homelessness was imposing great psychological strain on him and that hostel accommodation, where his history was known, would be inappropriate. Camden applied the *Bowers* formula, as found in successive Codes of Guidance, and decreed that he was not vulnerable, as past addiction did not necessarily create current vulnerability under the Act. The judge was satisfied that their approach was correct and that they had not become enmeshed in the *Ortiz* test. On the facts, there was nothing to suggest that he would meet particular difficulties in finding accommodation or, indeed, was any less capable of fending for himself.

The latest Code of Guidance stresses the need for flexibility in assessing the scope of the important residual phrase 'other special reason'. Paragraph 12.12 states:

> Authorities must keep an open mind and should avoid blanket policies which assume that particular groups of applicants will, or will not, be vulnerable for a special reason. Where an authority considers that an applicant may be vulnerable for a special reason, it will be important to make an in depth assessment of the circumstances of the case; significant factors in determining vulnerability may only emerge over a period of time and once a rapport has been established with the applicant.

AIDS and vulnerability

Local authority practice, in many areas, is to draw the line between the vulnerable priority applicant and the more resilient at the point of symptomatic/asymptomatic HIV. The latest Housing Research Report suggests that, as a minimum, people with severe HIV illness or AIDS should qualify as vulnerable or, at any rate, as a high priority for transfer or placement on a housing waiting list. The report concludes: 'Local authorities should review their allocation policies to ensure that people with AIDS or HIV illness are treated fairly compared to other people with similar levels of illness or disability' (p 11).

(d) Emergency

Perhaps, the most predictable and non-contentious of the statutory obligations relates to various emergencies and disasters and the imposition of such duties can be traced back to the National Assistance Act 1948. As with other sections of the 1985 Act, the pressure in terms of litigation is on the vague concluding formula, in this instance, 'or other disaster'. The Code of Guidance is curiously silent on the interpretation of this category and simply restates the criteria. In *Noble v South Herefordshire DC* (1983) 17 HLR 80, it was held that the similar wording 'or any other disaster' had to be read in context and required something comparable to flood or fire. On that reckoning, a demolition order did not qualify. It may be that a lawful eviction also falls outside this category, but what of unlawful eviction? The high incidence of harassment and illegal eviction in the private sector make this an important question and it was tackled in the recent case of *R v Bristol City Council ex p Bradic* (1995) 27 HLR 584. While the tenant was abroad, the landlord broke into his room, removed and stored his belongings and changed the locks. On his return, the tenant learnt that the landlord was in mortgage arrears and that the occupants of the house were liable to be evicted in a few weeks. He claimed priority need status, but Bristol decided that the illegal eviction did not constitute a 'disaster' and rejected his application. On application for judicial review, Sir Louis Blom-Cooper, who has consistently pushed at the frontiers of the legislation, held that 'disaster' should not be interpreted restrictively and could not have been limited to natural disasters. In any case, floods and fires could be caused by social conditions and personal intervention. In his opinion, each case would depend on its particular facts, but Bristol had misdirected itself in precluding consideration of the claim.

Unsurprisingly, the Court of Appeal upheld Bristol's appeal against that decision. The argument was that Parliament could not have intended that every emergency that caused homelessness could also generate a priority need. Where there was an unlawful eviction, some groups (families with children, for example) would still qualify under another segment of priority need. On the point of statutory interpretation, the Court were impressed that, in the 1985 Act, the word 'any' before 'other disaster' had been omitted. This suggested a clear connection between the event and emergencies and disasters and characterised the sort of event admissible. Lord Justice Roch did indicate that Parliament must have had in mind, along with natural disasters, emergencies, such as deliberately or accidentally started fires. The demarcation point had to be the inclusion of all emergencies caused by physical damage leaving the accommodation uninhabitable. So, unlawful eviction was not an emergency within s 59.

This reasoning seems peculiar in admitting claims by persons violently evicted by arson, but not by more peaceable unlawful means. Mr Bradic was just as homeless as a burnt out case. Is there some implicit deference to the greater trauma attendant on violent destruction, including, presumably, loss of belongings? At any rate, the impact is clear in that, for instance, many single persons, otherwise struggling to attain priority status, have no prospects of gaining accommodation after the ordinary relatively non-violent form of illegal eviction.

SUMMARY OF THE IMPACT OF THE 1996 ACT

The categories of priority need are untouched, save for minor drafting amendments, such as the omission of the second reference to pregnant women. Various supplementary categories, such as the blind, young people aged 16 or 17 years old, young people leaving care and the HIV positive, were suggested at Committee stage in the House of Commons, but proved unacceptable. Obviously, leaving aside the phraseology, the question is what members of a priority group can expect under the revamped legislation and this will shortly be examined.

INTENTIONAL HOMELESSNESS

Of all the criteria found in the legislation, this is by far the most litigated and contentious, with periodic requests from pressure groups for its abolition. Intentionality (to adopt the ugly, but serviceable shorthand) is the product of the arguments surrounding, and one of the prices of passage of, the 1977 Bill and expresses the conflict between allocation on the basis of need and allocation on the basis of preconceptions about merit. The deserving homeless are, supposedly, homeless through no fault of their own, but the feckless or the reckless and other categories are deemed undeserving. The significance of a finding of intentionality is crucial because, traditionally, it reduces entitlement from permanent to temporary housing, despite priority need status. There is evidence of great regional variation in the finding of intentionality, but, in some authorities, it is surprisingly high, presumably through lack of suitable accommodation or lack of sympathy with the legislation. In the case of the widespread problem of rent arrears, some authorities virtually adopt a blanket approach and assume intentionality from the very existence of arrears. Such an approach should be vulnerable to attack as an unlawful fettering of discretion.

The Code of Guidance and the judges have been forced into immense detail without approaching any clarity, as the basic questions of causation and responsibility are so difficult. How far back should causal analysis go? What if the outcome of a causal analysis conflicts with moral intuitions about fault? An instance of this last difficulty is *R v Barnet London Borough Council ex p Rughooputh* (1993) 25 HLR 607. The Court of

Appeal held that a mortgagor who secured a mortgage by false pretences was intentionally homeless when the business financed by the fraudulent application collapsed and the mortgagee recovered possession. However, the homelessness was not caused by any dishonesty, but by the collapse of the business, which was believed to be a sound investment.

The statutory definition of intentionality

Section 60 of the 1985 Act states:

(1) A person becomes homeless intentionally if he deliberately does or fails to do anything in consequence of which he ceases to occupy accommodation which is available for his occupation and which it would have been reasonable for him to continue to occupy.

(2) A person becomes threatened with homelessness intentionally if he deliberately does or fails to do anything the likely result of which is that he will be forced to leave accommodation which is available for his occupation and which it would have been reasonable for him to continue to occupy.

(3) For the purposes of sub-s (1) or (2) an act or omission in good faith on the part of a person who was unaware of any relevant fact shall not be treated as deliberate.

(4) Regard may be had, in determining whether it would have been reasonable for a person to continue to occupy accommodation, to the general circumstances prevailing in relation to housing in the district of the local housing authority to whom he applied for accommodation or for assistance in obtaining accommodation.

Guidance from the Code of Guidance

The Code attempts to exonerate the following from being deemed intentional:

(1) Where it is plausible that the applicant is incapable of managing his/her affairs, for instance, through old age, or mental illness or handicap.

(2) Where genuine financial difficulties occasioned by unemployment or family breakdown or other factors have led to the loss of accommodation. In relation to the common phenomenon of mortgagors in difficulty, the Code expects authorities to assess whether they overextended themselves financially in their initial commitments.

(3) Where an owner-occupier faced with foreclosure or possession proceedings sells before possession is recovered.

In addition, the Code identifies action, such as getting into arrears in ignorance of the availability of housing benefit, as less than deliberate in terms of sub-s (3).

The Code also provides a non-exhaustive list of the types of act and omission which should be deemed deliberate. These are:

(1) Selling a home when there is no risk of losing it, or 'wilful and persistent refusal to pay rent or mortgage payments'.

(2) Neglecting affairs after disregarding advice from experts.

(3) Voluntarily leaving accommodation in the UK or abroad which it would have been reasonable to continue to occupy.

(4) Eviction because of a record of anti-social behaviour such as harassment.

(5) Voluntarily leaving a job with tied accommodation when it would have been reasonable to stay on.

How intentional is intentional?

As can be seen from the wording of the statute, it is the deliberate act or omission leading to homelessness that is subject to scrutiny, rather than any intention to become homeless. As Goodall J characterised it in *Robinson v Torbay Borough Council* [1982] 1 All ER 726:

> In my judgment, if a person deliberately does an act the reasonable result of which is his eviction, and the act is in fact the cause of his eviction, then he becomes homeless intentionally even though he did not appreciate that it would be the cause. Similarly, if a person deliberately does an act and eviction is the likely result of what he deliberately does, then he becomes threatened with homelessness deliberately, even though he may not have appreciated that it would be the likely result.

The difficulties of analysis that are forced on authorities and the judiciary are illustrated by the case of *R v Wandsworth London Borough Council ex p Hawthorne* [1994] 1 WLR 1442. It concerned the common problem of rent arrears. The applicant had five children and was separated from her husband. She was evicted from her secure tenancy because of rent arrears and applied to Wandsworth for assistance. The authority determined that she was intentionally homeless as she had 'wilfully and persistently' failed to pay rent and her reasons for non-payment had been taken into account. In the Court of Appeal, the issue was whether, in assessing how 'deliberate' her actions were, the authority should have considered whether she simply could not make ends meet and could not afford to cover the rent and maintain her children.

Wandsworth had been arguing that her actions had been sufficiently deliberate because she had made a considered choice between two options, to pay or not to pay the rent. Lord Justice Nourse was not impressed by this argument. If consistently applied, it would rule out consideration of causation and basic factors, such as poverty. On a fault based analysis, it was not proper to refuse to house people whose resources were simply inadequate. Therefore, a blanket policy of stigmatising rent arrears as deliberate is unlawful. However, so long as an authority investigates financial circumstances and goes through the process of causal analysis in the individual case, a successful challenge via judicial review is almost inconceivable.

In this connection, another aspect of s 60 is also relevant; the question of reasonable continued occupation. If poverty, rather than profligacy, is the underlying cause, then some mileage can be extracted from the following dictum of Mr Justice Kennedy in *R v Hillingdon London Borough Council ex p Tinn* (1988) 20 HLR 305, where he said:

> As a matter of common sense, it seems to me that it cannot be reasonable for a person to continue to occupy accommodation when they can no longer discharge their financial obligations in relation to that accommodation, that is to say, pay the rent and make the mortgage repayments, without so straining their resources as to deprive themselves of the ordinary necessities of life, such as food, clothing, heat, transport and so forth.

Whose intention is it anyway?

One of the difficulties confronting an authority with family units and other groups is the possibility that an innocent party may apply to be housed and claim to be untainted by the intentionality of another family member. Some notion of acquiescence has, therefore, been established to discriminate between those who could have effectively protested against conduct leading to homelessness and those who appear to have condoned it. As the Code of Guidance puts it, in connection with rent and mortgage payments:

> ... if the applicant was aware of his/her partner's failure and did all he/she could reasonably be expected to do to prevent it, he/she should not normally be regarded as intentionally homeless. Careful consideration in this connection will however, need to be given to cases involving former joint tenants or mortgagors where both are legally responsible for the rent or mortgage payments, regardless of who actually makes the payments.

In the landmark case of *Lewis v North Devon District Council* [1981] 1 All ER 27, the court had to assess the likely intention behind the legislation. Was the purpose to treat someone living with a person who had become homeless intentionally as though tainted or was it better to allow the unintentional actor benefits which the undeserving might share? Mr Justice Woolf enunciated the following general principles; he did not consider that:

> ... a housing authority should close its eyes to the conduct of the other members of the family. On the contrary, in my view, the fact that the Act requires consideration of the family unit as a whole indicates that it would be perfectly proper in the ordinary case for the housing authority to look at the family as a whole and assume, in the absence of material which indicates to the contrary, where the conduct of one member of the family was such that he should be regarded as having become homeless intentionally, that that was conduct to which the other members of the family were a party.
>
> So, for example, where the husband is a tenant and gives notice in circumstances where he is properly to be regarded as having become homeless intentionally, the wife, even though she was not the tenant and she did not give the notice, can be regarded in the same way. In normal circumstances this would be treated as a joint decision. If however, at the end of the day, because of material put before the housing authority by the wife, the housing authority is not satisfied that she was a party to the decision, it would have to regard her as not having become homeless intentionally.

The mark of Cain(e)

A recent illustrative case is *R v Nottingham City Council ex p Caine* (1996) 28 HLR 374. An assured shortholder decided to withhold rent from his landlord because the premises were dilapidated. He received housing benefit during the period that rent was withheld. After eviction by the landlord, he and his partner were found to be intentionally homeless. Their applications were then considered separately and the Director of Housing reported to the relevant council committee that:

> ... there is no evidence that Ms Caine was aware that Mr Coombs had failed to pay the rent on the tenancy or that she knew about the arrears, as she was not the tenant or the claimant of housing benefit. It has to be decided whether she colluded in his withholding rent.

Ms Caine seized on the apparent finding of fact in the first sentence quoted and argued that the committee should have been bound by it. However, both at first instance and on appeal, the court were satisfied that a finding of acquiescence on her part could be justified. She had not made any statements which were adverse to her interest, but the council were entitled to conclude, as a matter of inference, that she had acquiesced. Consideration of the likely course of events in the family unit, such as the receipt of housing benefit of £238.33 per month when the rent was being withheld, made it reasonable to suppose that she knew about and consented to the money being used for the family, rather than for the rent. Similarly, the state of disrepair of the cottage was so obvious that it was unlikely that she was unaware that he was withholding the rent in protest.

This indicates that lying low and saying nothing is not going to exculpate people. The onus is, in effect, on the dissenting partner to prove their opposition. So, the notion of acquiescence assumes great importance; if a person attacks a partner when learning of a debt (*R v West Dorset District Council ex p Phillips* (1985) 17 HLR 336) or is on record in an affidavit that she disassociated herself from her husband's failure to pay the mortgage instalments, then she will not be tainted. Obviously, if someone belatedly learns of some profligacy they cannot be said to have acquiesced in it. For instance, where a partner learns too late of a burden of debt which is catastrophic, she or he cannot be blamed for inactivity in the face of inevitable homelessness.

Causation

Another perennial question is the range and extent of causal enquiries necessitated by the investigation of the reasons for ultimate homelessness. How far back in time is it reasonable to expect authorities to explore in search of the relevant cause? When people are unsettled, there could be many different sets of circumstances to consider. A compromise solution endorsed in the Code of Guidance has been to look back to the last period of settled accommodation and move the analysis forward from there. However, the *Awua* decision has destabilised conventional wisdom here, as elsewhere, and cast doubt on the proposition that settled accommodation is a prerequisite. In future, the test will be simply whether it was reasonable to remain in accommodation, however temporary.

The case law prior to *Awua* indicates that authorities can delve back in time beyond various periods of unsettled accommodation to the important precipitating event, the cause of subsequent homelessness. In *Din v Wandsworth London Borough Council* [1983] 1 AC 657, the family left accommodation which was suitable for all of them without waiting for any possession action for arrears of rent. They then moved to temporary accommodation and were held to be intentionally homeless because they had left the earlier accommodation after being advised to remain. For the family, it was argued that they would have become homeless in any event and there was no causal connection between their initial departure and ultimate homelessness. The House of Lords had no patience with this line of argument and the elaborate counterfactual speculation involved in considering what might have happened if they had not moved.

In *R v London Borough of Harrow ex p Fahia* [1998] 1 WLR 1396, the House of Lords had the opportunity to make a more definitive statement about the circumstances in which the causal chain might be broken. In *Awua*, Lord Hoffmann had stated that he wanted to reserve the question whether occupation of a settled residence was the only way to break the chain and, in *Fahia*, their Lordships again declined to grasp the nettle, since Harrow had conceded that its approach was wrong in only considering the issue of intervening settled accommodation. Mrs Fahia was arguing that there had been a material change in her circumstances since Harrow's decision that she was intentionally homeless. She and her family had been placed in a guest house, initially for a month, but then Harrow allowed her to stay for almost a year at a housing benefit cost of over £500 a week. When Harrow decided to halve her benefit, she faced eviction from the guest house and argued that she faced a materially different set of circumstances warranting fresh investigation of her status. This point was upheld, with some reluctance, in the House of Lords. Lord Browne-Wilkinson indicated that some legislative intervention might be advisable to create a more streamlined method of handling second and subsequent applications.

The meaning of 'available for his occupation' within s 60

Section 75 of the Act qualifies this phrase as follows:

> For the purposes of this Part accommodation shall be regarded as available for a person's occupation only if it is available for occupation both by him and by any other person who might reasonably be expected to reside with him.

The case of *Re Islam* [1983] 1 AC 688 reveals some interesting judicial reasoning on the proposition of availability for occupation. Mr Islam came to the UK from Bangladesh in 1965. Until 1979, he lived in a single room. In 1968, he went back home and married and on subsequent visits fathered four children. When the family came over in 1980, he had nowhere suitable for them and they were evicted from his room. He was deemed to be intentionally homeless and this decision was upheld in the Queen's Bench Division and the Court of Appeal. The Court of Appeal reasoning, in particular, is noteworthy. According to Lord Denning, the applicant was intentionally homeless because he had deliberately given up 'available' accommodation in Bangladesh. Sir Denys Buckley took the view that bringing the family over made the single room unavailable for his occupation. Alternatively, the combined accommodation in Uxbridge and Bangladesh should be considered 'available accommodation'. This seems to be taking 'two homes' split family logic too far. The House of Lords reluctantly conceded that he could not be intentionally homeless, as he had never abandoned accommodation adequate to house him and his family – those who might reasonably be expected to reside with him.

Because of housing pressure, virtually every conceivable aspect of the legislation has been explored in the quest for accommodation. In *R v Newham LBC ex p Dada* (1994)

The Times, 29 July, Sir Louis Blom-Cooper advanced the proposition that an unborn child could constitute a 'person' as in 'any other person who might reasonably be expected to reside with him' in s 75. Mrs Dada was pregnant when she approached Newham under Pt III of the Act. They naturally conceded priority need and offered her one room accommodation on a permanent basis. She refused the offer as she considered it unsuitable. The attitude of the council was that, as two bedroom accommodation was in shorter supply than one bedroom, she should be offered somewhere to live for the time being and could always apply for a transfer when the baby was born.

Sir Louis Blom-Cooper acknowledged that 'person' normally meant a living person, but claimed that it could include an unborn child on a purposive reading of the statute. The policy was to bring families together, if not keep them together, and a couple in similar circumstances to the Dadas were entitled to expect that the accommodation offered would accommodate the extra person. He thought it strange and unnecessarily disruptive to expect people to move into accommodation that would almost immediately become unsuitable and then have to wait for a transfer. This was another valiant attempt to go against the grain of constraints in allocation and, presumably, prioritise families with children within the priority group collective. However, on any orthodox linguistic analysis, the attempt is doomed to failure, since, surely, babies are more than persons 'who might reasonably be expected to reside' with applicants? What was presumably intended by the formula in s 75 was split families, as in the *Islam* case, other close relationships and carers. In March 1995, the Court of Appeal reasserted the status quo and reversed Sir Louis's judgment ([1996] QB 507). They could find nothing in Pt III of the Act to alter the interpretation of 'person' from its ordinary and natural meaning: that of a living person; someone alive at the time when the offer of accommodation was made.

Intentionality and mental illness

The concept of intention is difficult enough without enmeshing it with that of mental illness. What should the position be where a person is presumably in priority need by virtue of vulnerability occasioned by the illness, but is also alleged to be intentionally homeless? In *Ex p B (Homelessness)* (1994) *The Times*, 3 May, the court explored this connection. Mr Justice Harrison followed the Code of Guidance in finding a distinct difference between vulnerability making people relatively less able to cope and a finding of intentionality based on an applicant's ability to manage her own affairs. It may seem paradoxical that someone can be prioritised by mental illness, but downgraded by method in their madness, but it confers some flexibility on authorities in tackling such cases. The policy aspiration, in such instances, is to provide long term accommodation where possible, rather than expect the individual to take the initiative in finding somewhere to live.

Adequacy of reasons for a finding of intentionality

An important issue in respect of all decisions notified to applicants under the Act is the intelligibility and quality of the relevant reasons. There is a trend, in administrative law, towards greater transparency and accountability in areas such as this, although, clearly, it is difficult for authorities under pressure not to keep applicants waiting for decisions to come up with highly polished ratiocination. As the Code of Guidance puts it in para 4.8, 'inquiries should be careful but not over elaborate'. The statute itself, in s 64, simply requires the local authority to notify the applicant of the reasons for the decision, but says nothing about the quality of any reasons. There is no statutory requirement to give reasons in other areas of the homelessness rules, such as 'suitability' of accommodation under s 69 and, in *R v Kensington and Chelsea Royal London Borough Council ex p Grillo* [1995] NPC 85, the Court of Appeal refused to impose a general common law duty.

In *R v London Borough of Islington ex p Hinds* (1996) 28 HLR 302, a familiar pattern emerged of Sir Louis Blom-Cooper attempting to refine the quality of reasoning and the Court of Appeal coming to the rescue of the local authority. In the present instance, Sir Louis thought that it was necessary for decisions to separate out fact from value judgment and for the facts to be explicitly stated as findings, rather than merely matters taken into account. This requirement would facilitate the process of judicial review. On the facts, he was satisfied that the decision letter contained the faults indicated: 'Its primary failure is to mix up findings of fact, other relevant factual considerations and the conclusions reasonably to be drawn from fact; and to leave the reader puzzled as to the reasoning process.'

However, the Court of Appeal dissented and said that less demanding principles were well established. In *City of Gloucester v Miles* (1985) 17 HLR 292, Lord Justice Parker had settled the requirements as follows. The notice must state:

(1) That the authority is satisfied that the applicant became homeless intentionally.

(2) When he is considered to have become homeless.

(3) Why he is said to have become homeless at that time, that is, what is the deliberate act or omission in consequence of which it is concluded that at that time he ceased to occupy accommodation which was available for his occupation.

(4) That it would have been reasonable for him to continue to occupy it.

Lord Justice Otton also analysed the approach in *R v London Borough of Croydon ex p Graham* (1994) HLR 286, where it was stated (p 291):

> I readily accept that these difficult decisions are decisions for the local authority and certainly a pedantic exegesis of letters of this kind would be inappropriate. There is, nonetheless an obligation under the Act to give reasons and that must impose on the council a duty to give reasons which are intelligible and which convey to the applicant the reasons why the application has been rejected in such a way that if they disclose an error of reasoning the applicant may take such steps as may be indicated.

On the strength of these pronouncements, the Court of Appeal confirmed the soundness of the reasons given, although there did seem to be some factual confusion in the decision letter about which accommodation constituted the 'settled' accommodation and a lack of separation of fact from value judgment. The court preferred a realistic and pragmatic approach to the idealistic attitude taken by Sir Louis and the message to local authorities is, therefore, that a far from ideal presentation of reasons will be acceptable.

This latitude to authorities in notifying reasons does, however, have its limits. Sometimes, authorities will give reasons subsequently found to be defective and then attempt to substitute cogent ones. In *R v Westminster City Council ex p Ermakov* [1996] 2 All ER 302, the council justified a finding of intentional homelessness and then sought to have different reasons taken into account at judicial review stage. The Court of Appeal disagreed with the surprisingly hard line taken at first instance by Sir Louis Blom-Cooper against the applicant and stressed the significance of the conclusion to s 64(4) of the 1985 Act: 'they shall, at the same time, notify him of their reasons.' There was no objection to elucidation of reasons in court, but no justification for complete alteration.

Intentional homelessness and criminality

Just as in the area of general allocation policy, there are official concerns expressed in successive Codes of Guidance that investigation of intentionality must be individualised and not based on general policy preconceptions. In recent times, the media focus on paedophilia and the dangers posed to local communities has certainly not facilitated the task of local authorities required to apply the test of 'the fair minded bystander' in determining whether homelessness following incarceration is intentional. In *R v Hounslow London Borough Council ex p R* (1997) 29 HLR 939, the applicant had been given seven years imprisonment after various indecent assaults on children. He had to end his council tenancy, as he could not keep up the rent payments. On release, he applied to Hounslow, who found him to be intentionally homeless because the offences were deliberate acts in consequence of which he lost his original accommodation.

The language of s 60 would appear to require a straightforward analysis in terms of causation, but the test has been refined in various cases, such as *Robinson v Torbay BC* [1982] 1 All ER 726. The judge relied on the following commonsensical quotation from that case:

> I think that, if a man has been evicted, then he became homeless intentionally if the fair minded bystander could say to himself 'He asked for it'. If his conduct is such as to drive his landlord to evict him and if the fair minded bystander could say of the person evicted, 'Well I'm very sorry, but he asked for it'.

On such a test, it is not surprising that the judge dismissed the application for judicial review. The circumstances of this case are relatively clear cut, but, presumably, the same logic could be applied to offenders who are evicted after their past is discovered. Some commentators did not think that the unfavourable outcome spelled disaster for future applicants with such criminal convictions. The Chartered Institute of Housing, for example, argued that the onus would still be on the local authority to show that the person was involved in criminal activity, knowing that a conviction would attract a long custodial sentence, but that does not seem to be an enormous evidential burden on an authority.

THE HOUSING ACT 1996 AND INTENTIONALITY

As indicated earlier, the apparatus of intentionality is retained, although the difference in the practical outcome of successful applications as between the intentional and unintentional is slight. One innovation, in s 202, of the right to request review of any decision, entails the production of reasons for a decision on review. This requirement does not appear to involve the production of a full set of reasons for the original decision, but, possibly, a statement of satisfaction that the inquiries were properly conducted and the correct view taken of the available evidence. There is a further right of appeal to the county court on points of law.

There are two modifications to the definitional criteria designed to tighten up the law still further. 'Sham evictions' are specifically targeted in s 191(3), which states:

> A person shall be treated as becoming homeless intentionally if:
>
> (a) he enters into an arrangement under which he is required to cease to occupy accommodation which it would have been reasonable for him to continue to occupy; and
>
> (b) the purpose of the arrangement is to enable him to become entitled to assistance under this Part, and there is no other good reason why he is homeless.

The righteous indignation at this perceived social evil – including family expulsions – is obvious, but it is not clear that the case of collusion cannot be handled by the existing criteria in sub-s (1). It is also questionable whether people will bother to collude to become entitled to temporary accommodation. The latest Code of Guidance (draft March 1999) stresses that the onus is on local authorities to satisfy themselves about any collusion and that hearsay or unfounded suspicions will be insufficient.

Sub-section (4) of s 191 introduces a new category of intentional homelessness, where other suitable accommodation is available and the requisite advice and assistance have been given and the applicant fails to obtain accommodation when it would have been reasonable to secure it and then re-applies. This could be important as, if suitable accommodation is of a low standard because of local housing conditions, applicants can simply be referred to short term lets available in the local newspaper.

Local connection

When the Housing (Homeless Persons) Bill was going through Parliament in 1977, one of the moral panics was about 'magnet' authorities at airports, railway termini and attractive seaside towns being swamped by applicants who had no links with the authorities in question, but were simply attracted to them. These lodestone local authorities were bailed out by the focus on local connection. The ambition was also to stop applicants being shuttled between authorities indefinitely. It is only full duty applicants, those who are unintentionally priority need homeless, who are eligible for transfer in this way.

Transferring the duty

Section 67 of the 1985 Act states:

(2) The conditions for referral of an application to another local housing authority are:

(a) that neither the applicant nor any person who might reasonably be expected to reside with him has a local connection with the district of the authority to whom his application was made;

(b) that the applicant or a person who might reasonably be expected to reside with him has a local connection with the district of that other authority; and

(c) that neither the applicant nor any person who might reasonably be expected to reside with him will run the risk of domestic violence in that other district.

Definition of local connection

Section 61 states:

(1) References in this Part to a person having a local connection with the district of a local housing authority are to his having a connection with that district:

(a) because he is, or in the past was, normally resident in that district, and that residence is or was of his own choice; or

(b) because he is employed in that district; or

(c) because of family associations; or

(d) because of special circumstances.

A typical instance is the case of *Re Betts* [1983] 2 AC 613. The applicants became unintentionally homeless when they were living in Eastleigh in Hampshire. Prior to that, they had lived in Blaby in Leicestershire. Both authorities agreed that Blaby should have the responsibility for housing the couple, as they had lived there for several years and only around six months in Hampshire. The Betts wanted to stay in Hampshire. The Court of Appeal, in allowing the appeal against the rejection of the application for judicial review of the decision to return to Blaby, took the view that too rigid an interpretation of 'normally resident' had been applied. The House of Lords, however, thought differently and emphasised the importance of focusing on the existence of a local connection. Local connection meant far more than normal residence. In the words of Lord Brightman, 'It must be built up and established; by a period of residence; or by a period of employment; or by family associations which have endured in the area; or by other special circumstances which spell out a local connection in real terms'.

A recent illustration of how not to apply the criteria is to be found in *R v Slough Borough Council ex p Khan* (1995) 27 HLR 492. The decision letter stated that the was no local connection with Slough 'because the applicants had not secured accommodation for six months or more in the borough'. There were, however, long standing connections with the borough through a number of relatives. The application for judicial review was granted because the decision was flawed by lack of reference to family associations.

There is a national Agreement on Procedures for Referrals of the Homeless and a system of arbitration in the event of disagreement.

This Local Authority Agreement came under scrutiny in the case of *R v London Borough of Ealing ex p Fox* (1998) 95(11) LSG 35, where the definition of the elusive phrase in s 61, 'employed in that district', had to be considered. According to the Agreement, any employment had to be more than casual to qualify, but did that also connote paid, rather than unpaid, work? The judge was satisfied that an extended ordinary language approach to 'employed' was appropriate and ruled that Ealing had been mistaken in supposing that voluntary work in their area fell outside the definition. The applicant was granted judicial review of Ealing's decision to refer him to Solihull in Birmingham, since he had never lived there and it was inconsistent to count his voluntary work there in the past as constituting a local connection. So far as 'family associations' within s 61 were concerned, it was ruled that an uncle was less than sufficient; what was required on the authority of *R v Hammersmith and Fulham LBC ex p Avdic* (1998) 30 HLR 1 was a closer connection, such as parent, child or sibling.

LOCAL CONNECTION AND THE 1996 ACT

The criteria in the 1996 Act have necessarily become more elaborate to accommodate other innovations, such as the new reduced duty under s 197, where other suitable accommodation is available, but the fundamental structure appears unchanged. Full duty persons meeting the basically unaltered criteria for referral to another local housing authority do not initially have to go through the filter in s 197. By virtue of s 200 of the Act, where an authority tells an applicant that it intends to or has already duly notified another authority, it ceases to be under any interim duty to accommodate under s 188 and it is not subject to the main housing duty in s 193, but has to secure that accommodation is available for occupation while the outcome of the proposed referral is determined.

If the referral conditions are not met, the notifying authority has to secure that accommodation is available until it has settled the s 197 question, whether other suitable accommodation is available in the district. If there is, in its estimation, such suitable accommodation, the duty dwindles to the provision of such advice and assistance 'as the authority consider is reasonably required' to enable the applicant to get accommodation. If there is apparently no such suitable accommodation in the district, then the full duty, under s 193, becomes operative. The notified authority is required to proceed in the same fashion.

Protection of property of homeless persons and persons threatened with homelessness

A duty which is of practical importance, but whose legal limits have not been investigated in litigation is that of safeguarding the personal property of applicants. It arises, characteristically, where there is reason to believe that a person is homeless or threatened with homelessness. It can involve entering, at reasonable hours, the applicant's usual or most recent residence and taking steps to protect property by storing it or arranging for it to be stored. The obligation is re-enacted virtually identically in the Housing Act, ss 211 and 212.

The content of the various duties

Having outlined the various criteria and categories of central importance, it is necessary to describe the implications of particular findings within the Pt III structure and ways of challenging particular determinations and even gaining compensation in some circumstances. Once again, the implications of *Awua* and the impact of the Housing Act will have to be examined.

Initial duties of investigation

Under s 62 of the 1985 Act, where an authority is approached and they have reason to believe that the applicant is homeless or threatened with homelessness, they have to make the inquiries necessary to determine status. If the applicant is believed to be in a priority need category, the authority has a duty to make accommodation available pending the outcome of the full inquiry. When the inquiries are complete, the authority must give the applicant a reasoned notification of their findings.

Outline of various duties

In respect of full duty applicants (priority need unintentionally homeless), s 65 then spells out the obligation 'to secure that accommodation becomes available for his occupation'. For the intentionally homeless in priority need, the duty is to 'secure that accommodation is made available for his occupation for such period as they consider will give him a reasonable opportunity of securing accommodation for his occupation' and to furnish him with appropriate advice and assistance to that end. The intentionally homeless not in priority need have merely the entitlement to appropriate advice and assistance.

For full duty persons threatened with homelessness, the duty in s 66 is 'to secure that accommodation does not cease to be available for occupation'. Other ranks of those threatened with homelessness, such as those not in priority need or the intentionally homeless, are merely entitled to advice and assistance.

To complete this thumbnail sketch, authorities, under s 69, may perform their duties as outlined either by providing suitable accommodation themselves, securing it from some other person or by giving such advice and assistance as will so secure it. In assessment of suitability, authorities must have regard to the provisions in the 1985 Act relating to slum clearance, overcrowding and multiple occupation.

Interim duty to accommodate

The interim duty to accommodate the possibly priority need homeless is an integral part of any welfare safety net and the proposal to abolish the duty, pending the outcome of any decision, led to a flurry of opposition as the Bill was being processed and, eventually, the duty was reintroduced. It is in s 188 and it is specified there that the duty arises irrespective of any possibility of referral to another authority. The duty, however, ceases when the authority's decision is notified to the applicant, even if the applicant requests a review of the decision under the new provisions in s 202. The authority has the option, but not the obligation, to continue to secure that accommodation is available pending the outcome of the review.

R v London Borough of Camden ex p Mohammed (1998) 30 HLR 315 confirmed that it was lawful for an authority, save in exceptional circumstances, to refuse to continue to provide interim accommodation on cessation of the duty and pending the outcome of any review.

It is stated in s 197(6) that the suitable alternative accommodation filter has no application to the s 188 and other interim duties, so, at least, there are no gaping holes in the safety net (save for persons from abroad and asylum seekers).

In *R v London Borough of Ealing ex p Surdonja* [1999] 1 ALL ER 566, it was established that the specifications in s 206 of the 1996 Act apply also to the execution of the interim duty in s 188, since the duty forms part of 'housing functions', as stipulated in s 206. In this instance, Ealing had offered a family 'split accommodation' – rooms some distance apart – and had contravened the Act. The arrangement also fell foul of s 176, which specifies that accommodation is only available for occupation if it can also house those who normally live with the applicant or might reasonably be expected to live with him/her.

Erosion of the full duty

Although, as was emphasised ultimately in the *Awua* case, the Housing Act 1985 contains no reference, in crucial sections, to accommodation being permanent or settled, that assumption underpinning the Code of Guidance and some adjudication for many years. The Code of Guidance stated that the legislation made it clear that the accommodation secured had to be 'long term settled accommodation, commonly referred to as "permanent"'. This is, clearly, an optative interpretation. More realistically, the judiciary have narrowed the ambit of the duty, over the years, to the proposition that the obligations of authorities are indefinite, but that, as suitable long term accommodation may not be immediately available, the duty on authorities can be satisfied by the provision of staging post accommodation – a series of temporary lettings, if necessary, before any more permanent accommodation is secured.

The case of *R v Brent London Borough Council ex p Macwan* (1994) 26 HLR 528 shows how far the law had come before the denouement in *Awua*. The applicant had three children and was clearly a full duty person. She told Brent that she wanted to live in the northern part of the borough, where the waiting time on the general waiting list was two years. Brent offered her immediate council accommodation on an estate, but she refused. Thereafter, it was agreed that the offer would be withdrawn and a further offer made following a medical report. While the report was being compiled, the applicant requested and was granted 'second stage accommodation' in the private sector.

So, the policy of leaving people in temporary accommodation (in this case, three years), unless there were strong medical or social reasons for granting more permanent accommodation, came under scrutiny. For the applicant, it was argued that the policy contravened the Code of Guidance and was too inflexible as it took insufficient account of the needs of individual applicants. Brent claimed that the duty on authorities fell short of the immediate provision of permanent accommodation and was simply to provide housing that was suitable in terms of s 69. Staging post accommodation on the way to ultimate permanent accommodation was, therefore, legitimate.

In the Court of Appeal, Lord Justice Leggatt said that, although s 65 did not state that the accommodation had to be permanent or immediately available, it had to be secured without any time limit and was, therefore, indefinite. 'Suitable', in s 69, had to be given a very flexible interpretation to embrace questions of fact and degree and could include such factors as the size of the applicant's household, the applicant's preferences for location and type of accommodation and the general availability of accommodation within the authority's area. Competition from others for scarce resources was another factor. In the circumstances, therefore, Brent's policy was not irrational in that they had around 2,000 homeless families on their books and were, in fact, making sensible and flexible use of scarce resources.

The applicant's accommodation was accordingly suitable and the length of the lease would give her a period of stability before the eventual move into permanent accommodation. Thus, there is no problem on this reasoning in staging post accommodation. If Brent had been more inflexible and had ruled out the possibility of early transfer from temporary accommodation, even with strong medical or social evidence, its policy might have been deemed unlawful as too much of a blanket approach, but they incorporated the requisite flexibility.

Another case which shows how comprehensively the ground was cleared in partial preparation for *Awua* is *R v Wandsworth BC ex p Crooks* (1995) 27 HLR 660. With the diminution of local authority housing stock and the lack of other alternatives, housing in the private sector is the reality for many homeless persons. In *Crooks*, some of the arguments about such provision reached their logical conclusion. Was it sufficient, in terms of s 65, and was satisfaction of the full duty for assured shortholds to be provided?

Wandsworth met its obligations to full duty applicants by organising private sector assured shorthold tenancies for 12 to 18 months, with a reasonable expectation that the tenancies would be renewed. This picks up on a section of the Code of Guidance which suggests that the prospect of renewal for a reasonable duration could well make the accommodation 'settled'. However, that part of the Code is concerned with circumstances in which assured shortholds could be considered settled for the purposes of intentionality. Sir Louis Blom-Cooper was in more pragmatic vein than usual and accepted that 'permanent' was an unhelpful word, as it suggested an obligation to guarantee tenure or at least provide very long undisturbed occupation. 'Settled' was the more appropriate word and encompassed not only sustained occupation, but also more short term residence. So, an assured shortholder, paradoxically, could obtain 'settled' accommodation, either within the terms of the initial agreement or via the expectation of continuity. On this reading of the Act, the Code of Guidance is mistaken in saying that local authorities should not require homeless people to spend a specified period in temporary accommodation as a matter of policy. However, the shorthold initial periods were longer than the norm of six months, so there could be a cut off point where insecurity makes it impossible to say the accommodation is settled.

The impact of Awua

The significance of this decision, the facts of which have already been outlined, is largely in dispelling any lingering assumptions about permanent or even settled accommodation. In the post-1996 Act world, its importance will be diminished, but not extinguished, as pre-Housing Act 1996 cases will continue to filter through and there are wide ranging pronouncements in the case affecting elements other than the full duty, such as intentional homelessness.

Lord Hoffmann, giving the sole judgment (unfortunate echoes of *Street v Mountford*), pinpointed the fact that there is no reference to 'settled' in s 60, the definitional section on homelessness. He outlined the history, including *Puhlhofer*, that led to the insertion of the reasonable continuity of occupation requirement and commented on the interaction between the concepts of unintentional and intentional homelessness. He continued:

> If the accommodation is so bad that leaving, for that reason, would not make one intentionally homeless, then one is in law actually homeless. But, there is nothing in the Act to say that a local authority cannot take the view that a person can reasonably be expected to occupy accommodation which is temporary.

There could be a cut off point, as in *Puhlhofer*, where it might no longer be reasonable, but there was nothing in the legislation either in s 58 or s 60 to suggest that accommodation had to be 'settled'.

Where did the presupposition of 'settled' come from? Lord Hoffmann traced its origins to cases on intentionality, such as *Dyson v Kerrier District Council* [1980] 1 WLR 1205 and *Lambert v Ealing Borough Council* [1982] 1 WLR 550. The upshot of these cases was that, if there were a causal link between leaving settled accommodation and ultimate homelessness, that link would not be broken by intervening periods of temporary occupation. Thus, in the *Lambert* case, the applicant had a couple of holiday lets after uprooting himself and family from home in France. As Lord Denning put it, 'they were in no way settled so as to entitle them to ignore the original cause of their homelessness'.

Having disposed of the requirement of settled or permanent accommodation for the purposes of ss 58 and 60, Lord Hoffmann continued by asserting that the same proposition applied to the full duty obligations under s 65(2), knowing that he was going against the settled opinions of the courts and the Code of Guidance. Again, he attempted to locate the source of the misconception about the duty. The first contributory factor was the line of authorities already mentioned, such as *Dyson*, but he was satisfied they had nothing to do with the meaning of accommodation elsewhere in the Act. The second source of error was judicial attempts to summarise the difference between duties to the unintentionally and intentionally homeless. Through this route, with statements, such as that of Lord Brightman in *Puhlhofer*, p 512: 'indefinite accommodation if not intentionally homeless, temporary accommodation if intentionally homeless,' the illusion of permanence for the full duty developed.

According to Lord Hoffmann, the distinction lay in limited duties versus potentially unlimited duties. He continued:

> At the end of the period which the council considers enough to give the intentionally homeless person a reasonable opportunity to find accommodation, the council can require him to leave. If he consequently becomes homeless, he will not on that account have any claim under the Act. An unintentionally homeless person, on the other hand, cannot be required to leave the accommodation provided under s 65(2) unless he is either provided with alternative accommodation or there is a reason why his consequent homelessness will not give rise to a further duty under s 65(2). In this sense the duty to accommodate is indefinite, but it is not in my view legitimate to construe it as a duty to provide permanent accommodation.

So, the full duty, as conceived by Lord Hoffmann, appears to be a permanent duty to provide, if necessary, impermanent accommodation. He was, ironically, scathing about the artificiality involved in accepting the staging post approach – temporary accommodation with a commitment to more permanent in future – as satisfying that duty. In his view, it made it difficult to tell when authorities duties began and ended.

The traditional emphasis on permanence was the product of confusion between general housing duties and lifeline legislation. He endorsed the comment of Lord Brightman in *Puhlhofer* where he said:

> It is an Act to assist persons who are homeless, not an Act to provide them with homes. It is intended to provide for the homeless a lifeline of last resort, not to enable them to make inroads into the local authority's waiting list of applicants for housing. Some inroads there are probably bound to be, but in the end the local authority will have to balance the priority needs of the homeless on the one hand and the legitimate aspirations of those on the housing waiting list on the other hand.

So, the full duty was as baldly stated in s 65(2): simply to secure that accommodation became available for occupation. Admittedly, that accommodation had to be 'suitable' within s 69(1), but that had nothing to do with permanence, but rather more to do with the physical state of the property and possibly with its affordability. He concluded:

> If the tenure is so precarious that the person is likely to have to leave within 28 days without any alternative accommodation being available, then he remains threatened with homelessness and the council has not discharged its duty. Otherwise it seems to me that the term for which the accommodation is provided is a matter for the council to decide.

Merits of the Awua *decision*

Can Lord Hoffmann's approach to the homelessness legislation be justified? At the level of pragmatism and sympathy with the drift of government policy, it is faultless and, as demonstrated, it is the culmination of a process of erosion of traditional attitudes and interpretations. From a legalistic approach to statutory interpretation, it can also be seen as impeccable, as none of the magic words, like 'permanent' or 'settled', have ever appeared in the legislation and it is open to and, perhaps, even incumbent on, the House of Lords to eradicate errors of interpolation. However, from a purposive perspective, mindful of the initial desire in 1977 to get away from the plight of those in temporary accommodation or shuttled between different departments of the same authority, it is bizarre. What is the point of constructing the apparatus of full and lesser duty and penalising intentionality so harshly if the first prize in the shape of 28 days is not worth pursuing and, possibly, less valuable than the second prize: temporary accommodation for the intentionally homeless? If there is provision in s 22 of the Housing Act 1985 requiring reasonable preference to be given to certain categories, including the statutorily homeless, why bother with Pt III of the Act, save to define certain candidates for reasonable preference?

Strictly speaking, the pronouncements about the nature of the full duty are *obiter dicta* and persuasive, rather than binding because the precise legal issue in *Awua* involved the interpretation of intentional homelessness. In practice, only the House of Lords will be in a position to revert to the previous legal criteria and it is unlikely that a different view of the 'lifeline' legislation will be taken in the present political climate.

The impact of Mansoor

Since many of the pronouncements of Lord Hoffmann might, at first blush, appear to be *obiter*, it is instructive to see how *Awua* has been subsequently applied in the Court of Appeal, especially in *R v Wandsworth LBC ex p Mansoor* (1997) 29 HLR 801. There are still some doctrinal loose ends in the wake of *Awua*, notably the minimum or threshold that would satisfy the law's requirements – described by Lord Justice Evans as 'the temporal element in the offer of accommodation'.

The agreements under review were relatively lengthy assured shorthold tenancies: one for 18 months with a clause for renewal if both parties agreed; and one for 12 months with the possibility of insertion of a renewal clause. The claimants argued that such tenancies were inadequate in terms of the duty in s 65(2) of the 1985 Act.

The Master of the Rolls, Sir Thomas Bingham, had no patience with arguments that Lord Hoffmann's remarks about permanence and the full duty were *obiter*, since *Awua* turned on intentionality. He was sure that it was correct to read 'accommodation' in the same way throughout the statute and, in any case, asserted that the decision was of high persuasive authority and correct in principle. He was convinced that the terminology of 'permanent' or 'indefinite' was inappropriate, 'but it could, in any event, be said that the offers made to these appellants were of indefinite duration'.

Of all the adjectives bandied about in this context, 'indefinite' is, perhaps, the most unfortunate, as it is irredeemably ambiguous and worthy of closer judicial scrutiny. At one level, it can be interpreted, as suggested by Lord Hoffmann, that the *obligation* never ends if the preconditions continue to be met, so that, in that sense, 'indefinite' means 'infinite', but the *accommodation* supplied could take the form of successive short lets in different locations. Another sense, as apparently deployed in *Mansoor*, is that of the offers being of indefinite duration, since it was uncertain whether they would last for 18 months or two years or whatever. This second sense obviously creates a lower threshold for satisfying the full duty than the prior interpretation.

At any rate, the Court of Appeal were satisfied that the *Awua* approach was not based on ignorance of previous authority or relevant parts of analogous legislation. There was, moreover, nothing objectionable about rewriting the Code of Guidance, and there was no point in rehearsing on the basis of *Pepper v Hart* [1993] AC 593 any justifications to be found in Hansard debates on earlier legislation, such as the Housing and Planning Bill 1986 or the Asylum and Immigration Appeals Bill 1993 and, even, the Housing (Homeless Persons) Bill 1977.

The temporal element in the offer of accommodation

One of the judges, Lord Justice Evans, was, however, anxious that the total acceptance of the logic of *Awua* should not obliterate all analysis of expectations of authorities under s 65(2). Even if 'permanent, settled or indefinite' accommodation was a thing of the past:

> ... this does not mean that there can never be cases where it is *Wednesbury* unreasonable to offer something less than what has been meant, as I understand the authorities, by 'settled' accommodation. One example could be a young family with dependent children of school age who could reasonably expect to remain in the same area, if not the same home, for a period of years.

This, therefore, represents a moderating principle on the apparent *carte blanche* given to authorities by *Awua*. The Lord Justice supported this approach by contrasting the terms of s 65(2) with the incontestably temporary duty in s 65(3), 'for such period as they will consider will give him a reasonable opportunity of securing accommodation for his occupation'.

What about 'interim' accommodation? On a pessimistic reading of *Awua*, the rejection of permanence could imply that a short term offer satisfied the full duty and, therefore, 'interim' accommodation might become redundant. Lord Justice Evans was reluctant to accept this argument. 'If there is some minimum requirement as to security of tenure, which is dependent on the circumstances of each case and, in particular, on the ground or grounds on which the applicant has established a priority need, then there may be cases where an offer which is sufficient to discharge the duty cannot be made at once.'

The content of the new full duty, as amended in 1997

The unintentionally homeless priority need applicant – the full or main duty person – is treated rather differently under the new rules, the 1996 Act, as amended by the incoming Labour administration. Broadly speaking, where the authority is satisfied that there is other suitable accommodation available for the applicant in the district, the duty in s 197, is merely to provide the applicant with such advice and assistance as will be reasonably necessary to help the applicant secure it. The accommodation in question must be suitable for the applicant and his/her household and, as pointed out earlier, the Homelessness (Suitability of Accommodation) (Amendment) Order 1997 SI 1997/1741 states that accommodation must be available for occupation for two years at least, to be suitable. This means that the rights of applicants under old and new rules are substantially the same.

Where a local authority is, however, satisfied that suitable accommodation of this duration is not available in the district, it must secure that accommodation is available for the applicant for a period of two years. The most recent Code of Guidance seeks to offset the discrimination against the homeless in access to long term housing that was inherent in the 1996 Act, by urging authorities to consider whether the applicant should be processed via the general allocation criteria from the outset. Section 194 of the 1996 Act permits local authorities to grant further periods of two years if certain preconditions are met, but the aspiration is to re-house people more permanently before the initial two year period has elapsed.

One of the questions that has emerged since the introduction of the 'full duty' in s 193 of the Act relates to the lack of any time constraints in the Act on fulfilment of the duty. In *R v London Borough of Southwark ex p Anderson*, 11 February 1999, it was held that it was impossible to demonstrate that the council was failing in its duties merely through lapse of time, as an unresolved offer was still being processed. Another feature of this case and the more recent *R v Merton London Borough Council ex p Sembi* (1999) *The Times,* 9 June is judicial discussion of the relationship between the prospect of judicial review and the mechanisms in ss 202 and 204 of the 1996 Act for a county court challenge to any adverse decision. In *Sembi*, it was strongly affirmed that, once a local authority's decision had become reviewable under s 202, a claimant should go down that procedural route, rather than seek an application for judicial review. Ms Sembi was confined to a wheelchair and had to leave previous accommodation with her brother on his death. Merton put her in temporary accommodation in a home for the elderly and the terminally ill, while attempting to find somewhere more suitable. Mr Justice Jowitt considered that the provision of accommodation that was adequate for the time being, though, arguably, not 'suitable' in terms of the statute, as she was only 52, was sufficient to discharge the statutory duty. The implication of this is clearly that county courts considering appeals on matters of law will also find the conduct of authorities unexceptionable in such circumstances.

Periodic review of circumstances

There may, however, be persons who are accommodated by the authority for longer than a year or two and there has to be further provision in the Act for filtering out those who do not deserve such extended occupation. Accordingly, in s 194, it is decreed that, in such situations, a local authority must carry out a review of the applicant's circumstances at least every two years. It may commence a review after two years have elapsed. The drafting of the section is particularly cumbersome, but boils down to the proposition that the authority has to satisfy itself, periodically, that the applicant wants to stay on and still qualifies for preferential treatment under the original criteria. At this point, there might appear to be discretion for local authorities unsympathetic to the aims of the legislation to keep applicants in the same accommodation for some time, although subsisting on short commons as opposed to the beggar's banquet of the 'old' homelessness legislation. However, this generosity is precluded in s 207(1).

Ways of discharging the duty to secure accommodation

There is some continuity in this respect in that, as before, authorities can, under s 206, provide their own accommodation or secure that it is provided by someone else or provide sufficient advice and assistance to ensure that accommodation is so available. However, s 207 also says that an authority must not discharge its duty by providing accommodation for more than two years (either continuously or in aggregate) in any period of three years, other than hostel accommodation or accommodation leased to the local authority with vacant possession for use as temporary housing. Therefore, there is here a definite prohibition of any authority inclination to be more generous than statutorily presupposed and grant a secure tenancy for some years. There is, however, provision in s 207(4) for the Secretary of State to relax the restrictions 'if it appears to him that the authority will not otherwise be able reasonably to discharge their housing functions'. Any longer term housing is more likely to be provided by making more generous arrangements for authorities to use leasing from the private sector.

Duties in the case of threatened homelessness

The emphasis in housing policy is often on prevention of homelessness in the first place and there is provision in the Act in s 195 for duties to those so threatened to be complementary to those already outlined. Thus, there is the usual emphasis where the full duty is pending to take reasonable steps to ensure that the accommodation is not lost. However, this clause also has to be read subject to s 197 and the availability of other suitable accommodation. Does this mean that people can be allowed to become homeless because there is other accommodation which they can take up? The wording of s 197 suggests that, in such circumstances, there is a duty to provide appropriate advice and assistance for an applicant 'to enable him to secure such accommodation', that is, the fresh accommodation. So, it would seem that the duty is to help people find somewhere else, rather than attempt to safeguard their continued occupation if there is no scarcity of suitable accommodation. If the authority decides that there is some scarcity and accommodates the applicant elsewhere, then the time limits and other criteria for the operation of the full duty come into play.

Duties to the intentionally homeless

Priority need intentionally homeless persons are, under the present law, entitled both to advice and assistance and to accommodation for long enough to give them a reasonable opportunity of finding accommodation for themselves. What constitutes a reasonable period fluctuates with local housing conditions, but, outside areas of housing stress, it could be weeks, rather than months, as might be appropriate in London. Those not in priority need and intentionally homeless have the right to advice and assistance only.

Impact of the Act

Any accommodation duties, however temporary, towards the intentionally homeless are also affected by the preoccupation in the Act with relieving authorities from obligations to accommodate if they are satisfied that other suitable accommodation is available. Section 197, again, comes to the rescue in appropriate circumstances, so the duty would dwindle to one of providing appropriate advice and assistance. Where there is the perception that suitable alternative accommodation is available and the appropriate advice and assistance have been given, under s 196(4), people will be treated as becoming threatened with homelessness intentionally if they fail to obtain accommodation which they could reasonably have been expected to obtain.

Co-operation and liaison with other agencies

As the Code of Guidance points out, there is a great need for liaison and co-operation with agencies, such as social service departments, health authorities and the probation service, in order to prevent and tackle the problems of homelessness. Many of the issues that arise are not directly legal, but discretionary: priority and resource allocation arguments in an era of retrenchment. It has, for example, been contended that the mentally ill should be given a clearer prioritisation for access to housing and that local authorities should be compelled to state how many residential places they have available for those seriously ill.

In the absence of clear legal issues in relation to health and community care matters, the focus, here, will be on a legislative attempt to define the relationship between the homelessness legislation and the Children Act 1989. Both codes are obviously concerned with the protection of vulnerable children and one of the ambitions behind the framing of the 1989 Act, as with the original homelessness legislation, was to prevent families being shuttled between departments. Section 27 of the 1989 Act placed an obligation on housing authorities to respond to a request for help from social services and 'comply with the request if it is compatible with their own statutory or other duties or obligations and does not unduly prejudice the discharge of any of their functions'. Section 20 of that Act places the obligation on social services to accommodate children in need in certain circumstances.

The formula in s 27, at first sight, does not make massive inroads into pre-existing housing authority duties and this impression was confirmed by the verdict of the House of Lords in *R v Northavon District Council ex p Smith* [1994] 2 AC 402. In 1992, Northavon determined that the applicant and his family were intentionally homeless. Accordingly, they were placed in temporary accommodation for a few months and put on the general housing waiting list. Before the expiry of that arrangement, Mr Smith approached Avon social services authority under s 17 of the Children Act 1989 for help towards a deposit for a tenancy. The social services department declined to exercise its powers under s 17 and, instead, invoked s 27 to get the district council to assist in providing housing. It wrote to the council asking if some form of secure tenancy were available and urging them not, at any rate, to evict from the temporary accommodation. The district council responded by saying there was no question of a long term tenancy being available, since that would contradict their previous finding of intentionality. At first instance, where the application for judicial review of the decision by the housing authority not to co-operate was considered, the application was rejected, but the Court of Appeal took the view that housing authorities could be required via s 27 to undertake more than their perception of Housing Act duties and provide more long term housing. In the view of the court, there should be no shuffling of responsibilities between authorities and, in the words of Lord Justice Bingham, 'if children in need do not command protection under one code, they will command it under the other'.

However, the House of Lords reaffirmed a separatist approach to the two Acts. Lord Templeman noted that a practical compromise solution had already been reached, with Avon paying the deposit on a private sector tenancy and Northavon taking responsibility for rent obligations. He then examined the justifications advanced for the Court of Appeal decision. First, it was argued that the housing authority was under a duty to provide permanent accommodation on request. Secondly, the housing authority should, at least, have further considered providing permanent accommodation. Thirdly, the authority should, at least, have provided or considered providing temporary accommodation, but the response did not mention temporary accommodation. Fourthly, the authority should have justified its refusal to supply permanent accommodation.

Lord Templeman disapproved of this approach, as he felt it blurred the functions of different authorities or, indeed, two departments of the same authority. He preferred the approach of the first instance judge where he said:

> Section 27 imposes a duty of co-operation but co-operation is one thing; the preservation of the separation of powers between public authorities is another. Nothing in s 27 as a whole, or in s 27(2) in particular, enlarges or otherwise amends the powers and duties of the requested authorities under other statutes. Moreover, the duty to co-operate is not unlimited. On the contrary, s 27(2) guarantees the separation of the functions of the different public authorities. Section 27(2) expressly provides that the request must be compatible with the requested authority's own statutory or other duties and obligations, and that the request must not unduly prejudice the discharge of any of their functions.

Therefore, the housing authority were not obliged to co-operate in the manner suggested and social services would have to shoulder the burden of protecting the interests of the children under the 1989 Act. The consequence of this decision is that housing authorities unable or unwilling to co-operate have only to quote the 'unduly prejudice' formula to cover any non-compliance with a s 27 request. The formal legal position is a different matter from good practice and some of the judges stressed the value of informal co-operation, but the *Smith* decision does not give social services much leverage in negotiation. The implication is that s 27 is virtually redundant.

What impact will *Awua* and the Housing Act have here? Clearly, once the extent of housing authority duties is dramatically reduced, either judicially or legislatively, there can be little point in requesting permanent accommodation as that is beyond the call of duty. In certain circumstances, it might be advisable to seek what little help there is available for such groups as the intentionally homeless, since there will be an obligation to accommodate for a reasonable period. With the emphasis in the Housing Act on progress via the general allocation criteria on a housing register and the downgrading of the homelessness legislation, the points systems in the new improved s 22 of the Housing

Act 1985 – s 167 of the 1996 Act – will be crucial. The Smiths, with a large family, fell squarely within the current 'reasonable preference' criterion in s 22, but, with 2,630 people on the waiting list, their prospects of permanent housing were remote.

Damages for breach of duties

A successful challenge to a decision by judicial review may sometimes result in remission of a case to a local authority and confirmation of the original decision. However, there may be other instances where the authority is clearly in breach of duty and the question arises whether damages are recoverable for breach of some private law duty. The judiciary have developed a distinction between decision making functions which are a public duty and executive functions, which involve private law functions and where damages are in principle available. A decision making function would be, for instance, a determination on homelessness status or intentionality. An executive function would be where a duty has been acknowledged by an authority, but not fulfilled, as where persons in admitted priority need are turned away without even bed and breakfast accommodation. In those circumstances, the quarrel is not with the decision, but with the failure to implement it.

In *R v Northavon District Council ex p Palmer* (1995) 27 HLR 576, the issue of damages for breach of statutory duty was given its most recent airing. The applicant, who was squatting in Avon, applied for accommodation under Pt III in January 1992. Her family consisted of her husband, who was very ill, three grown up sons and a mentally handicapped adult daughter. Her application was erroneously treated as a request to go on the general waiting list. In October 1992, the Palmer family were evicted from their squat and moved to a dilapidated caravan on an unauthorised site. In April 1993, Northavon determined that the family was not homeless because Avon had not obtained possession of the site where the caravan was standing. After Avon did get a possession order, Northavon eventually, in May 1993, acknowledged a full duty and housed the family.

The applicant sought judicial review, asking for a declaration that Northavon had been in breach of statutory duties to make the requisite inquiries in 1992 and house her. She claimed damages for the inconvenience and suffering caused by the council's failure, between January 1992 and May 1993, to investigate her case and house her and her family. Under s 31(4) of the Supreme Court Act 1981, in an application for judicial review, it is open to the court to award damages to the applicant if a claim for damages in an action by writ could have been made at the time of the application. At first instance, the application for judicial review and claim for damages were dismissed.

In the Court of Appeal, a long litany of alleged breaches of ss 62 and 63 was described. Northavon contended that all such breaches fell exclusively in the domain of public law and did not give rise to any private law rights. A number of breaches, in the opinion of the Master of the Rolls, fell squarely behind the public law boundary, such as the failure to recognise the applicant as an applicant under Pt III. He relied on the judgment of Lord Bridge, in *Cocks v Thanet District Council* [1983] 2 AC 286, as establishing the public/private demarcation in this sphere. On that reckoning, one of the alleged breaches of duty was the duty to house her under s 63. However, the logical difficulty was that a decision to house had to be made before the duty to house originated and the decision was not made until May 1993. The condition precedent to the creation of a statutory duty was, therefore, not satisfied until that date, even if it should have been satisfied in January 1992. Therefore, even if it was incontestable that action should have been taken earlier, there had been no concession of this point by the authority.

Lord Justice Bingham refuted the claim that an action for damages would lie by quoting from Lord Bridge in the *Cocks* case (p 293):

> After reference to *Thornton v Kirklees Metropolitan Borough Council*, in *De Falco v Crawley Borough Council* [1980] QB 460, p 480, I said:
>
> 'If an ordinary action lies in respect of an alleged breach of duty, it must follow, it seems to me, that in such an action the plaintiff as well as claiming damages or an injunction as his remedy for the breach of duty can claim any declaration necessary to establish that there was a relevant breach of duty, and in particular, a declaration that a local authority's decision adverse to him under the Act was not validly made.'
>
> In the light of the dichotomy between a housing authority's public and private law functions, this is a *non sequitur*. The fallacy is in the implicit assumption that the court has the power not only to review the housing authority's public law decision but also to establish the necessary condition precedent to the housing authority's private law liability.

So, the fundamental problem was that the private law duty could not be established until the public law decision making activity had happened. This conclusion was reached with regret, not surprisingly, as it gives authorities a perverse incentive not to decide – to drag their feet before making a decision which could lead to private law liability. It is reminiscent of ideas about repairing obligations which give landlords the incentive to let property deteriorate so far that they cannot be called upon to put matters right.

Is the conclusion reached by the Court of Appeal inescapable? The quotation from the *Cocks* case about the fallacy of substituted judgment seems directed at the situation where a decision, presumably adverse to the applicant, has been made. The presence of an adverse judgment is hardly the same as the absence of a favourable one. On these facts, it is difficult to avoid the conclusion that the council were *Wednesbury* unreasonable in failing to apply the relevant legal criteria for over a year and some form of mandatory injunction requiring the processing of the application via s 63 would have been available early in 1992. However, the delay in enforcing rights and establishing the position, under Pt III of the Act, appears fatal to the damages claim.

If a claim for damages linked to judicial review is unavailing in these circumstances, what of other possible avenues, such as the law of negligence? The latest principles to emerge from the House of Lords, in this sphere, could contain some hope for applicants in the position of Mrs Palmer. The case in question is *X (minors) v Bedfordshire CC, M (a minor) v Newham London BC, E (a minor) v Dorset CC, Christmas v Hampshire CC, Keating v Bromley London BC* (1995) 26 BMLR 15. Three general propositions emerge from the judgment of Lord Browne-Wilkinson:

(1) A breach of statutory duty does not inherently give rise to any private law cause of action. To prove the opposite, it must be shown that the statutory duty was, in fact, imposed for the protection of a limited class of the public and that Parliament intended to confer a private right of action for breach of duty on that class. In this connection, regulatory or welfare legislation (such as homelessness) is not to be treated as for the benefit of individuals, but for society at large.

(2) In the event of careless exercise of statutory powers and duties, it has to be demonstrated that the circumstances are such as to raise a duty of care at common law. In relation to discretion it was stated that (p 29):

> Most statutes which impose a statutory duty on local authorities confer on the authority a discretion as to the extent to which, and the methods by which, such statutory duty is to be performed. It is clear both in principle and from the decided cases that the local authority cannot be liable in damages for doing that which Parliament has authorised. Therefore, if the decisions complained of fall within the ambit of such statutory discretion they cannot be actionable in common law. However, if the decision complained of is so unreasonable that it falls outside the ambit of the discretion conferred upon the local authority, there is no *a priori* reason for excluding all common law liability.

Lord Browne-Wilkinson picked up on this statement from Lord Reid in *Dorset Yacht Co Ltd v Home Office* [1970] 2 All ER 294, p 301, where he said 'there must come a stage when the discretion is exercised so carelessly or unreasonably that there has been no real exercise of the discretion which Parliament has conferred'. These *dicta* appear to be getting uncomfortably close to the actions or inaction of the authority in the *Palmer* case.

(3) It is established that the courts cannot adjudicate on 'policy' matters where social values or the allocation of finite resources or equivalent matters are involved. The argument continues as follows (p 32):

> If the decision complained of falls outside the statutory discretion, it can (but not necessarily will) give rise to common law liability. However, if the factors relevant to the exercise of discretion include matters of policy, the court cannot adjudicate on such policy matters and, therefore, cannot reach the conclusion that the decision was outside the ambit of the statutory discretion. Therefore, a common law duty of care in relation to the taking of decisions involving policy matters cannot exist.

Where does all this leave the question of liability in negligence in the *Palmer* case? It can, surely, not be argued that the failure to exercise the discretion was non justiciable because it was based on policy matters. The failure to exercise the discretion stemmed from a careless failure to identify the significance of the facts presented, which should have resulted in action under Pt III being taken.

This decision clearly predates the *Awua* case's redefinition of statutory duties into dramatically reduced obligations. The Housing Act 1996 is, perhaps, more generous than *Awua* in some respects, but is unlikely to encourage litigation.

Any hopes that claimants might have nurtured about damages for breach of homelessness duties appear to have been scotched by the recent decision of the House of Lords in *O'Rourke v Mayor and Aldermen of the London Borough of Camden* [1998] AC 188. Mr O'Rourke applied to Camden on release from prison, claiming to be homeless and in priority need because of vulnerability. After initially rejecting his application, the council agreed to conduct the inquiries specified in s 62 of the 1985 Housing Act and housed him in temporary accommodation for 12 days, at which point, he was evicted by them with no further offer of accommodation. He sought damages for breach of statutory duty, specifically the obligation in s 63(1) of the 1985 Act:

> If the local housing authority have reason to believe that an applicant may be homeless and have a priority need, they shall secure that accommodation is made available for his occupation pending a decision as a result of their enquiries under s 62.

The claim for damages was rejected at first instance, had some success in the Court of Appeal, but was again rejected in the House of Lords on the authority of Lord Hoffmann, with whom the rest of their Lordships concurred. He naturally referred back to the pointers given in the *X* case and emphasised that judicial review was always available to those with the requisite *locus standi.* He found a number of indicators to support the proposition that Parliament did not intend to confer private rights of action in this area. The first such indicator was that:

> Public money is spent on housing the homeless not merely for the private benefit of people who find themselves homeless, but on grounds of general public interest; because, for example, proper housing means that people will be less likely to suffer illness, turn to crime or require the attention of other social services. It is not simply a private matter between the claimant and the housing authority.

It should be interpolated here that formulation of general utilitarian considerations of this type, summarising the indirect benefits of various aspects of welfare provision, could be used to scupper virtually claims for breach of statutory duty. The second pointer, identified by Lord Hoffmann, was the fact that so many of the functions to be discharged by the local housing authority had important elements of discretion incorporated in them, as by reference to 'reason to believe'. Therefore, it would be odd if errors of judgment in broad discretionary areas, nevertheless, incurred some liability to compensate.

What of the supposed distinction between decision making functions, beyond the scope of private action, and executive functions, relating to the implementation of an acknowledged duty? This distinction stems from cases like *Cocks v Thanet District Council* [1983] 2 AC 286 and Lord Hoffmann was unhappy about it, arguing that it was illogical. Why should the law differentiate between the poor performance of an acknowledged duty, where damages might be available, and a perverse refusal to recognise a particular duty, where damages would not be feasible?

The conclusion was that no private law cause of action existed, and, therefore, that *Thornton v Kirklees MBC* [1979] QB 625, was wrongly decided.

CHAPTER 4

ALLOCATION OF SECURE TENANCIES

The political and ethical dilemmas about allocation of council housing and concomitant difficulties of legal interpretation are as long standing as the provision of public sector housing itself. In recent years, pressure has intensified with the marginalisation of council housing and its depletion through the right to buy and large scale voluntary transfer. It is symptomatic that, in some areas, the decline of local authority housing has led to aspirants to housing looking elsewhere and local authorities may themselves have little or no stock to allocate and be forced to rely on nomination rights to housing associations or agreements with the private sector. The role of local authorities as direct providers of housing by building themselves has virtually disappeared. In 1995, authorities built 600 new properties in England, as against 25,000 by housing associations. In 1975, by contrast, authorities built over 130,000.

The legal framework for allocation of council housing has undergone subtle changes, in recent years, with refinement of the degree of discretion enjoyed by local authorities and, in the case of the recent Conservative administrations, a desire to be more stipulative and interventionist about eligibility. Recent reforms have led to intensive debates about the legality of such measures as 'blanket bans' on classes of person, such as those with rent arrears or a criminal record. The various changes made in the 1996 Housing Act have, as elsewhere, been marginally changed by the incoming Labour administration, rather than radically reconstructed. The most recent contribution has been a new draft Code of Guidance on allocation and homelessness dating from March 1999 and this will be explored in due course.

The 'old' law in s 22 of the Housing Act 1985

As in many other contexts, it will be necessary to give an outline of the old law in this sphere, now superseded by the provisions of the 1996 Housing Act. This makes sense not just for historical interest, but because there is a large measure of continuity in regard to such factors as the retention of the notorious 'reasonable preference' formula, litigation on which has, therefore, no natural expiry date in terms of relevance.

The traditional formula enshrined in s 22 is that, in the selection of tenants, authorities are required to give reasonable preference to those in unsanitary or overcrowded houses, large families, people subject to unsatisfactory housing conditions and certain statutorily homeless persons under ss 65 and 68 of the 1985 Act. It is noteworthy that licensees are excluded from the operation of this discretion and that it contains a strong emphasis on the physical characteristics of dwellings, rather than the social attributes of applicants. The emphasis on physical qualities goes back to the 1930s, whereas, as already hinted, the focus on behavioural characteristics, such as anti-social behaviour or rent arrears, is more recent.

The obvious justification for such a vague formula and generally non-directive set of criteria is that there is legitimate scope for regional variation and adaptation of policy to local needs. However, for some time, commentators have also suggested that the 'reasonable preference' formula is too protective of the exercise of discretion and renders decisions non-justiciable, save in flagrant cases of fettering of discretion or corruption or bad faith. There have been some recorded instances of successful challenge by way of judicial review, but those are rare and characteristically pathological cases. For example, in *R v Canterbury City Council ex p Gillespie* (1987) 19 HLR 7, Canterbury was found wanting because of their inflexibility in refusing to admit on to the waiting list or select for housing someone with a secure tenancy elsewhere, in a situation where consideration of individual circumstances would have shown that it was unrealistic to expect the applicant to terminate her tenancy. Similarly, where there is evidence of corruption in allocation for local party political reasons, a challenge is likely to succeed. In *R v Port Talbot BC ex p Jones* [1988] 2 All ER 207, a borough councillor obtained a three bedroomed house as a matter of priority in the area where she was to stand for election when, in the normal course of events, she would have had to wait several years for even a one or two bedroomed flat. Mr Justice Nolan gave an early indication of his instinct for rooting out corruption in public life by stigmatising the council's action as an unlawful abuse of power.

However, more recent cases display the characteristic reluctance of the courts to interfere with the operation of local discretion. In *R v London Borough of Newham ex p Dawson* (1994) 26 HLR 747, it was even accepted that, in the absence of any statutory requirement, no duty to give reasons arises from a decision under s 22. The underlying justification was that the powers of authorities in this sphere are those of general management and create no rights for individuals and, in any case, the decision was not so startling or aberrant as to require explanation.

Watters and a 'reasonable head start'

R v Wolverhampton MBC ex p Watters (1997) 29 HLR 931, from which the above quotation comes, is an instructive recent examination of the degree of flexibility and individualised reference necessary to rescue what otherwise might appear to be an absolute bar from susceptibility to judicial review. The problem which continually falls to be analysed is how far countervailing considerations, such as a bad record on rent arrears, can erode or even nullify any notional 'reasonable preference' derived from satisfying one or more of the categories in s 22.

The Watters had five children and had been evicted from council accommodation because of rent arrears of over £2,000. Wolverhampton did provide them with temporary housing, but with one less bedroom than they needed, so Mrs Watters applied, without success, to go on the housing waiting list. She sought judicial review of that rejection.

Both the trial judge and the Court of Appeal concluded that it was lawful to exclude from consideration for housing a family which, nevertheless, fell within the first three categories in s 22. The idea, perhaps surprisingly, was that factors, such as rent arrears, could diminish and even nullify any preference and 'reasonable' signalled the possibility and legality of such a subtraction exercise. In the words of Lord Justice Leggatt: 'No preference is to be given except reasonable preference. That involves balancing against the statutory factors such factors as may be relevant.'

There are also useful pronouncements on the related issue of the degree of flexibility inherent in the published policy on rent arrears. In this instance, there was enough leeway to avoid any finding of an unlawful fettering of discretion. According to the first instance judge, Mr Justice Dyson:

> In the present case, the policy adopted by the council gives considerable negative weight to non-payment of rent. The council has, however, mitigated this where substantial efforts have been made by a tenant to reduce the arrears. The council has also decided that even those tenants owing arrears of rent who have not made substantial efforts to reduce them should be allocated housing if they have a substantial social or medical need or if other exceptional circumstances exist. This seems to me to be a perfectly reasonable response to the statutory obligation imposed upon it by s 22.

The conclusion from this judicial analysis is that the 'reasonable head start' can be relatively easily offset by a suitably individuated policy and can, ultimately, lead to disqualification from the race itself, in terms of access to the waiting list. The degree of flexibility in a policy is a question to be re-examined later in this chapter in the context of the latest draft Code of Guidance on allocation. In this connection, it should be added that are statements from the lower echelons of the judiciary suggesting that it is better, indeed incumbent on authorities, to try to keep people in the race. In *R v Lambeth LBC ex p Njomo* (1996) 28 HLR 737, excessive rigidity in policy application resulted in a successful application for judicial review and the statement from Mr Justice Sedley, as he then was, that an authority must not 'eclipse or distort the priority which s 22 accords'. This would suggest that the head start cannot be so easily outweighed by countervailing factors. In *Njomo*, the damning rigidity or inflexibility was summarised as follows by the judge:

> Although the respondent council's transfer policy, with its built in exceptions, is not in itself an unlawful fetter on the council's discretion under Pt II of the Housing Act 1985, the way in which it has been applied is unlawful. The respondent, by treating the policy exceptions as exhaustive, has failed to take into account a potential ground for waiving or mitigating the operation of the legitimate principle that arrears will count against a tenant seeking a transfer under Pt II, namely that the arrears were being disputed in action for their recovery and now that the action itself is gone beyond recall.

The conclusion is, therefore, that, although the ambit of any discretion can in principle be wide, its exercise must not be fettered by inflexible application. A comparable example of inflexibility is to be found in *R v London Borough of Islington ex p Aldabbagh* (1994) 27 HLR 271, where the policy assailed was one of refusing any transfer application by a person with rent arrears, unless the applicant had made an agreement to pay the current rent and some commitment to reduce the arrears.

Anti-discrimination legislation

The rather vague and reluctant judicial encroachments on authorities' freedom of action are not of course the whole story. There is a raft of anti-discrimination legislation, such as the Race Relations Act 1976 and the Sex Discrimination Act 1975, which have, for decades, outlawed discrimination on grounds of race or sex in housing as elsewhere. It is conceivable that any equality of opportunity arguments derived from subjection to the Human Rights Act 1998 will also have an impact.

There is, lamentably, no shortage of documentation of racism or racial bias in the allocation of housing, just as recently racial harassment has been identified as a powerful constituent of harassment more generally defined. In some localities, it has been demonstrated that certain ethnic groups are discriminated against in access to houses and are more likely to be allotted accommodation in flats, usually above a certain floor level. The anti-discrimination legislation attempts to combat racial bias in allocation by outlawing both direct and indirect discrimination. 'Direct' involves treating persons less favourably in applications on the grounds of race and inherently introduces difficulties of proof. However, in some investigations, such as that conducted by the Commission for Racial Equality on Race and Council Housing in Hackney (1984), it was shown, through overwhelming statistical evidence, that the council had practised unlawful direct discrimination against black applicants and tenants who had been allocated housing from the waiting list.

'Indirect' discrimination is a useful concept because it goes beyond or behind any ostensible objectivity and even handedness in allocation. By definition, it involves the universal application of a criterion, but a criterion which, of itself, disadvantages certain groups because proportionately fewer members of such groups can satisfy the criterion. A classic example would be the universal application of some residence requirement in the locality as a precondition for access to the housing waiting list, thereby disadvantaging recent immigrants. Another example would be giving less favourable treatment to those with very large families, as such an approach might disproportionately penalise those from particular ethnic groups. The most recent draft Code of Guidance on allocations warns further that, in some locales, the specification of owner-occupiers as a non-qualifying class for eligibility for the housing register could constitute indirect racial discrimination for the same reasons.

THE 1996 HOUSING ACT AND ALLOCATIONS

In the words of the Code of Guidance that accompanied the Act:

> Part VI of the 1996 Act introduces a new legislative regime which, for the first time, places a duty on local housing authorities to set up and maintain a housing register and to make most allocations from their register to qualifying persons through an allocation scheme.

As will have become apparent from the previous chapter, one of the underlying aims was to exclude from 'reasonable preference' status those statutorily homeless persons traditionally within the ambit of s 22, in an effort to remove the 'perverse incentive' of substantial rights under the homelessness legislation and concentrate on a single track into social housing. In the 1996 Act, we find a very broad definition of the various prioritised 'reasonable preference' groups and the original intention was to allow, in the words of the initial Code of Guidance, 'ample scope to operate discretionary elements within the scheme'. What was, however, non-negotiable was the exclusion of statutory homelessness from the categories prioritised in s 167 of the 1996 Act.

The advent of the Labour administration in 1997 prompted the restoration of the old rules under which the unintentional priority need homeless qualified for reasonable preference and that will shortly be examined in detail. The picture is, therefore, that the preference categories have with the exception of homelessness remained unaltered since 1997, but the slant which authorities are expected to take on exclusion policy and interpretation of the categories could well take different forms in successive Codes of Guidance. The available evidence suggests that some authorities have taken quite sweeping steps to exclude large categories of applicant from the register.

The new allocation structure and criteria

Section 159 of the 1996 Act explains the scope of the new allocation criteria. Affected are: selection by authorities of secure and introductory tenants of their own housing; nominations to other authorities of such tenants; and nominations to housing associations. All local housing authorities are compelled, by s 162, to establish and maintain a housing register, of qualifying persons. Under s 163, persons are entitled to be put on the register if they apply and appear to be a qualifying person. If an authority decides not to register an individual or remove him or her from the register, it must so notify the individual, giving reasons. Those rejected then have 21 days to request an internal review of the decision.

It is clear that the reformed criteria are applicable to new applicants and not those already in the system. Sub-section (5) of s 159 states that the provisions of Pt VI do not apply to a person who is already a secure or introductory tenant, an assured tenant (other than an assured shortholder of a registered social landlord) or an assured tenant of housing allocated by a local housing authority.

The general justifying aim of the reforms to s 22 was expressed as follows in the 1996 consultation document:

> The provisions governing priorities in allocations will enable local authorities to devise allocation schemes which make the best use of resources to meet long term needs in the light of local circumstances. They will operate at two levels: they will ensure that the most vulnerable individuals receive first priority in the allocation of housing stock; they will also ensure that the claims of everyone else on the register receive proper consideration, according to underlying need.

The next stage is to enumerate the new criteria in s 167, incorporating the changes made by the Allocation of Housing (Reasonable and Additional Preference) Regulations 1997 SI No 1902. Thereafter, it will be useful to see how the guidance on fleshing out the categories has changed with successive administrations and particular problems, such as the determination of classes of qualifiers and non-qualifiers and the legality of blanket bans, will have to be scrutinised in some detail.

The new 'reasonable preference' categories

Section 167(2), as amended, privileges the following categories of applicant:

> As regards priorities the scheme shall be framed so as to secure that reasonable preference is given to:
>
> (a) people occupying insanitary or overcrowded housing or otherwise living in unsatisfactory housing conditions;
>
> (b) people occupying housing accommodation which is temporary or occupied on insecure terms;
>
> (c) families with dependent children:
>
> (d) households consisting of or including someone who is expecting a child;
>
> (e) households consisting of or including someone with a particular need for settled accommodation on medical or welfare grounds;
>
> (f) households whose social or economic circumstances are such that they have difficulty in securing settled accommodation.
>
> The scheme shall also be framed so as to secure that additional preference is given to households within para (e) consisting of someone with a particular need for settled accommodation on medical or welfare grounds who cannot reasonably be expected to find settled accommodation for themselves in the foreseeable future.

1997 additions

1 Those owed a duty under s 65(2) or 68(2) of the Housing Act 1985. This is a (vanishing) breed of those whose applications predate the commencement date of the 1996 Act, 20 January 1997 and the duty has not yet been discharged.

2 Those owed a duty under s 193 or 195(2) of the 1996 Act. These are the comparable provisions in the new law for full duty homeless persons and those threatened with homelessness.

3 Where the authority are exercising their power under s 194 of the 1996 Act. This brings in the idea in the 1996 legislation that, after the two year minimum period specified in s 193, if persons are still in priority need and want to keep on depending on the council for accommodation, the authority has the power to continue to secure accommodation 'and they shall not continue to do so for more than two years at a time unless they are satisfied on a further review' about essentials, such as priority need.

4 Where persons have, within the previous two years, been provided with advice and assistance by an authority under s 197(2) of the 1996 Act or who are occupying accommodation obtained through such assistance.

Before considering the complexities of local authority discretion to determine the qualifying classes for social housing, it is advisable to consider the general criteria outlined above, as it is these that could be undercut by too inflexible a policy. It is significant that the latest Code of Guidance (draft, March 1999) does not always go into great detail in fleshing out the often vague and nebulous categories of reasonable preference, being content to allow for broad discretion. The latest code, perhaps, concentrates more on general policy exhortation, as when in the introductory chapter it stresses that local authorities have to integrate their allocation policy with transfer policy, with 'their wider objectives in meeting housing needs in the area' and with other areas of welfare provision (para 1.6). By contrast, the previous codes issued by the Conservative administration sometimes contained quite detailed prescription about the fostering of certain moral preferences, such as for married couples over cohabitees.

(a) People in insanitary or overcrowded or otherwise unsatisfactory housing

The antiquity of a word like 'insanitary' shows the longevity of criteria of this type, which are relatively uncontroversial. This factor merely reproduces the wording in the 1985 Act and the latest Code of Guidance is content to describe the category as 'self-explanatory'.

(b) People in temporary or insecure accommodation

The original conception of this novel category, which, of course, covers those, in a sense, threatened with homelessness, was relatively narrow, encompassing tied accommodation. However, the proliferation of short term agreements in both the private and public sector probably makes it a growing category in some areas. The latest Code of Guidance has this to say about (b):

> [It] covers two types of cases. The first is accommodation occupied by the occupant which is of a temporary nature, for example, a temporary shelter, hostel, women's refuge or a dwelling due to be demolished. The second is accommodation occupied on insecure terms by the applicant. This might cover forms of tenure such as an assured shorthold tenancy or a licence (express or implied). This category is not intended to cover only cases where people are at risk of losing their accommodation, although it is open to an authority to give a higher priority weighting in such cases.

(c) and (d) Families with dependent children and households expecting a child

The latest Guidance confines itself to pious platitudes about the importance of a stable home environment, whereas the original framers of the criteria were more specifically moralistic in privileging married couples and denigrating cohabitees and single mothers. In its 1996 consultative document, the Conservative government linked the importance of stability, already identified, to the belief that 'local authorities should give priority to ensuring that families, particularly married couples, with dependent children or who are expecting a child have access to settled accommodation'. Somewhat naively, the 1996 document also exhorted authorities to give consideration to 'the needs of those who have delayed starting a family because of the inadequacies of their accommodation'. There was no further explanation of the way to identify the socially responsible couples who genuinely had delayed, as opposed to others happy to use the inadequacy argument as a means of increasing their chances of getting housed.

It should, however, be added that the latest plans unveiled by the Social Exclusion Unit contain proposals for 'quasi-independent' accommodation for single mothers, presumably in the form of hostels, so there is more continuity between old Conservative and new Labour approaches than might be imagined.

(e) People with a particular need for settled accommodation on medical or welfare grounds

This category is again relatively non-controversial and the original purpose behind this formulation was to identify circumstances where a settled home is necessary to meet other needs. The latest code offers examples, such as physical or learning disability or multiplesclerosis, or those with behavioural problems, such as addiction. It is stressed that the category includes households who need accommodation 'to give or receive care'.

'Welfare grounds' is also to be broadly interpreted to include 'not only care or support needs, but also other social needs which do not require continuing care and support, such as the need to provide a secure base from which a care leaver (that is, someone being resettled by a social services authority under s 27 of the Children Act 1989) or other vulnerable person can build a stable life'. Children could well come into this category under either medical or welfare grounds and close co-operation with social services is anticipated in fulfilment of duties under the Children Act, such as the obligation in s 17 'to safeguard and promote the welfare of children within their area who are in need'.

(f) Households having difficulty in securing settled accommodation

The pervasiveness of assured shortholds must increase the constituency of private tenants, in this category, but successive Codes of Guidance have confined themselves to brief explanations about the particular problems of those with low incomes. A novelty in the latest Code of Guidance is the exhortation that such households should, perhaps, be given priority in any strategy to prevent homelessness and there is much more attention in the latest code to such pro-active intervention.

The 'new' homelessness categories

The resurrection of the reasonable preference for the full duty homeless, of course, takes place in an altered climate, since the devaluation of the full duty towards the homeless to the two year period under Pt VII of the 1996 Act puts more pressure on the long term route into social housing. The latest Code of Guidance can only offer the advice that allocation schemes should 'balance' the needs of households who are homeless with those qualifying for reasonable preference under other criteria. It is, of course, acknowledged that homeless households will often have attributes that would lodge them in other preference categories, in any event.

Reasonable preference and the quantification of need

The favoured formula of reasonable preference, as the latest Code of Guidance notes, does not confine authorities to assessment in terms of the stated criteria, which are not intended to be exhaustive. What other factors can be introduced, and how, is a matter for discussion shortly in terms of such features as 'blanket bans'.

So far as extending the criteria is concerned, the latest code offers some illustrations of possible appropriate expansion, such as having regard to the needs of extended families and the significance of pets to many elderly people. There is, however, a sting in the tail of the advice, a formula that has been used before, that 'Authorities should not allow their own secondary criteria to dominate their allocation scheme at the expense of the statutory priority categories'.

The Code of Guidance also refers to a vexed question which has arisen from the practice of some local authorities of suspending the entitlements of people demonstrably within a reasonable preference category until, for example, evidence of some progress in paying off rent arrears. The advice is that there is no objection to a scheme which prioritises those without rent arrears over those with arrears and similar housing need. However (para 5.32), 'rent arrears in themselves would not remove a person who is in a category to whom reasonable preference has to be given under s 167(2) from such a category'. This advice is not necessarily an authoritative statement of the law and, certainly, it seems to go against the grain of the decisions previously analysed under the old law, where annulment of reasonable preference through one factor was perfectly permissible, so long as that annulment formed part of some suitably individuated policy. Presumably, this is what is meant by the prohibition of 'secondary factors' dominating any scheme?

Guidance on qualification for social housing

Now that the relatively generous preference framework in s 167 has been explored, it is appropriate to take a step back from the substantive categories and examine the general issue of classification of qualifiers and non-qualifiers for social housing. The obvious background is the vulnerability to judicial review of any policy which is too redolent of a blanket ban or undue inflexibility. However, as pointed out in the latest Guidance:

> ... s 161(4) only permits the authority to decide classes of persons who are, or are not, qualifying persons, and leaves no residual discretion to take account of individual circumstances where a person already falls within a class of qualifying or non-qualifying persons. An authority must therefore ensure that classes are carefully and clearly defined. The test of a properly defined class should be whether it is evident to any person from the description of the class whether he or she falls within its ambit.

The idea behind this instruction is tolerably clear; that applicants should be able to read off their status from the published criteria and this is easy to perceive if the classes are defined in terms of age limits and residence criteria. However, in other instances of criteria, such as anti-social behaviour or rent arrears, with a broad factual spectrum of degrees of misbehaviour and indebtedness, it is difficult to imagine how status could be read off a rule in this fashion, unless the criterion in question was as long as the 119th Psalm and much more complicated.

The Code of Guidance is aware of the pitfalls and urges authorities, for example, not to concentrate on defining the classes of non-qualifiers, since the corollary of this would be that the register would be very extensive. Another danger might be to define some qualifying classes and then independently some non-qualifying, which could result in the nightmare of people being neither qualifying nor non-qualifying, but in some sort of limbo.

The tentative solution advanced by the Code involves some sophisticated juggling with sets and classes reminiscent of the realms of higher mathematics. To quote para 3.13:

> However, it is possible, by careful design, for an authority to decide on a class of non-qualifying persons which incorporates exceptions within that class: these exceptions can be based on a range of categories of housing need. Thus, if an authority wish to establish a class of non-qualifying persons, (for example, people with a history of anti-social behaviour or persistent rent arrears) from which they wish to allow certain descriptions of persons (for example, people with a community care assessment) to be qualifying persons, they would need to:
>
> (i) describe the non-qualifying class in such a way that certain descriptions of person who would otherwise fall within that class are omitted from it; and
>
> (ii) ensure that the persons omitted from the non-qualifying class also fall within a class of qualifying persons.

Assuming that classes are defined with the requisite sophistication, the aspiration must be that excluding the vast majority of rent arrears cases, save those with the readily ascertainable escape route of a community care assessment, rescues any policy from vulnerability to judicial review. Is this aspiration likely to be fulfilled? A note of caution or pessimism can easily be sounded by reference to classic long standing principles of administrative law. In the words of one author (Craig, *Administrative Law*, 3rd edn, p 391):

> A public body endowed with discretionary powers is not entitled to adopt a policy or rule which allows it to dispose of a case without any consideration of the merits of the individual applicant who is before it.

Could not a person with a 'meritorious' rent arrears problem argue that exonerating only those with the objectively ascertainable community care assessment or other badge of housing need is too rigid and inflexible to withstand judicial scrutiny? There are some conflicting strains in administrative law doctrine in this sphere, as is demonstrated by contrasting judicial approaches in the benchmark case of *British Oxygen Co Ltd v Board of Trade* [1971] AC 610. The thinking appears to be that it is permissible to have some sort of stringent policy formulation, so long as there is sufficient flexibility in the actual implementation of the policy. So long as those exercising any discretion do not shut their ears to a particular application, then there is sufficient flexibility. However, the caveat entered by judges, such as Lord Reid, is 'provided that the authority is always willing to listen to anyone with anything new to say'. In the case of accumulated rent arrears, for instance, there may be little novelty. Perhaps, what will rescue a policy is the fact that, as in the case of allocations, there is the right to request an internal review of an adverse decision, in which case it is possible to argue, without too much cynicism, that an individuated focus is built into the exercise of any discretion.

In the case of rent arrears, the Code of Guidance suggests a rather complex formulation of the criteria for exclusion from the register. Automatic exclusion is not recommended, but, instead, a more tentative approach of designating a class of persistent defaulters, but including some housing need criteria in the definition of the class. A perpetual exclusion is also discouraged; instead, the emphasis should be on such redeeming features as undertaking to reduce the arrears. Such a cautious formulation is, however, likely to fail the 'test of a properly defined class' as outlined earlier – clarity of the scope of the class – since it would be difficult to exclude value laden terminology, such as 'reasonable' steps to reduce arrears, which would prevent persons being able to read their eligibility directly from the face of the published criteria. The conclusion is that the sort of refined policy adopted in the *Watters* case will meet any challenges about undue rigidity or inflexibility, but at the price of undermining one of the aspirations behind the determination of groups of qualifiers and non-qualifiers, transparency and ready intelligibility and applicability of the criteria themselves. The tension between the desire to escape the rigours of judicial review and the anxiety to give an instant picture of eligibility is likely to create headaches for framers and updaters of qualification criteria in the next few years.

INTRODUCTORY TENANCIES

Along with other measures aimed at anti-social behaviour, Pt V of the 1996 Housing Act contained proposals for allowing local authorities to impose introductory tenancies on newcomers. Authorities themselves have been divided on the merits of the idea, with some anxious to introduce probationary tenancies as widely as possible, but others opposed to any such destabilisation.

The basic framework is that local authorities and housing action trusts have the option of offering introductory tenancies to new tenants, with tenancies lasting a year and terminable by a court order for possession. The landlord has to give reasons for termination in the notice of proceedings for possession and the tenant has the right to a review of any adverse decision, so long as the request is made within a fortnight of the service of notice of proceedings. On the face of it, the court has no discretion to grant possession only if deemed reasonable or to assess the merits of any reasons given, but has no choice but to grant the possession order.

The relevant statutory provisions spell out this constriction of court discretion. According to s 127 of the 1996 Act:

> (1) The landlord may only bring an introductory tenancy to an end by obtaining an order of the court for possession of the dwelling-house.
>
> (2) The court shall make such an order unless the provisions of s 128 apply.

This, when read in conjunction with s 128, which bars the court from entertaining possession proceedings unless the landlord has duly served a notice of proceedings, would seem to exclude county court jurisdiction over matters of substance. This intuition was confirmed by the Court of Appeal, in *Manchester City Council v Cochrane* [1999] 1 WLR 809, where the 'remarkable constriction of the court's powers' was noted and where it was argued that the only real cope for intervention lay in the possibility of an adjournment if realistically leave to apply for judicial review might be forthcoming. There was no way in which the court could entertain a defence which basically consisted of a rebuttal of the charges that had provoked the service of the notice. The Court of Appeal was also impressed by the difference between this part of the legislation and the more generous wording and broader jurisdiction in s 204 of the 1996 Act in the case of homelessness.

So long as they survive, introductory tenants have the usual rights such as succession, repairs and information and consultation entitlements. The original idea was that, if possession had not been obtained by the end of a year, the tenancy would become secure, but that was altered in the Committee stage in the House of Commons to establish that, where a landlord has started proceedings before the end of the probationary period, the tenancy will not cease to be introductory until the date on which possession is finally ordered. If some automatic upgrading after a year had survived in the Act, landlords would then have had to rely on one of the specific statutory grounds for possession against secure tenants and would have had much less control over outcomes.

So far as the implementation of such schemes is concerned, the underlying principle is intended to be discretionary and permissive. Authorities are supposed to consult tenants on any proposed scheme. Tenancy agreements should contain information about the sort of behaviour that will cause failure of probation and, under s 136 of the 1996 Act, tenants are entitled to rudimentary information over and above what appears in the agreement. Housing associations are excluded from the operation of introductory tenancies because they can and do use assured shorthold agreements as a means of achieving the same end.

Are introductory tenancies necessary? In their favour, it can be said that there is consensus that anti-social behaviour on some estates has reached alarming proportions and that existing legal measures, even with increased ammunition under the Crime and Disorder Act 1998, are inadequate. However, opponents argue that these measures leave untouched the problem of anti-social behaviour by long established tenants and are an unwelcome erosion of security of tenure. It is conjectured that the virtually unlimited scope for terminating tenancies and the (as seen) rubber stamping by the courts create risks of abuse by communities resistant to newcomers, who might take to manufacturing evidence against newcomers or indulging in other forms of victimisation. When the 1996 Act was going through Parliament, there was considerable disquiet and moves to establish clearer and more accessible criteria for the granting of possession, but such attempts were unsuccessful.

CHAPTER 5

SECURE TENANCIES

INTRODUCTION

It is difficult to imagine, especially until recently, local authorities being trusted with the management of anything, let alone millions of council houses. However, until 1980, there was very little intervention in the relationship of landlord and tenant in the public sector, certainly so far as security of tenure was concerned, largely because it was assumed that local authorities would exercise their housing management functions responsibly and not indulge in capricious or vindictive use of discretion. In this connection, the case of *London Borough of Hammersmith and Fulham v Harrison* [1981] 2 All ER 588 is instructive. The Court of Appeal were faced with arguments that, as with the early Rent Acts, the impact of the 1980 Act should be retroactive, conferring security on those already subject to an expired notice to quit. Lord Justice Brandon rejected the comparison and said:

> By contrast, Chapter II of Pt 1 of the 1980 Act was not enacted in order to meet any immediate or urgent crisis in housing accommodation. Its purpose was rather the social one of giving to tenants in the public housing sector, so far as reasonably practicable, the same kind of protection from being evicted from their homes without good and sufficient cause as had been enjoyed by tenants in the private housing sector for many decades under the Rent Acts. This assimilation of rights as between public and private sector tenants, though no doubt regarded as desirable in the general interests of social equality and non-discrimination, was not an urgent matter, and no special reason for setting the earliest possible deadline for such assimilation existed. In this connection, it is to be observed that, for numerous years past, it had been thought safe and proper to give to local authority landlords a complete discretion with regard to the eviction of public sector tenants, and to rely on them to exercise such discretion fairly and wisely.

There is certainly a long history of the courts approving the utmost discretion for authorities, short of bad faith or the most glaring *Wednesbury* unreasonableness. In *Shelley v London County Council* [1948] 2 All ER 898, Lord Porter said, 'It is, to my mind, one of the important duties of management that the local body should be able to pick and choose their tenants at will'. Even model tenants, therefore, had no rights in this regard, as was demonstrated in *Cannock Chase DC v Kelly* [1978] 1 All ER 152. As Lord Justice Lawton put it:

> ... the duty to assess need and to allocate resources may necessitate notices to quit being given to persons who have paid their rent and complied with the terms of their tenancies. The giving of a notice to quit to such a tenant is consistent with proper management, regulation and control.

The change in 1980 to a more elaborate framework of rights sometimes dignified with the name of the 'tenant's charter' was, therefore not necessarily because the rights gap between private and public sectors was crying out to be filled, although, naturally, the *Kelly* approach attracted some criticism. The more cynical interpretation of the sudden change is that a framework was primarily needed to establish the right to buy that a clear constituency of prospective purchasers had to be identified. The main idea behind the 1980 Act can be seen in the flagship section, s 1, under which it is proclaimed that a secure tenant has the right to buy, long before the defining characteristics of a secure tenant are revealed.

Before examining the provisions of the right to buy, it is necessary to work through the familiar pattern of definition of status, security of tenure and rent rights. The governing statute is now the Housing Act 1985. The Housing Act 1996 has made some alterations to the grounds for possession.

The definition of a secure tenancy

Section 79 (1) states:

> A tenancy under which a dwelling-house is let as a separate dwelling is a secure tenancy at any time when the conditions described in ss 80 and 81 as the landlord condition and the tenant condition are satisfied.

The terminology of tenancy, dwelling-house and let as a separate dwelling is familiar from the Rent Act 1977 and the Housing Act 1988. One difference, however, is that the 1985 Act contains no provision comparable to s 22 of the 1977 Act or s 3 of the 1988 legislation, under which rights are safeguarded if there is partial exclusive occupation and sharing of other rooms such as kitchens. An occupier who shares a kitchen will not be able to be a secure tenant (*Central YMCA Housing Association Ltd v Saunders* (1990) 23 HLR 212).

The interpretation of 'let as a separate dwelling' also arose in the complicated circumstances of *Basingstoke and Deane Borough Council v Paice* (1995) 27 HLR 433, where a secure tenancy mysteriously blossomed from the lease, by a council, of a garage subsequently partially converted into a residential flat and let on a protected tenancy. When the intermediate landlord surrendered the lease of the main premises to the council, it was held that the tenant of the flat became a secure tenant by operation of law. There is no equivalent in the 1985 Act to the provisions in the s 137 of the Rent Act 1977 under which subtenants become tenants of the head landlord when the intermediate lease is determined, but the Court of Appeal decided that s 79 was flexible enough to admit of these rare circumstances. The particular difficulty alleged with 'let as a separate dwelling' was that, at the time of the surrender of the intermediate tenancy, the flat was not so let, since the only relevant premises at that point were the main premises held by the intermediate landlord.

Licences

By virtue of s 79(3) and a somewhat perplexing sub-section, licensees appear to acquire equivalent status to secure tenancies. It baldly states that:

> ... the provisions of this Part apply in relation to a licence to occupy a dwelling-house (whether or not granted for a consideration) as they apply in relation to a tenancy.

There is, on the face of it, a desire to transcend the wrangling over leases and licences that bedevilled the private sector for years and to confer basic rights on licensees. On the other hand, if authorities can be trusted not to indulge in the elaborate tactics required to create licences, since their licences tend to be genuine ones, unlike private sector landlords, why bother to upgrade certain licences in the mysteriously oblique fashion found in s 79(3)? If local authority licences are not shams, why not leave well alone? However, the generosity falls short of conferring the right to buy on licensees, since the reference to 'this Part' confine it to Pt IV, when the right to buy is in Pt V and a similar barrier operated in the 1980 Act.

The significance of s 79(3) was assessed in *Westminster City Council v Clarke* [1992] 1 All ER 695. The defendant was a full duty unintentionally homeless person, in priority need because of vulnerability. Westminster placed him in a room in a hostel under an agreement which stressed that it conferred a personal licence and non-exclusive occupation. After complaints about his conduct, steps were taken to evict him, but the initial possession order was reversed by the Court of Appeal, which held that he was a secure tenant. This is not at all like the traditional approach of the Court of Appeal to the lease/licence distinction and it can be conjectured that resentment of *Street v Mountford* prompted a mischievous desire to get rid of an allegedly bad law by overenforcing it and drawing attention to its apparent awkwardness in other contexts. At any rate, the significance of the Court of Appeal decision was that the occupant got substantially greater rights than contemplated, that possession would only be recoverable against him through one of the recognised grounds for possession.

The House of Lords and Lord Templeman, again in a solo judgment, failed to focus on the ostensible purpose behind s 79(3), which makes no mention of exclusive possession (or occupation) as a prerequisite for licences being equated with tenancies. The issue, then, is how far the general law established in *Street* is relevant to the different circumstances obtaining in the public sector. Lord Templeman took the view that s 79(3) did not alter the general principle that required exclusive possession if a licence were to be on a par with a secure tenancy. From what has already been established, it would be almost self-contradictory, in most instances, to suppose that a licensee could have exclusive possession. Perhaps, a way out would have been to invoke the exemptions listed in *Facchini v Bryson* [1952] 1 TLR 1386 and to argue that there was no intention to create a tenancy and, hence, no likelihood of exclusive possession. Another simpler approach would have been to assert that, in the circumstances, something like a lodger arrangement was created, since by its nature the agreement reserved and required genuine rights of control, supervision and access. In the event, Lord Templeman reached the pragmatic conclusion that Mr Clarke did not have exclusive possession of his room and stressed the peculiarities of the hostel arrangement, with a view to deterring any imitations from those anxious to avoid the Rent Acts (presumably, future Rent Acts).

Therefore, although the reasoning may be tortuous, the conclusion is clear enough: s 79(3) has no application unless exclusive possession has also been granted. This leaves it with very little scope, as likely candidates for exclusive possession licenses, such as service occupiers, are independently excluded from secure status anyway. The original purpose of s 79(3) could well be obscure, but it does not deserve to be pensioned off in this fashion.

Ex-squatter licensees

By virtue of s 79(4), sub-s (3) does not apply to a licence granted as a temporary expedient to a person who entered the dwelling-house or any other land as a trespasser. We now know that sub-s (3) does not apply unless exclusive possession has been granted, so does this mean that temporary licences to squatters without exclusive possession are ineligible anyway? The relationship between sub-ss (3) and (4) has been confused by the *Clarke* decision.

The tenant condition

According to s 81 of the 1985 Act, the tenant condition identified in s 79 will be met if the tenant is an individual and occupies the dwelling-house as his only or principal home, or in the case of a joint tenancy, all are individuals and at least one joint tenant so occupies. This clearly inspired the preconditions for assured tenancies under the 1988 Act and has the obvious purpose in the public sector of precluding the proliferation of security in different premises and multiple purchases under the right to buy.

The landlord condition

Section 80(1) describes the prescribed public bodies. They are limited to: a local authority; a new town corporation; a housing action trust; an urban development corporation; the Development Board for Rural Wales; and certain housing co-operatives. The list of prescribed landlords shrank significantly in 1988 when it was determined to 'privatise' housing associations and charitable housing trusts and, as already seen, locate them with private sector assured landlords under the Housing Act 1988. The obvious consequence of this is that housing association tenancies predating 15 January 1989 are likely to be secure. In addition, s 35 of the 1985 Act decrees that some tenancies entered into after the commencement date for 1988 can still be secure. These include the obvious, such as tenancies granted pursuant to a contract predating 15 January and tenancies granted to a person who immediately prior to the grant was a secure tenant. They can also originate where possession has been granted on a suitable alternative accommodation ground and the court considers that an assured tenancy does not provide sufficient security.

Exclusions from secure tenancy status

The predictable list of exceptions is found in Sched 1 to the Housing Act 1985.

(1) Long leases

These are defined in s 115 of the Act as tenancies for a term certain exceeding 21 years. There may be possibilities of enfranchisement or extension of the lease under the

Leasehold Reform Act 1967 or the Leasehold Reform, Housing and Urban Development Act 1993 for leaseholders of houses and flats respectively.

(2) Premises occupied in connection with employment

A tenancy is not secure if the tenant is an employee of the landlord or of various listed public bodies and his contract of employment requires him to occupy the dwelling-house for the better performance of his duties. Members of the police force and fire services are specifically excluded, in the former case, where subsidised housing is provided and, in the latter, where the purpose of the letting is to ensure close proximity to a fire station.

If the drafting of an employment contract is careful, it will be difficult for an employee to claim secure status. In *Elvidge v Coventry City Council* [1993] EGCS 140, there was originally no requirement, but, after promotion, a new contract incorporating the formula in para 2 was accepted and secure status was, therefore, unattainable.

In *Hughes v Greenwich London Borough Council* [1994] 1 AC 170, on the facts, there was no requirement of occupation for the better performance of duties. A headmaster was able on retirement to exercise the right to buy a house built for him about a quarter of a mile from his school. It was not essential for him to occupy the house in order to do his job, although it was certainly convenient. In such circumstances, the court was not prepared to imply any term into the contract. As Lord Lowry put it in the House of Lords:

> In order that a term may be implied, there has to be a compelling reason for deeming that term to form part of the contract, and that compelling reason is missing in this case, unless it was essential that Mr Hughes should live in the house in order to do his job, but the facts found contradict that proposition.

By contrast, in the case of *South Glamorgan County Council v Griffiths* (1992) 24 HLR 334, it was held that, even if there was no express term in the contract of employment, it was legitimate to imply an occupational requirement if it was essential for the employee to occupy for the better performance of his duties. In that case, the implication was easier on the facts than in *Hughes*, since the employee in question was a school caretaker and the house was next to the school. Mr Griffiths also produced an argument that was never likely to succeed, namely, that, on retirement, he fell outside para 2 and, hence, was a secure tenant. The Court of Appeal were understandably unsympathetic to this approach, but did stress that authorities should not prejudice outcomes by significant delay in seeking possession.

(3) Land acquired for development

A tenancy is not secure if the dwelling-house is on land which has been acquired for development and the dwelling-house is used by the landlord as temporary housing accommodation pending that development. Development has the traditional meaning ascribed to it in the Town and Country Planning Acts. This paragraph does not specify that the landlord who originally acquired the land has to be the same as the current landlord, so the exclusion operates where the landlord's predecessor actually acquired it. If any plans for development fall through the exception will cease to apply.

(4) Accommodation for homeless persons

We have already seen how certain temporary accommodation provided for homeless persons cannot be an assured tenancy. The same principles operate in relation to secure tenancies, where the authority has to house pending the outcome of inquiries, but there is no intention to create a secure tenancy. The circumstances outlined in this exclusion fall under s 63 (duty to house while investigating apparent priority need), s 65(3) (temporary duties to the priority need intentional homeless) and s 68(1), where the housing duty arises in respect of local connection investigation. Any tenancy granted in such circumstances cannot be secure until a year has elapsed, so authorities have to diary ahead. It is always possible, though unlikely, that the tenant will be notified before the year is up that the tenancy has become secure. The 1996 Act modifications to the homelessness rules do not affect the position here.

(5) Temporary accommodation for persons taking up employment

The idea behind this exclusion is the straightforward one of assisting people from outside a district to take up employment there, but without creating a secure tenancy. The preconditions for exclusion are that the tenant must be informed in advance about the exception and that the tenancy was to meet the need for temporary accommodation in order to work and to find somewhere more permanent to live. As with the previous exception, there is a time limit of one year.

(6) Short term arrangements

This paragraph states:

> A tenancy is not a secure tenancy if:
>
> (a) the dwelling-house has been leased to the landlord with vacant possession for use as temporary housing accommodation;
>
> (b) the terms on which it has been leased include provision for the lessor to obtain vacant possession from the landlord on the expiry of a specified period or when required by the lessor;
>
> (c) the lessor is not a body which is capable of granting secure tenancies; and
>
> (d) the landlord has no interest in the dwelling-house other than under the lease in question or as a mortgagee.

Such arrangements are designed to give guarantees of repossession to private sector landlords letting to authorities who then sublet. Prior to the 1980 Act and the advent of secure tenancies, such triangular arrangements were straightforward since the temporary occupants could not claim protection under the Rent Acts against a public sector landlord.

What is the position if the local authority is granted a licence, rather than a lease, in these circumstances, and creates licences for temporary occupiers? At this point, the difficult sub-s 79(3) resurfaces, stating that the provisions of Pt IV of the Act apply to a licence to occupy a dwelling-house in the same way as they apply to a tenancy. In that case, the occupier under the double licence arrangement would have a secure licence unless the arrangement fell within para 6.

In *Tower Hamlets London Borough Council v Miah* [1992] 2 All ER 667, the court made heavy weather of analysing such a transaction. On a strict interpretation of the exception, an obvious paradox arises: that a licence obtained from a local authority licensee confers greater security on an occupant than a licence from a local authority tenant. Is it, therefore, justifiable, on common sense pragmatic grounds, to argue that 'leased' in (a) includes 'licensed', as the greater includes the lesser? The Court of Appeal decreed that it was and so the exception was applicable.

(7) Temporary accommodation during works

> A tenancy is not a secure tenancy if:
>
> (a) the dwelling-house has been made available for occupation by the tenant (or a predecessor in title of his) while works are carried out on a dwelling-house which he previously occupied as his home; and
>
> (b) the tenant or predecessor was not a secure tenant of that other dwelling-house at the time when he ceased to occupy it as his home.

The purpose of this is clear, but what is not so obvious is the type of insecure tenancy envisaged where the tenant or predecessor occupies premises as his home before being temporarily accommodated elsewhere. Are other inhabitants of Sched 1 what the draftsman had in mind or, rather situations where the landlord condition is not satisfied?

(8) Agricultural holdings

A tenancy is not secure if the dwelling-house is comprised in an agricultural holding (as defined by the Agricultural Holdings Act 1986) and is occupied by the person responsible for the control of the farming of the holding. Such an exception has counterparts in the Rent Act 1977 and the Housing Act 1988 and is unlikely to affect many tenancies.

(9) Licensed premises

A tenancy is not secure if the dwelling-house consists of or includes premises licensed for the sale of intoxicating liquor for consumption on the premises. Comparison should be made with s 11 of the 1977 Act and para 5 of Sched 1 to the Housing Act 1988.

(10) Student lettings

The underlying purpose, here, is equivalent to the comparable sections in the 1977 and 1988 Acts, but there are more procedural formalities for public sector landlords to observe. There has to be prior notice specifying the educational establishment in question and warning the student of the significance of the exception. There are two eventualities that the exception specifically caters for. The first, comprises the situation where the course has finished, in which case the tenancy cannot be secure for six months after the student has ceased to attend. The second, 'in any other case', presumably where the student does not stay the course, the exclusion will prevail until six months after the grant of the tenancy.

(11) Business tenancies

A tenancy is not a secure tenancy if it is one to which Pt II of the Landlord and Tenant Act 1954 applies (tenancies of premises occupied for business purposes).

(12) Almshouses

The charitable impulses do not extend to conferring secure status on licensees. It is stated that a licence to occupy a dwelling-house is not a secure tenancy if the licence was granted by an almshouse charity in certain circumstances. This exception, therefore, makes further, but not massive, inroads into an already etiolated s 79(3).

Overall, the list of exceptions to secure status is tightly drafted, not only to maximise the constituency of those with tenant's charter rights, but also to facilitate the right to buy.

SECURITY OF TENURE FOR SECURE TENANTS

Repossessions by local authorities are often processed rapidly by the courts, quite often because tenants are unrepresented, absent or unclear of their rights or a combination of such factors.

The grounds for possession in Sched 2 to the 1985 Act contain some principles common to private sector legislation, but other elements which are unique to the public sector and reflect the authority's housing management role. There is provision in the 1996 Housing Act to strengthen the grounds for possession still further against anti-social behaviour. These measures will be analysed in detail in due course.

The starting point in the 1985 Act is s 82, which, in sub-s (1), stipulates that neither periodic nor fixed term tenancies can be brought to an end by the landlord, save by obtaining a court order. A tenancy can be terminated by the tenant in accordance with the notice to quit requirements if it is periodic and by surrender or other methods if it is fixed term.

Section 84(1) ordains that the court cannot make a possession order, save on one or more of the grounds set out in Sched 2 to the Act. Before court proceedings can commence, the landlord has to serve a 'notice seeking possession' on the tenant in accordance with s 83 of the Act. The notice must give particulars of the ground(s) relied on to give the tenant a chance to make amends if possible. If, for example, arrears of rent constitutes the ground, the amount of arrears should be specified. The notice has to be in the form specified by Regulations made by the Secretary of State (at present, the

Secure Tenancies (Notices) Regulations 1987 SI 1987/755). The provisions for the subsequent recovery of possession vary, as frequently happens, between periodic and fixed term tenancies.

Fixed term tenancies

Where there is provision in the lease for re-entry or forfeiture, under s 82(3), if forfeiture would otherwise have happened, the court has to make an order terminating the tenancy. At this point, a periodic tenancy springs up by virtue of s 86, just as it would if the tenancy expired by the passing of time. The only exception to this is if the tenant is granted another secure tenancy of the same dwelling-house to begin at the end of the first tenancy.

Periodic tenancies

The procedural requirements in s 83 govern secure periodic tenancies, whether original or imposed by s 86. The notice must specify a date after which proceedings for possession may be begun and only remains in force for 12 months.

Impact of the 1996 Act: new s 83

Section 147 of the Act substitutes a new s 83, substantially reproducing the old. However, one innovation is the opportunity for an authority to start possession proceedings at an earlier stage than previously where Ground 2 and anti-social behaviour are involved. The court can entertain possession proceedings as soon as the notice of intention to seek possession has been served. In addition, the court has jurisdiction analogous to that in other contexts to dispense with the requirement of the issuing of such notices if it appears just and equitable to do so. This will be welcomed by authorities with a cavalier approach to procedural niceties.

A new s 83A is also added and is similar to the formalities for assured tenancies in this sphere. Where possession is sought on the ground of domestic violence and notice is served on the tenant and the departed partner is not the tenant or party to the proceedings, the court has to be satisfied that a copy of the notice has been served on the departed partner or that reasonable steps have been taken to achieve that end.

The problems of joint tenancies and notices to quit

At this point, it is appropriate to dwell on some of the difficulties occasioned by the interaction of the law on the termination of tenancies in the broad context of matrimonial and related disputes. Cases, such as *London Borough of Harrow v Johnstone* [1997] 1 WLR 459, show the House of Lords coming to grips with various important themes, such as the doctrine that unilateral acts are effective to determine a joint tenancy and concerns about actions to regain possession against a sole remaining spouse being in contempt of court. The notorious *Spycatcher* case (*Attorney General v Times Newspapers Ltd* [1992] 1 AC 191) was even invoked (unsuccessfully) in this latter connection.

The precise history of the breakdown of the Johnstone household now has to be sketched. The Johnstones had a joint secure tenancy from Harrow of some years standing, with four weeks notice stipulated in the agreement. In 1994, the wife left the matrimonial home, taking the children. The husband obtained a 'prohibited steps' order under the Children Act 1989 and another order under the Domestic Violence and Matrimonial Proceedings Act 1976, forbidding the wife to use violence against him or otherwise harass him or 'to exclude or attempt to exclude' him from the matrimonial home.

The wife's predicament in seeking housing was, naturally, the fact that her continuing tenancy disqualified her from any right to new accommodation. Harrow therefore advised her to serve the appropriate notice to quit on them and she complied. When told of the imminent termination of the tenancy, the husband refused to vacate and relied on the above mentioned injunction. Nevertheless, Harrow persisted with proceedings for possession against him and lost both at first instance and in the Court of Appeal, on the grounds that such circumvention of the 1976 Act injunction was a contempt of court.

In the House of Lords, due attention was given to what could be styled the preliminary issue, the validity of any unilateral notice to quit and the merits of the decision in *Hammersmith London Borough Council v Monk* [1992] 1 AC 418. The basic problem confronted by the judges in both cases was the relationship between the traditional common law doctrine of determination of tenancies and the modern climate of protective social legislation. Should the fact that unilateral termination can deprive the other spouse of 'vested' statutory rights steer the courts towards reassessment of traditional doctrine? In *Monk*, Lord Bridge had refused to muddy the waters through consequentialist reasoning of this type. His view was:

> This may appear an untoward result and may, consequently, provoke a certain reluctance to hold that the law can permit one of two joint tenants unilaterally to deprive his co-tenant of 'rights' which both are equally entitled to enjoy. But, the statutory consequences are, in truth, of no relevance to the question which your Lordships have to decide. That question is whether, at common law, a contractual periodic tenancy granted to two or more joint tenants is incapable of termination by a tenant's notice to quit unless it is served with the concurrence of all the joint tenants.

This, of course, is based more on assertion than argument, but Lord Mustill, in *Johnstone*, accepted this approach and concluded that, in the absence of the special procedural context of the case, the wife's notice to quit did have the desired effect and terminated the joint tenancy. What, then, could be made of the argument that the wife, by giving notice to quit, was in breach of the relevant injunction and that that tainted the later actions of herself and the council? Given that the order actually granted to the husband, in this instance, was some sort of non-molestation order under the 1976 Act, what was the effect of the wife's subsequent actions? Lord Mustill's analysis, again heavier on assertion than argument, was as follows:

> It is, in my view, absolutely plain that the prohibition order against excluding the husband was not intended to be a mandatory order, requiring the wife to co-operate in maintaining in force the rights created by the joint tenancy, pending the adjustment of these rights on a future date in proceedings not yet started. The application was made at a

> time of crisis when the husband had been locked out of the house and wanted to get back in. His concern was that his wife had excluded him from the exercise of the rights of occupation which he undoubtedly possessed under the joint tenancy. There is no sign in the documents of an apprehension on his part that the rights themselves were under threat and would require protection by an order requiring the wife to keep the tenancy in being.

The logic of this argument is that the husband is heavily penalised for lack of foresight and preoccupation with enjoyment of, rather than perpetuation of, tenancy rights. It also suggests that a typical emergency prompted injunction gained under the 1976 Act is of no avail against the simplest possible manoeuvre – the service of a notice to quit. What of the other argument adduced by the husband, relating to the integrity of the judicial process and the possibility of a contempt of court? It is at this point that the media cases, such as *Spycatcher,* become marginally relevant. The *Spycatcher* litigation is distinguishable in that there was a clear intention to act defiantly and interfere with the course of justice by publishing forbidden information to get other papers off the hook. However, there were pronouncements from the House of Lords in *Spycatcher* to suggest that the courts will intervene to avert destruction of certain vested interests when, as Lord Oliver put it:

> The gratuitous intervention of a third party intended to result in that purpose being frustrated and the outcome of the trial prejudiced must manifestly interfere with and obstruct what the court has determined to be the interests of justice.

The problem with identifying such acts and interests in the *Johnstone* case was that, at the time the wife served the notice to quit, there were no proceedings in train involving such matters as adjustment of proprietary rights. Why should Harrow be expected to delve beneath the surface of the scenario presented to it of the departure of the wife and the need for separate accommodation? If there were no proceedings pending, then how could Harrow be thought to conspire or collude to frustrate such proceedings? According to Lord Mustill, there were clear reasons for rejecting the *Spycatcher* approach and any assumptions about contempt of court:

> There, the newspaper defiantly acted in detriment to the obvious interests of justice. Here, the council simply carried through the logic of its housing policy, that one person could not have two council tenancies at the same time. I find it impossible to hold that, by putting its statutory duty as housing authority before the interests of a matrimonial relationship of which it was not the guardian, the council contemptuously subverted the authority of the court or intentionally nullified the aims of any legal proceedings. So, the council was entitled to possession.

Different types of ground for possession

As has been seen, private sector grounds, particularly in the 1988 Act, often lean heavily towards the mandatory to facilitate recovery of possession. There are no mandatory grounds in the 1985 Act, although there was an attempt to insert one in the recent Housing Bill and, instead, there is, in s 84, a tripartite division of the 16 current grounds. Possession will not be granted in the case of Grounds 1–8 unless the court considers it reasonable to make the order. For Grounds 9–11 the only prerequisite is that the court is satisfied that suitable accommodation will be available for the tenant when the order takes effect. So, Grounds 9, 10 and 11 are the closest to mandatory the public sector criteria get. Grounds 12–16 operate on combined criteria, with both reasonableness and availability of suitable accommodation required. Many of the grounds are identical to private sector grounds or closely equivalent and more detailed attention will be paid to those which are unique to the public sector.

Grounds on which the court may order possession if it considers it reasonable

Ground 1: rent arrears or breach of obligation

> Rent lawfully due from the tenant has not been paid or an obligation of the tenancy has been broken or not performed.

This corresponds to Case 1 of the 1977 Act. Characteristically, in the case of rent arrears, a possession order will be granted and suspended on certain conditions. Local authorities have to be careful when negotiating with tenants after certain orders have been granted, in case they inadvertently re-negotiate a new tenancy and have to begin possession proceedings *de novo*. This point was illustrated in the case of *Burrows v Brent London Borough Council* (1995) 27 HLR 748. Brent had obtained a final possession order for non-payment of rent and an order for payment of arrears. When the arrears were not forthcoming within 14 days, the council then agreed with Ms Burrows that she could continue to live in her flat so long as she paid a sum equivalent to rent and made regular payments towards the arrears. She failed to comply with this further agreement and the council sought to enforce its possession order. Brent argued that the agreement was simply to suspend the operation of the possession order on certain conditions and did not involve any intention to create a legal relationship or grant her exclusive occupation. However, the Court of Appeal disagreed and concluded that the obvious purpose of the agreement was to allow her to stay in exclusive occupation of the property at a rent and, therefore, conferred on her either a tenancy or a licence to occupy. It was unnecessary to decide which, as either would give her secure status by virtue of the notorious s 79(3).

By contrast, in *Greenwich London Borough Council v Regan* (1996) 28 HLR 469, it was established that re-negotiation of terms is not so perilous for landlords where it is overshadowed by a suspended, rather than final, order for possession. Mr Regan was subject to a suspended order for several years and eventually agreed to pay a more substantial sum towards the arrears in addition to the usual weekly rent. The Court of Appeal considered that it was, in every case, a question of fact whether the conduct of parties was consistent with modification of their existing relationship or whether a new relationship was created. They placed emphasis on the statement from Lord Justice Auld in *Burrows*: 'It all depends what the parties intended in the circumstances.' This ostensibly objective test, in fact, gives scope for the courts to impose their own version of events. Landlords re-negotiating after suspended orders are likely to be viewed favourably and saved from commencing possession proceedings all over again, but there are logical difficulties about fresh negotiations when a tenancy is defunct after a final possession order.

These logical problems, however, did not dissuade the House of Lords in *Burrows* from allowing the appeal by Brent ([1996] 1 WLR 1448). The central notion used in the House of Lords, that of the 'tolerated trespasser', is not, however, one which looks doctrinally respectable or, indeed, conceptually distinct from that of the licence it is designed to replace. The pragmatic justification for the notion is, however, very clear, that the effect of the Court of Appeal judgment would be to create a new tenancy or licence whenever there was by agreement any variation of a possession order. Lord Browne-Wilkinson in the leading judgment deplored the idea that 'humane and reasonable landlords' acting with generous impulses should be penalised in this way. If the Court of Appeal argument were upheld, then councils would be wary of making concessions or would have to apply to the court for variation of an existing order and His Lordship found it 'impossible to believe that Parliament intended to produce such an unreasonable regime, penalising sensible agreements out of court and requiring repeated applications to an already overstretched court system'.

What, then, was the legal approach endorsed by the House of Lords? As has happened previously, the court is thrown back on a vague test of intention – in traditional language, *quo animo* – with what intention – the parties acted. This test gives ample scope for finding the real intention in the collective will of the local authority's functionaries, rather than in the mind of the struggling tenant who, presumably, did not intend to act detrimentally to her own interests. In the particular context, secure tenancies were *sui generis* – in a class of their own – and the actions of the local authority signalled a willingness not to terminate the tenancy if certain conditions were met. In such a context, doctrine about the impact of a tenant holding over on termination of an ordinary tenancy was inappropriate and it was unnecessary to attribute to the parties any intention to create a new tenancy or licence, since the old tenancy could be seen as being in limbo or suspended animation. Accordingly, the correct designation of the occupant was a trespasser whom the landlord has undertaken not to evict – a 'tolerated trespasser'.

However congenial to hard pressed local authorities, this decision does betray a rather cavalier approach to traditional doctrine. Of course, it is not the fault of the House of Lords that the rather mysterious s 79(3), which privileges licensees in a rather spectacular fashion, has remained on the statute book for so long. If that section were to be repealed or refashioned, then the obvious finding of a licence would not be so catastrophic for landlords. Another possible solution would be to add to the list of exclusions from secure tenancy status.

The interaction of eventual eviction for rent arrears and continuing responsibility for defaulters under the homelessness rules, albeit intentional homelessness, has also to be considered.

So far as breach of other covenants is concerned, a case illustrative of the discretion operative is *Wandsworth London Borough Council v Hargreaves* [1994] EGCS 115, where the covenant in question was 'not to permit to be done anything which may increase the risk of fire'. A visitor to the flat made a mistake in petrol bomb manufacture and caused a serious fire. The tenant had not participated. The Court of Appeal held that it was not reasonable to make a possession order. By contrast, where tenants are in persistent breach of apparently minor covenants, such as those prohibiting the keeping of dogs, they could well be evicted (*Green v Sheffield City Council* (1993) 26 HLR 349). Again, such tenants are presumably intentionally homeless.

Ground 2: misconduct or conviction

> The tenant or a person residing in the dwelling-house has been guilty of conduct which is a nuisance or annoyance to neighbours, or has been convicted of using the dwelling-house or allowing it to be used for immoral or illegal purposes.

This formulation echoes Case 1 under the 1977 Act and Ground 14 of the 1988 Act, although 'neighbours' is preferred to 'adjoining occupiers'. Dissatisfaction with the slowness of the machinery for recovery of possession has led to the use of injunctions to restrain action more speedily. The alarm about nuisance and anti-social behaviour has prompted substitution of this ground in the Housing Act 1988, s 144. It reads:

> The tenant or a person residing in or visiting the dwelling-house:
>
> (a) has been guilty of conduct causing or likely to cause a nuisance or annoyance to a person residing, visiting or otherwise engaging in a lawful activity in the locality; or
>
> (b) has been convicted of:
>
> (i) using the dwelling-house or allowing it to be used for immoral or illegal purposes; or
>
> (ii) an arrestable offence committed in, or in the locality of, the dwelling-house.

As comparison of the two grounds demonstrates, the net is to be cast wider in future. The emphasis on conduct likely to cause a nuisance allows for the possibility of evidence from third parties not themselves affected, such as local authority officers. This, in turn, has raised the problem of the possibility of eviction through uncorroborated evidence. In the original draft of the Bill, 'vicinity of the dwelling-house' was preferred to locality, but the latter has been chosen to reflect the ambition to cover as wide an area as possible. 'Neighbourhood' was also considered and rejected. The courts were bound to get their teeth into the semantics of 'locality' before long.

In *Manchester City Council v Lawler* (1999) 31 HLR 119, the Court of Appeal took the opportunity to endorse a broad and flexible interpretation of 'locality', allowing an appeal by the council against the view of the trial judge that the terms of the tenant's undertaking, including reference to 'in the locality of' her property, were unclear. Ms Lawler had given various undertakings following an application for a possession order and Manchester sought to commit her to prison for breach of them after an incident involving the threatening of a child with a knife in a shopping precinct three streets away from her home. The appellate court were satisfied that 'in the locality' was sufficiently precise and that it was up to the courts to determine their precise scope on the facts. Here, it was obvious that the scene of the incident was 'in the locality'.

New Ground 2A: domestic violence

Section 145 of the 1996 Act introduces the following new ground at this point:

> The dwelling-house was occupied (whether alone or with others) by a married couple or a couple living together as husband and wife and:
>
> (a) one or both of the partners is a tenant of the dwelling-house;
>
> (b) one partner has left because of the violence of the other towards:
>
> (i) that partner; or
>
> (ii) a member of the family of that partner who was residing with that partner immediately before the partner left;
>
> (c) the court is satisfied that the partner who has left is unlikely to return.

As already discussed in relation to the comparable innovation for assured tenancies and housing associations, any initiative against domestic violence is broadly supported, but there are claims that the scope of this ground is still too narrow.

Ground 3: deterioration in condition of dwelling-house

> The condition of the dwelling-house or any of the common parts has deteriorated owing to acts of waste by, or the neglect or default of, the tenant or a person residing in the dwelling-house and, in the case of an act of waste by, or the neglect or default of, a person lodging with the tenant or a subtenant of his, the tenant has not taken such steps as he ought reasonably to have taken for the removal of the lodger or subtenant.

This wording has already been encountered in Case 3 under the Rent Act 1977. The tortuous wording cries out for greater brevity and the presence of the archaic doctrine of waste is incongruous in modern social legislation. The Law Commission has recently recommended abolition of the doctrine and replacement with some more sensible formula. (Report No 238: *Landlord and Tenant: Responsibility for State and Condition of Property*.)

Ground 4: deterioration of furniture

> The condition of furniture provided by the landlord for use under the tenancy, or for use in the common parts, has deteriorated owing to ill treatment by the tenant or a person residing in the dwelling-house and, in the case of ill treatment by such a person lodging with the tenant or a subtenant of his, the tenant has not taken such steps as he ought reasonably to have taken for the removal of the lodger or sub tenant.

Another ground virtually identical to a Rent Act Case 4, but whose purpose in the public sector is not so clear. How often do local authorities provide furniture for tenants, as opposed to insecure licensees and hostel dwellers?

Ground 5: false statement by tenant

> The tenant is the person, or one of the persons, to whom the tenancy was granted and the landlord was induced to grant the tenancy by a false statement made knowingly or recklessly by the tenant.

This is the ground borrowed by the Act for housing association assured tenancies. The 1996 Act also substitutes for the last three words 'by – (a) the tenant; or (b) a person acting at the tenant's instigation' (s 146). An instance of such a falsehood is *Rushcliffe BC v Watson* (1991) 24 HLR 124, where a person obtained a secure tenancy by concealing the existence of her housing association tenancy and claiming to be staying with family and friends. The false statement has to be made by the tenant, so there could be circumstances where there has been a misrepresentation of fact by a member of the tenant's household at no risk to the tenant's security.

Ground 6: premium paid on assignment by virtue of exchange

> The tenancy was assigned to the tenant, or to a predecessor in title of his who is a member of his family and is residing in the dwelling-house, by an assignment made by virtue of s 92 (assignments by way of exchange) and a premium was paid either in connection with that assignment or the assignment which the tenant or predecessor himself made by virtue of that section. In this paragraph, 'premium' means any fine or other like sum and any other pecuniary consideration in addition to rent.

This ground relates only to exploitation of official exchange and does not touch on the widespread practice in some areas of extracting 'key money' as the price of an informal assignment.

Ground 7: misconduct by employee

> The dwelling-house forms part of, or is within the curtilage of, a building which, or so much of it as is held by the landlord, is held mainly for purposes other than housing purposes and consists mainly of accommodation other than housing accommodation, and:
>
> (a) the dwelling-house was let to the tenant or a predecessor in title of his in consequence of the tenant or predecessor being in the employment of the landlord, or of:
> a local authority;
> a new town corporation;
> a housing action trust;
> an urban development corporation;
> the Development Board for Rural Wales; or
> the governors of an aided school; and
>
> (b) the tenant or a person residing in the dwelling-house has been guilty of conduct such that, having regard to the purpose for which the building is used, it would not be right for him to continue in occupation of the dwelling-house.

This elaborate ground requires some deciphering. It is unique to the 1985 Act and is aimed rather obliquely at situations, such as misconduct by a school or hospital caretaker, hence the laborious references to purposes other than housing purposes. How common such evictions are is not known, but they are unlikely to be numerous given the special circumstances. Points of interpretation which could prove awkward if the higher courts become involved are the position of service occupiers who are licensees. Presumably, because they are likely to fall foul of the exclusion of service occupancy by virtue of Sched 1, para 2, they cannot be drawn into this ground by the operation of the ubiquitous s 79(3). And is that what the vague formulation 'in consequence of being in the employment' is intended to convey? Is it something less than a prerequisite for the better performance of duties? But, how likely is that if the occupation is in part of or within the curtilage of the school or hospital in question?

Ground 8: temporary occupation while works are carried out

> The dwelling-house was made available for occupation by the tenant (or a predecessor in title of his) while works were carried out on the dwelling-house which he previously occupied as his only or principal home and:
>
> (a) the tenant (or predecessor) was a secure tenant of the other dwelling-house at the time when he ceased to occupy it as his home;
>
> (b) the tenant (or predecessor) accepted the tenancy of the dwelling-house of which possession is sought on the understanding that he would give up occupation when on completion of the works, the other dwelling-house was again available for occupation by him under a secure tenancy; and
>
> (c) the works have been completed and the other dwelling-house is so available.

The purpose of this ground is more obvious and the court retains discretion to confirm occupation in the new temporary accommodation if the authority is dragging its feet.

Grounds on which the court may order possession if suitable alternative accommodation is available

Ground 9: overcrowding

> The dwelling-house is overcrowded within the meaning of Pt X, in such circumstances as to render the occupier guilty of an offence.

Ground 10: demolition or reconstruction

> The landlord intends, within a reasonable time of obtaining possession of the dwelling-house:
>
> (a) to demolish or reconstruct the building or part of the building comprising the dwelling-house; or
>
> (b) to carry out work on that building or on land let together with, and thus treated as part of, the dwelling-house,
>
> and cannot reasonably do so without obtaining possession of the dwelling-house.

One of the advantages of this ground is that it gives scope for evicting people where misconduct is difficult to prove. This version is much simpler than that found in the mandatory Ground 6 in the Housing Act 1988. An indicative case on judicial attitudes to a landlord's professed intentions is *Wansbeck District Council v Marley* (1987) 20 HLR 247. The works in question entailed no more than the construction of a doorway and the Court of Appeal was not satisfied that it could not reasonably be built without obtaining possession. In addition, they were unconvinced that there was a clearly defined and settled intention.

Ground 10A: redevelopment scheme

> The dwelling-house is in an area which is the subject of a redevelopment scheme approved by the Secretary of State or the Corporation in accordance with Pt V of this Schedule and the landlord intends within a reasonable time of obtaining possession to dispose of the dwelling-house in accordance with the scheme.
>
> or
>
> Part of the dwelling-house is in such an area and the landlord intends within a reasonable time of obtaining possession to dispose of that part in accordance with the scheme and for that purpose reasonably requires possession of the dwelling-house.

This ground was inserted by the Housing and Planning Act 1986 to facilitate redevelopment. Tenants must be consulted before a redevelopment scheme is initiated.

Ground 11: landlord a charity

> The landlord is a charity and the tenant's continued occupation of the dwelling-house would conflict with the objects of the charity.

This appears, primarily, applicable to housing association tenants whose agreements predate Housing Act 1988 reforms. Actual examples of the use of this ground are rare, but, hypothetically, it would apply to persons who have lost their religious faith, if that was one of the preconditions for the exercise of the charity or, more realistically, if they lose single parent status or no longer have children or win the lottery.

Grounds on which the court may order possession if it considers it reasonable and suitable alternative accommodation is available

Ground 12: accommodation required for new employee

> The dwelling-house forms part of, or is within the curtilage of, a building which, or so much of it as is held by the landlord, is held mainly for purposes other than housing purposes and consists mainly of accommodation other than housing accommodation, or is situated in a cemetery, and:
>
> (a) the dwelling-house was let to the tenant or a predecessor in title of his in consequence of the tenant or predecessor being in the employment of the landlord or of:
> a local authority;
> a new town corporation;
> a housing action trust;
> an urban development corporation;
> the Development Board for Rural Wales; or
> the governors of an aided school;
> and that employment has ceased; and
>
> (b) the landlord reasonably requires the dwelling-house for occupation as a residence for some person either engaged in the employment of the landlord, or of such a body, or with whom a contract for such employment has been entered into conditional on housing being provided.

This ground is not dependent on any misconduct on the part of the tenant and operates merely to free accommodation when employment has ceased and the dwelling is 'reasonably' required for a new employee. It is similar to Case 8 under the Rent Act 1977. Obviously, school and hospital and cemetery caretakers were thought difficult to prise out of accommodation crucial to various undertakings.

Ground 13: accommodation required for physically disabled person

> The dwelling-house has features which are substantially different from those of ordinary dwelling-houses and which are designed to make it suitable for occupation by a physically disabled person who requires accommodation of a kind provided by the dwelling-house and:
>
> (a) there is no longer such a person residing in the dwelling-house; and
>
> (b) the landlord requires it for occupation (whether alone or with members of his family) by such a person.

This is a straightforward housing management ground designed to maximise the use of specially adapted accommodation.

Ground 14: accommodation for those in especially difficult circumstances

> The landlord is a housing association or housing trust which lets dwelling-houses only for occupation (whether alone or with others) by persons whose circumstances (other than merely financial circumstances) make it especially difficult for them to satisfy their need for housing, and:
>
> (a) either there is no longer such a person residing in the dwelling-house or the tenant has received from a local housing authority an offer of accommodation in premises which are to be let as a separate dwelling under a secure tenancy; and
>
> (b) the landlord requires the dwelling-house for occupation (whether alone or with members of his family) by such a person.

Another ground unique to the 1985 Act, this caters for various mental and physical disorders and is exceptionally broadly drafted in general, save for the reference to 'family' in conclusion rather than a more neutral term like 'household'. It only applies to tenancies predating the 1988 Act reforms.

Ground 15: accommodation for people with special needs

> The dwelling-house is one of a group of dwelling-houses which it is the practice of the landlord to let for occupation by persons with special needs and:
>
> (a) a social service or special facility is provided in close proximity to the group of dwelling-houses in order to assist persons with those special needs;
>
> (b) there is no longer a person with those special needs residing in the dwelling-house; and
>
> (c) the landlord requires the dwelling-house for occupation (whether alone or with members of his family) by a person who has those special needs.

An example of such a special facility would be a day care centre.

Ground 16: under-occupation

> The accommodation afforded by the dwelling-house is more extensive than is reasonably required by the tenant and:
>
> (a) the tenancy vested in the tenant by virtue of s 89 (succession to periodic tenancy), the tenant being qualified to succeed by virtue of s 87(b) (members of family other than spouse); and
>
> (b) notice of the proceedings for possession was served under s 83 more than six months but less than 12 months after the date of the previous tenant's death.
>
> The matters to be taken into account by the court in determining whether it is reasonable to make an order on this ground include:
>
> (a) the age of the tenant;
>
> (b) the period during which the tenant has occupied the dwelling house as his only or principal home; and
>
> (c) any financial or other support given by the tenant to the previous tenant.

As already demonstrated, the curtailment of statutory succession in the private sector has left many erstwhile carers for previous tenants with dramatically reduced rights as assured tenants, especially in connection with rent. Ground 16 appears to angle the court's discretion in precisely the opposite direction and enable dedicated carers to stay in the family home on the same terms, in certain circumstances, despite the fact of underoccupation. With less deserving cases, the presence of grounds such as this can be used as leverage to persuade people to accept a transfer without recourse to court proceedings.

Attempted new grounds in the Housing Bill

The opposition attempted to introduce some additional grounds at the Committee stage of the Bill to strengthen the response to anti-social behaviour. It was proposed to introduce the following Ground 17 and to make it mandatory:

> The tenant or a person residing in the dwelling-house has been convicted of an offence under s 4 of the Misuse of Drugs Act 1971 (production or supply of controlled drugs) and the offence was committed in the dwelling-house or within the vicinity of the dwelling-house.

There was also an attempt to introduce a special expedited possession procedure for the new Ground 17, for Grounds 2–4 and the non-monetary part of Ground 1. However, the amendments were withdrawn on assurances that the reformed nuisance and annoyance ground might be refashioned to deal with the problem of drug dealers in particular. The inclusion of reference to arrestable offences in the 1996 Act presumably reflects that assurance.

Suitable alternative accommodation

The private sector version of these criteria has already been analysed and some of the case law is relevant to the Housing Act rules. However, in some respects, the establishment of suitability is easier for local authorities, as might be expected in view of their housing management functions and constraints on options for transferring tenants. 'Character', which figured prominently in the private sector formulation, is missing from the public sector equivalent, indicating that, other things being equal, people can legitimately be moved to less select areas which the private sector environmental emphasis might preclude.

The criteria are set out in Sched 2, Pt IV to the Housing Act 1985. So far as comparable security of tenure is concerned, other secure tenancies or protected tenancies not subject to a mandatory ground for possession are acceptable, as is an assured tenancy not vulnerable under Grounds 1–5 of the 1988 Act. The court has to determine whether the accommodation is reasonably suited to the needs of the tenant and his family and has to have regard to the following factors:

(a) the nature of the accommodation which it is the practice of the landlord to allocate to persons with similar needs;

(b) the distance of the accommodation available from the place of work or education of the tenant and of any members of his family;

(c) its distance from the home of any member of the tenant's family if proximity to it is essential to that member's or the tenant's well being;

(d) the needs (as regards extent of accommodation) and means of the tenant and his family;

(e) the terms on which the accommodation is available and the terms of the secure tenancy;

(f) if furniture was provided by the landlord for use under the secure tenancy, whether furniture is to be provided for use in the other accommodation, and if so the nature of the furniture to be provided.

As in the private sector, local authority certification that it will accommodate is conclusive, although this naturally applies to assistance to other agencies, like housing associations, rather than where the landlord is a local authority. Comparison with the private sector criteria shows more emphasis on objectively ascertainable factors in the 1985 Act, such as needs as regards extent of accommodation and little opportunity to contemplate the fate of luxuries like the tenant's spiritual needs. 'Character' is, as stated, the main difference between the two sets of principles.

RIGHTS OF SECURE TENANTS

Rights to information

Along with more substantial rights, the Housing Act makes it clear that secure tenants are entitled to certain information and consultation. Section 104, therefore, requires authorities to publish information about its secure tenancies 'in such form as it considers best suited to explain in simple terms and so far as it considers it appropriate' and, in particular, to elucidate any express terms, the right to buy and repairing obligations under the Landlord and Tenant Act 1985. It would be difficult to think of a more paternalistic formulation than that quoted. Under s 105, there is provision for consultation on matters of housing management which are, however, defined to exclude rents and service charges.

Assignment

The general principle enunciated in s 91 is, predictably, that any secure tenancy is not capable of being assigned, save in narrowly defined circumstances. The exceptions are an assignment in accordance with s 92 (official exchanges), property adjustment orders made under s 24 of the Matrimonial Causes Act 1973 and an assignment to a statutory successor. The first two exceptions are self-explanatory, but the third enables a person to assign a tenancy to someone who would be qualified to succeed if the tenant died immediately prior to the assignment – that is, they fulfil any residence or other requirements. A recent illustration of this possibility is the case of *Camden London Borough Council v Goldenberg and Another* (1996) 28 HLR 727. A person who had gone to live with his grandmother was held to have fulfilled the residential requirements after she moved into a nursing home after assigning her tenancy to him. If more than one person is so qualified, this exception enables the tenant to choose his assignee.

Subletting and lodgers

Under s 93 of the 1985 Act, it is a term of every secure tenancy that the tenant may allow any persons to reside as lodgers in the dwelling-house, but will not sublet or part with possession of part of the dwelling-house without the written consent of the landlord. Consent cannot be unreasonably withheld and the onus is on the landlord to demonstrate that refusal was reasonable. Factors to be taken into account, if the tenant asks for a declaration that the refusal is unreasonable, are the possibility of overcrowding and the imminence of any works on the premises which could affect the subtenant.

If a secure tenant sublets the premises totally, irrespective of consent, the tenancy will cease to be secure and cannot become secure subsequently. In *Monmouth Borough Council v Marlog* (1995) 27 HLR 30, a tenant underoccupying a three bedroom house allowed the defendant and her two children to occupy the other two bedrooms. When the tenant gave up possession, the defendant claimed a tenancy, but the Court of Appeal held that she was a lodger within s 93, since it would be ludicrous to suppose that the intention of the parties had been to create a tenancy.

Repairs

Apart from the general law of repairs analysed elsewhere, there is some specific provision for secure tenants to expedite 'qualifying repairs', as where the authority is under an obligation under the Landlord and Tenant Act 1985. Section 121 of the Leasehold Reform, Housing and Urban Development Act 1993 enabled the Secretary of State to introduce regulations to this effect and the relevant principles are now found in the Secure Tenants of Local Housing Authorities (Right to Repair) Regulations 1994 SI 1994/133. Tenants requesting the execution of qualifying repairs are entitled to a repair notice from the authority specifying the nature of the repair, the identity of the contractor and the date for completion of the works, failing which the tenant is entitled to compensation. It is not clear how much this procedure adds to existing legal remedies for secure tenants in this sphere.

Improvements

Section 97 of the 1985 Act states that it is an implied term of every secure tenancy that the tenant shall not make improvements without the written consent of the landlord, such consent not to be unreasonably withheld. 'Improvement' is broadly defined in s 97(2) to include any alterations or additions to the dwelling-house or to the fixtures and fittings.

Variation of terms

Sections 102 and 103 indicate the ways in which the terms of secure tenancies can be varied. Apart from agreement between landlord and tenant or rent variation in accordance with any term of the lease, there is broad scope in s 103. This applies to periodic tenancies and involves four weeks notice and prior consultation, save in the case of rent and services, where no consultation is necessary. If a tenant does not like the variation, the only option extended by s 103 is to give a notice to quit.

These provisions, therefore, go some way to offset security of tenure, and private sector tenants are more comfortably off in this respect.

Rent

The history of the public rented sector is one of formal legal autonomy for local authorities against a background of repeated attempts by central government to force up rent levels by way of various forms of financial constraint, such as manipulation of subsidy, and ring fencing of housing revenue accounts. Rent levels have risen dramatically in recent years, although the rises are now tapering off, partly because of the implications for housing benefit.

The legal position can be relatively simply stated. Section 24 says:

> (1) A local housing authority may make such reasonable charges as they may determine for the tenancy or occupation of their houses.
>
> (2) The authority shall from time to time review rents and make such changes, either of rents generally or of particular rents, as circumstances may require.

Section 162 of the Local Government and Housing Act 1989 put a more interventionist gloss on these rules by inserting a new sub-s (3) which requires authorities in determining rents to 'have regard, in particular, to the principle that the rents of houses of any class or description should bear broadly the same proportion to private sector rents as the rents of houses of any other class or description'. This idea of proportionality is very clumsily expressed, but appears to mean that distinctions of rank which are preserved in the private sector must be operative in council housing. Thus, if rents for substantial private sector houses are six times that of single rooms, the same ratio must be achieved and maintained in the public sector. This rapprochement of private and public sector rents goes back at least as far as the Housing Finance Act 1972, under which there was an attempt to impose the 'fair rent' system on council tenants.

Statutory succession

The rules, here, are less generous than the heyday of the private sector, since only one succession is possible. However, the definition of membership of a tenant's family is much more concrete and unequivocal than the 'broadly recognisable de facto familial nexus' so crucial in the private sector. Some element of controversy and uncertainty was injected at the Committee stage of the Housing Bill in the House of Commons, since a majority were persuaded to set succession by a homosexual partner on a par with heterosexual succession via spouse or cohabitee. However, that decision was rapidly reversed after the committee stage and the Housing Minister hopes to persuade authorities to operate on a basis of facilitating joint tenancies and, thereby, automatic succession in such circumstances, rather than have succession to a sole tenant an entitlement.

The basic principle is set out in s 87 of the 1985 Act:

> A person is qualified to succeed the tenant under a secure tenancy if he occupies the dwelling-house as his only or principal home at the time of the tenant's death and either:
>
> (a) he is the tenant's spouse; or
>
> (b) he is another member of the tenant's family and has resided with the tenant throughout the period of 12 months ending with the tenant's death,
>
> unless, in either case, the tenant was himself a successor, as defined in s 88.

This provision applies to periodic secure tenancies and overrides any contrary expression in a will or the operation of the rules of intestacy. Under s 113 of the 1985 Act, persons living together as husband and wife qualify, but not homosexual couples. In *Harrogate Borough Council v Simpson* (1984) 17 HLR 205, it was held that the survivor from a lesbian relationship was not qualified to succeed. Otherwise, the definition of family in the Act is generous enough to include relationships short of cousin, that is, grandparents, nephews and nieces are included, as are relatives of half blood and illegitimate children.

As demonstrated by the decision in the House of Lords in *Waltham Forest LBC v Thomas* [1992] 2 AC 198, the requirement of residence with the tenant has also been generously construed to cover occupation of any houses, whether or not council houses, provided it is for a year and they were co-resident in a council house when the tenant died. 'Resided' was assessed by the Court of Appeal in *Camden London Borough Council v Goldenberg* (1996) 28 HLR 727. Even though a grandson had moved out of his grandmother's flat in the year preceding her assignment of the tenancy to him, it was held that his actions in house-sitting elsewhere and planning to move into alternative accommodation when it became available were not enough to interrupt residence with the tenant for the purposes of s 87. The Court, by a majority, held that a period of absence did not necessarily break the continuity of residence. It was appropriate to consider the nature and extent of the connection with the premises during the period of absence and the grandson had kept the flat in question as his postal address and had left most of his belongings there. So far as the quality of the intention to return was concerned, there was no realistic chance of alternative accommodation becoming available, so the intention to return was more than just colourable.

As often happens with social legislation of this type, the framers of the law do not appear to have contemplated the following question: can minors succeed to a secure tenancy if they otherwise appear to have met the qualifying conditions? The Court of Appeal, in *Kingston on Thames Borough Council v Prince* (1999) 1 FLR 593, concluded that there was no reason to exclude minors, despite the fact that the Law of Property Act 1925 is emphatic in s 1(6) that 'a legal estate is not capable of being held by an infant'. The saving grace was that a minor could hold an equitable interest in a tenancy until attaining her majority.

The court was influenced by the following proposition, that 'The modern tendency of the law was to recognise that children were, indeed, people'. Although there were exceptions to this principle, such as the rule described elsewhere that minors were unable to use the homelessness provisions in their own right, there were no policy reasons for disentitling children, especially if secure tenancies could, in other contexts, such as the Matrimonial Causes Act 1973, be assigned to minors.

Only one succession is contemplated by the Act, which has never been as generous as the private sector equivalent. Fixed term tenancies devolve according to the will of the tenant or under the intestacy rules. Under s 90, the tenancy remains secure until it is vested or otherwise disposed of. In that eventuality, it will cease to be secure unless the disposal is in connection with matrimonial proceedings under s 24 of the Matrimonial Causes Act 1973 or is to a person qualified to succeed.

CHAPTER 6

THE RIGHT TO BUY

INTRODUCTION

The right to buy, according to one of its advocates, Michael Heseltine, signalled the most profound social revolution of this century. The ideological, economic and political ramifications of the right are immense and there is profound disagreement about the merits of the policy. In game show terms, it can be characterised, initially, as a combination of *The Sale of the Century* and *The Price is Right*, but, latterly, with the perils of negative equity, it has taken on the appearance of the *Wheel of Fortune*.

What is indisputable is the quantity of council housing stock sold off since the inception of the right to buy in 1980. Well over a 1,5000,000 properties have changed hands in England and Wales. The arguments advanced for the emancipation of council tenants when the Housing Act 1980 was passed ranged across the spectrum of buzzwords, such as 'freedom', 'choice', 'independence', 'initiative', 'variety' and 'opportunity'. Tenants would gain a stake in the property owning (on a mortgage) democracy and would have the freedom to exploit their proprietary rights by improvement and transfer into other forms of owner-occupation. Apart from individual gain, the quality of neighbourhoods would be enhanced by the diversification of tenure and the erosion of the monolithic council estate. Local authorities would gain from capital receipts and from relinquishing obligations, such as repair, far more than would be lost in projected future rent.

In general terms, the policy looked suspiciously like one where everybody stood to gain and none to lose. Against the policy, it was stated, though with diminishing vehemence from official opposition parties as the years went by, that municipal asset stripping of this type, however providential for individual purchasers, would detract from authorities' ability to house those in need and merely ensure that the most attractive properties disappeared and were not replaced. This, in turn, would produce marginalisation of council estates and more social polarisation between owners and tenants. These prophecies have been fulfilled and the collapse of the housing market in the late 1980s and early 1990s has proved catastrophic for many encouraged to buy and the momentum of sales has been lost. The emphasis has switched from encouragement of individual privatisation through the right to buy, to collective approaches, such as large scale voluntary transfer.

Nevertheless, the general underlying commitment to the extension of owner-occupation remains as strong as ever, as was demonstrated in the recent White Paper, *Our Future Homes, Opportunity, Choice, Responsibility*, 1995, and housing association tenants are singled out in the Housing Act as the next candidates for owner-occupation. Sections 16 and 17 will entitle certain assured tenants of registered social landlords to buy at a discount to be specified by the Secretary of State. Designated rural areas can be excluded from the right to buy and it is estimated that over 1,000 tenants a year will purchase.

It should be stressed that authorities are not constrained to operate within the framework of the right to buy if they choose to exercise the power to sell in certain contexts. The 'designated sales' policy adopted by Westminster Council, in recent years, is still under examination as an attempt to dispose of stock when vacant to suitable incomers to the area and to remove it from the pool available for general allocation.

Who qualifies?

The criteria are found in s 118 and the following sections of the Housing Act 1985. Secure tenants have, in principle, the right to buy, but licensees do not qualify, despite s 79(3), because the upgrading of licences with exclusive possession is confined to Pt IV of the Act and the right to buy is governed by Pt V. In the case of joint tenants, the right to buy belongs to all of them, provided that at least one of them occupies the dwelling house in question as his only or principal home. There is a differentiation of type of property to be acquired. In the case of houses where the authority owns the freehold, then the freehold is purchased, but, in the case of flats or any dwelling where the authority does not own the freehold, then only the leasehold is available. Only a minuscule percentage of flats have ever been purchased under the right to buy.

Irrespective of any joint tenant status, a tenant may enlist the assistance of up to three other family members in sharing the right to buy. Section 123 provides that those eligible are spouses, any other family member resident for the previous year and any other family member who has not so resided, provided the landlord agrees. The joint purchasers will then be treated as joint tenants of the property. This option must have facilitated the right to buy when perceived as a family asset.

How long is the qualifying period?

The basic qualifying period, under the Act, is only two years. This threshold can be passed in a number of ways; the crucial factor is the length of time as a public sector tenant, not necessarily a secure tenant. Intermittent periods as a public sector tenant count and neither the landlord nor the premises have to be the same throughout.

Exclusions from the right to buy

Schedule 5 to the Act specifies certain narrowly drawn exceptions to the right to buy. Some have been repealed, because it was recognised that there was no reason to exclude the disabled from the right to buy, unless there were countervailing considerations, such as being in a block of sheltered housing. The significant survivors are as follows.

Charities

(1) The landlord is a housing trust or a housing association and is a charity. (The Housing Act 1996 has altered this.)

Certain housing associations

(2) The landlord is a co-operative housing association.

(3) The landlord is a housing association which has at no time received various forms of grant aid from public funds.

Landlord with insufficient interest in the property

(4) The landlord has an insufficient interest in the property, either because it does not own the freehold or does not have a long enough lease (21 years for a house and 50 years for a flat, the time calculated at the date of the tenant's notice claiming to exercise the right to buy).

Dwelling-houses let in connection with employment

(5) The dwelling-house is part of or within the curtilage of a building held mainly for non-housing purposes and consists mainly of non-housing accommodation, or is in a cemetery, and was let to the tenant or predecessor in consequence of being in the employment of a public sector landlord.

Certain dwelling-houses for the disabled

(6) The dwelling-houses have substantially different features from those of ordinary houses, are designed for physically disabled persons, form part of a group and are near a social service or special facilities.

(7) The house is one of a group customarily let to people who are suffering from or have suffered from a mental disorder and a social service is, or special facilities are, provided.

Sheltered housing for the elderly

(8) The house is one of a group particularly suitable for occupation by elderly persons and customarily let to persons aged 60 years and over. Special facilities, such as a warden, must be provided. The Leasehold Reform, Housing and Urban Development Act 1993 altered the wording of this exception for notices served after 11 October 1993; prior to the change, it referred to 'persons of pensionable age' which had to be altered as it was sexually discriminatory.

(9) Individual sheltered housing for the elderly can also be excluded by the Secretary of State in response to a tenant's notice challenging an authority's refusal to grant the right. There are particular difficulties with this provision in rural areas where the desire to extend owner-occupation can seriously erode housing stock available for

the elderly. Much, in consequence, depends on the interpretation of 'particularly suitable, having regard to its location, size, design, heating system and other features' for the elderly/pensioners. One obvious significant factor is the availability of shops within reasonable walking distance. In *R v Secretary of State for the Environment ex p Oxfordshire District Council* (1994) HLR 417, the Secretary of State had determined that the right to buy was available for an elderly person because there were no shops reasonably near and therefore the house was not particularly suitable for such persons. The Council successfully sought judicial review of this decision because the determination had involved a departure from a previous Circular outlining the proposed method of applying the exception criteria.

Dwelling-houses let on crown tenancies

(10) The right to buy does not arise if the landlord is a tenant of the Crown, unless the landlord is entitled to grant a lease under the right to buy without consent or the landlord has been informed that consent has been given to the granting of such a lease.

Other circumstances in which the right to buy cannot be exercised

(11) By virtue of s 121, the right to buy cannot be exercised in two sets of circumstances. The first is if the tenant is obliged to give up possession of the dwelling-house in pursuance of an order of the court or will be so obliged at a specified date. The second operates if the purchaser, or one of them if it is a shared purchase, has a bankruptcy petition pending against him, has a receiving order against him, is an undischarged bankrupt or has made a composition or arrangement with creditors which has not been finalised. The second set of circumstances is self-explanatory, but the first has occasioned some difficulties of interpretation.

In *Enfield London Borough Council v McKeon* [1986] 1 WLR 1007, some of the procedural formalities for purchase had been completed. The tenant, who had succeeded her father, served the requisite notice claiming the right to buy and the landlords, in their turn, served a notice acknowledging the right. Thereupon, the authority served another notice indicating that they would seek possession on the grounds of underoccupation. Subsequently, they issued proceedings for possession, but not before they had served the notice required by s 125 of the Act and stated the price of the freehold and other matters. Was the tenant entitled to complete the freehold purchase or was she disqualified by s 121? The Court of Appeal noted the ambiguity of 'exercised' – was it a once and for all transaction, as when the s 122 notice was served or was it part of a continuous process? The latter interpretation was preferred and Lord Justice Slade said that 'in my judgment, the right is "exercised" each and every time when the tenant takes any step towards the implementation of his right to purchase'. So, she could not exercise the right to buy.

The harshness of this decision was mitigated in the ensuing Court of Appeal verdict in *Dance v Welwyn Hatfield DC* [1990] 1 WLR 1097. In the latter case, the facts were different, as negotiations were virtually complete and had reached the stage

> where they appeared to satisfy the demands of s 138(1) which says 'as soon as all matters relating to the grant and to the amount to be left outstanding or advanced on the security of the dwelling-house have been agreed or determined'. The purchasers had served a notice requesting completion, only to be met with a s 83 notice invoking Ground 10 and the intention to demolish/reconstruct. The Court of Appeal distinguished McKeon and held that the authority had to complete the sale.

The recent House of Lords decision in *City Council of Bristol v Lovell* [1998] 1 WLR 446 has, however, repudiated the approach in *Dance*, preferring to leave it to judicial discretion to determine whether a claim to buy the freehold could, in effect, be defeated at the last moment, since, in the words of Lord Hoffmann, 'it is the administrative discretion of the court to regulate its business and to decide when and in what order it will hear the cases which come before it'. In essence, that meant that the claim by the tenant for enforceability of the right to buy via injunction in s 138(3) of the Housing Act 1985 could be deferred and defeated by a council's claim for possession.

Such flexibility in juggling the order of claims is, therefore, very important in practice and could be used to defeat claims more meritorious than that of Mr Lovell, who was suspected of drug dealing and, indeed, of using the proceeds of dealing to make a cash purchase of his council house. According to Lord Hoffmann, lamentably virtually the sole mouthpiece in highest level judicial analysis of housing law in recent years, the house had 'steel grills over doors and windows, kennels for Rottweiler dogs, surveillance cameras to check visitors, a radio scanner tuned to a police frequency and equipment for locating covert listening devices'. In view of the obvious nature and purpose of these features, it is, perhaps, surprising that Bristol so belatedly took steps to recover possession.

Mr Lovell had, in fact, served the requisite notice to exercise the right to buy in April 1994. In June, the council acknowledged the right and stated the price and other details. It was only in July that they served notice of their intention to apply for a possession order against him under Ground 2 of Sched 2 to the Housing Act 1985. Proceedings for possession started in September, in October the tenant accepted the terms of the offer and in November he asked for the possession proceedings to be stayed. The council subsequently altered their particulars of claim to include allegations about drug dealing from the premises. Early in 1995, the tenant applied for an injunction to compel sale, but the trial judge decreed that the council's allegations had first to be investigated and rejected the application for a stay of proceedings and for an injunction. Mr Lovell succeeded on appeal at the two intermediate levels, but fell at the last hurdle, the House of Lords.

Lord Hoffmann's justification for denying the right to buy was derived from distinguishing between types of discretion which he felt had been judicially confused in previous cases. The discretion whether or not to grant any application when a case came to trial – and the language of s 138 is quite mandatory – had to be distinguished from the managerial/case handling discretion, determining the appropriate order of hearing different claims. That latter discretion does appear to be enshrined in Ord 13 r 3(1) of the County Court Rules 1981, which states that 'the court may at any time and from time to time, upon application or of its own motion, by order adjourn or advance the date of the hearing of any proceedings'. Accordingly, no tenant can feel safe until the conveyance has actually been executed and, conversely, councils can take their time about formulating reasons to oppose any purchase. This is hardly in the spirit of the original legislative purpose, which was to force through sales by recalcitrant local authorities and, yet, again, hard cases may make bad law, since completely 'innocent' tenants, such as Dance, are, henceforth, vulnerable to claims for repossession for development right up to the last minute.

The effect of the Lovell decision was apparent in *Tandridge District Council v Bickers*, 30 June 1998. In the latter case, the tenants, who were vulnerable in a possession action for neighbour nuisance and breaches of other terms of the tenancy agreement, initiated their claim to the right to buy after possession proceedings had been started. When the Bickers sought a court order to expedite the freehold purchase, the district judge rejected their concurrent application for the possession proceedings to be adjourned and decreed that both actions should be heard simultaneously. Unsurprisingly, the recorder faced with the two actions opted to take the possession order first and the Court of Appeal found nothing wrong in the exercise of such discretion. Proper consideration had been given to the fact that the obtaining of a possession order would defeat the right to buy and the recorder had reasonably concluded that tenants with nothing to fear would not be prejudiced if a possession action were taken first.

The calculation of the price

The basic formula in s 126 of the 1985 Act is that the price payable is the value of the property, on certain assumptions, less the discount to which the purchasing tenant is entitled. The value is the price obtainable on the open market by a willing vendor. In the case of freehold purchase, there are various assumptions: that the vendor is selling with vacant possession; that neither the tenant nor a resident family member is interested in buying; and that the property has the benefit and burdens that would ordinarily attach to it under a sale. When a long lease is being purchased, comparable assumptions are made.

Duty of care in valuation of properties

A besetting problem for local authorities and prospective purchasers in a fluctuating property market has been that of (pardonable) overvaluation by the authority, naturally creating difficulty and a desire for legal redress when values plummet and negative equity supervenes. Is it reasonable, in policy terms, to hold authorities liable in negligence if their assessment of the price under the 1985 Act proves too optimistic? Is the role of authorities as vendors and facilitators distinguishable from that of professional valuers when it comes to negligence? How much significance should be attached to the fact that prospective buyers are urged to obtain an independent valuation?

Unsurprisingly, these questions were answered in favour of local authorities in the test case of *Blake and Brooks v The London Borough of Barking and Dagenham* (1996) 30

HLR 963. As discussed elsewhere, the conceptual apparatus involved in determining the existence of a duty of care in tort is immensely cumbersome and riddled with criteria that enable the judges to dispense 'palm tree justice'. The plaintiffs placed reliance on the following statement from *Lord Bridge in Caparo v Dickman* [1990] 2 AC 605, p 617:

> What emerges is that, in addition to the foreseeability of damage, the necessary ingredients in any situation giving rise to a duty of care are that there should exist, between the party owing the duty and the party whom it is owed, a relationship characterised by the law as one of 'proximity' or 'neighbourhood' and that the situation should be one in which the law considers it fair, just and reasonable that the law should impose a duty of a given scope upon the one party for the benefit of the other.

The context was that the vast majority of aspirant purchasers never sought any second opinion under s 128 of the 1985 Act. So far as the crucial criterion of 'fair, just and reasonable' was concerned, the judge, Mr Justice Douglas Brown, was happy to employ the restrictive filter in the shape of the threefold categorisation by Lord Browne-Wilkinson in *X v Bedfordshire CC* [1995] 2 AC 633 of the circumstances in which a local authority might in general terms be liable. The first proposition was that a breach of any statutory duty (to state the price under s 125) did not, of itself, give rise to any private law cause of action. Such a cause could only materialise if it were shown that the duty in question was imposed for the protection of a limited class of the public and that there was a concomitant intention to confer a private right of action on such a class. This could not be demonstrated in this instance.

Secondly, if there were merely careless performance of the duty in question, no duty of care sprang up at common law and the bare assertion of the careless exercise of a statutory duty or power could not substantiate any cause of action. Thirdly, if a statutory duty did create a duty of care at common law, then the defendant, in any instance, would have to have brought about the sort of relationship between himself and the plaintiff as to justify the finding of a 'free standing' common law cause of action. The judge thought there was no justification for the imposition of such a duty on grounds of public policy.

The conclusion was that the terms of s 125, in any event, were inadequate to impose any statutory duty on the authority. The judge identified:

> ... a statutory scheme which provides in clear terms, communicated to the applicant both in the notice and in the helpful pamphlet, that he has a right to apply to an independent government valuer. In those circumstances, it does not seem to me just or reasonable that there should be a duty of care on the local authority.

Duty of care and substantial disrepair

Similarly, in *Payne v Barnet London Borough Council* (1998) 30 HLR 295 the Court of Appeal took a restrictive view of the obligations and liability of local authorities when it came to informing prospective purchasers of flats of potential disrepair problems. Admittedly, there was a duty in s 125(4A) to inform of any structural defects, but the doctrine of *caveat emptor* still constrained a purchaser to conduct the appropriate inquiries into the general issue of disrepair. There was no wider obligation of disclosure to be imposed on a local authority. The underlying problem for purchasers, in this sphere, is having to operate in what could, politely, be called a paternalistic framework of social legislation, with all sorts of information, such as guide price and structural defects, available as of right. However, beyond the specified obligations, the judiciary are naturally reluctant to enter into the spirit of the right to buy rules and extend the paternalistic provisions, preferring, instead, to resurrect the harsh doctrines of the common law such as *caveat emptor.*

The qualifying period for right to buy and discount

The original discount levels were altered in the mid-1980s and there was another surge of sales about the time of the general boom in the late-1980s. The discounts for flats are designed to be even more attractive than those for houses and the maximum discount can be reached through occupation for only half as long as that for houses. Section 129 of the Housing Act states:

> (2) The discount is:
>
> (a) in the case of a house, 32% plus 1% for each complete year by which the qualifying period exceeds two years, up to a maximum of 60%;
>
> (b) in the case of a flat, 44% plus 2% for each complete year by which the qualifying period exceeds two years, up to a maximum of 70 %.

No great mathematical ability is required to deduce that house buyers can benefit from up to 30 years of occupation, whilst flat purchasers reach the ceiling after only 15 years.

What is the position when a tenant initiates the purchase process and is agreed to be entitled to a certain level of discount, but dies before completion? Is a successor to the secure tenancy entitled to the same level of discount or must it be readjusted to meet the successor's length of residence? The statute is typically unhelpful in saying only that, in the event of such a succession, 'the new tenant shall be in the same position as if the notice had been given by him and he had been the secure tenant at the time it was given'. In *McIntyre v Merthyr Tydfil District Council* (1989) 21 HLR 320, the Court of Appeal had to adjudicate on the predictable set of facts, that the successor would be several years short of the occupation chalked up by her predecessor and, hence, *prima facie,* entitled to a more limited discount. The court concluded that the successor could claim the higher discount and did step into the predecessor's shoes in continuation of the process begun by the tenant's original notice.

Repayment of discount in certain circumstances

Section 155 of the Act establishes the general principle that a purchaser has to repay a certain amount of the discount if the property is sold within three years of exercising the right to buy. A simple sliding scale operates to claw back all the discount within the first year; two-thirds of it in the second; and one third in the third. So the repayment provision is not exactly a burden if a little patience is used. In addition, various disposals are exempted by ss 160 and 161 from the repayment obligations. Chief among the exemptions are where someone takes the property under a will or intestacy or where there has been a disposal under s 24 of the Matrimonial Causes Act 1973 (property adjustment orders in connection with matrimonial proceedings).

Procedure

Not all the elements in the complicated procedural framework will be explored in equal depth, but the most important and recent features will be mentioned. It is noteworthy that the mechanism operates on a fairly strict timetable, unlike private sector equivalents in relation to leasehold reform where, often, there is a vested interest for a landlord in delay and prevarication. Expropriation of a public sector landlord is implicitly deemed more meritorious than private sector enfranchisement, which has attracted accusations of breach of human rights.

A tenant wishing to exercise the right to buy must serve a notice in prescribed form. This is not an irrevocable commitment, as the notice can be withdrawn at any time before completion. Thereafter, the landlord has normally only four weeks in which to serve a notice in reply either acknowledging the right to buy or offering reasons for its ineligibility. The tenant has the right to apply to the county court for a ruling if rejected.

Assuming that the claim is accepted or approved by the county court, the landlord then has eight weeks for houses and 12 weeks for flats to serve notice of the purchase price in accordance with s 125 of the 1985 Act. In this notice, apart from details of the asking price and explanation of its calculation there should be information about such matters as service charges and any structural defects. More recent purchasers (after 11 October 1993) now have to serve another notice on the landlord within 12 weeks of receipt of the s 125 notice. The tenant has to state whether he intends to persevere with the purchase. Alternatively, if the right to acquire on rent to mortgage is sought, a different form of notice must be used.

As already seen, once everything has been satisfactorily arranged in terms of s 138, the landlord is obliged to convey the freehold or grant the lease as appropriate. When landlords drag their feet, there are several ways in which the transaction can be accelerated. The Housing Act 1988 introduced measures for tenants to take through the service of yet more notices, an 'initial notice of delay', followed by an 'operative notice of delay' if the landlord fails to respond appropriately. The sanction is that rent payments can then be credited against the ultimate purchase price when the landlord sees reason. The Secretary of State also has wide powers to intervene where it is apparent that 'tenants generally, a tenant or tenants of a particular landlord have or may have difficulty in exercising effectively or expeditiously the right to buy' (s 164).

Long leaseholders and the right to buy

Around 200,000 leaseholders have bought their leases under the provisions of the right to buy. Many of them have been particularly afflicted by high service charges. Along with protection against forfeiture, there is provision in the Housing Act 1996 for levels of charge to be reduced proportionally where central government funding is involved and there is an overriding reasonableness requirement.

Designated sales policy and wilful misconduct

Although the actions of the ruling Conservative group in Westminster involved the exercise of discretion to sell council property, rather than the right to buy, it is still advisable to focus on the litigation generated by the 'designated sales policy', which still awaits some resolution in the House of Lords (see *Porter v Magill* (1999) 96(21) LSG 39). The fate of the policy is also important for analysis of the scope of the duty to house certain preference groups under s 22 of the Housing Act 1985 and its successor, s 167 of the Housing Act 1996. The precise legal issue to which over £10 million of public money has already been devoted is whether the actions of Dame Shirley Porter and her colleagues constituted 'wilful misconduct' within s 20(1)(b) of the Local Government Finance Act 1982. The auditor found that massive losses had been caused by such misconduct and imposed surcharges on five of those involved. The Divisional Court exonerated three of the five, but rejected the appeals by Dame Shirley Porter and her deputy David Weeks, who then appealed successfully to the Court of Appeal.

The factual background is the decision of the ruling Conservative group in *Westminster* in the aftermath of the local elections in 1986 to formulate a policy of 'building stable communities', including a programme of increasing the level of discretionary designated sales, which operate outside the provisions of the right to buy. Supposedly, this scheme was motivated by a desire to increase the numbers of prospective Conservative voters in marginal wards in Westminster. *Prima facie*, it might be thought that such a policy of favouring incomers of friendly political persuasion as first option for empty council properties was in clear contravention of the duty in s 22 of the Housing Act 1985 to give reasonable preference in housing allocation to certain priority groups, such as the statutorily homeless. Nevertheless, advice was obtained from learned counsel that any extension of a designated sales policy coupled with capital grants for house purchase would not be unlawful. In July 1987, the Housing Committee voted by majority to extend the programme in such a fashion, attracting the wrath of the minority Labour group, media attention and the lengthy investigation by the auditor.

One of the points of critical legal significance was, therefore, the effect of expanding a policy to make it 'dressed up in city wide clothes', thereby disguising any apparent targeting of marginal wards and alleged gerrymandering. In the Divisional Court, the arguments for and against the finding of wilful misconduct were neatly encapsulated as follows:

> The essence of the case against Dame Shirley was that, as leader of the majority party, she was instrumental in pursuing the political policy of targeting designated sales in the marginal wards, despite the absence of support from council officials or independent consultants and in the absence of any legitimate local government reasons, for the improper purpose of electoral advantage by seeking to introduce more electors who might vote Conservative.
>
> The essence of her case is that political considerations inevitably play a part in local government, but that there is a divide well understood by councillors between party proposals and council policy and there was nothing improper in the council or housing committee implementing a policy founded on party political considerations, provided these were not dominant and there were other legitimate reasons for the policy; further,

> she was entitled to rely on the advice of leading counsel, based on information provided to him by officials, which she believed would include all relevant matters, as a complete answer to any allegation of lawful misconduct.

It can be seen from this last paragraph that the courts could easily get bogged down in casuistry comparable to the doctrine of double effect. It could be asserted that some 'aim' of providing diversity or a better social mix on certain estates was perfectly legitimate (indeed, it finds echoes in current rumblings and prognostications about future national housing policy) and reprieved any improper motivation that could have dominated the attitude of Council leaders to the policy. The accepted legal definition of 'wilful misconduct' is, moreover, the awkward formula produced by Mr Justice Webster in *Graham v Teesdale* (1981) 81 LGR 113, p 123, where he described it as 'deliberately doing something which is wrong, knowing it to be wrong or with reckless indifference as to whether it is wrong or not'. This sets a high threshold of proof, even on the civil balance of probabilities, since, on the face of it, the receipt of favourable counsel opinion on legality would remove any taint of deliberate or even reckless conduct, since presumably, councillors do not then have to shop around for another less favourable barrister's interpretation.

The issue of causation also persuaded the Court of Appeal that no wilful misconduct as defined had, in fact, occurred. Whatever might ultimately have been in the minds of the architects of the policy, the crucial Committee vote, in July 1987, had been prefaced by a properly balanced assessment of the merits and demerits of any designated sales policy in which case the majority vote in favour could not be considered to be improperly motivated. As there had been no manipulation of the Committee's votes, the arguments about wilful misconduct had simply not been substantiated. Accordingly, any judgment, as in the inferior court, that the misconduct lay in the attempt 'to achieve unlawful electoral advantage' was misguided and close to a circular argument.

Are the House of Lords likely to perceive the pattern of events differently from the Court of Appeal? If the shades of *Street v Mountford* are invoked and a more robust approach taken to the 'real' purpose of the policy, it might be possible to argue that the underlying political motivation tainted and vitiated the whole policy. However, that still leaves the stumbling block of counsel's opinion sanctioning pursuit of the policy and the probably intractable difficulty that, in terms of causation, any 'malice aforethought' harboured by the protagonists could not taint the deliberations and voting patterns of the crucial Housing Committee. The only non-contentious conclusion to emerge is that the protracted and prohibitively expensive process of inquisition by auditor is unlikely to survive, as there are moves afoot in the wake of the Nolan recommendations to create a new criminal offence of 'misuse of public office' to replace the unwieldy notion of 'wilful misconduct'. The final piece of conjecture, apart from haruspication about the decision in the House of Lords, is whether Dame Shirley would have been convicted of the new offence. It would appear plausible that the obtaining of favourable opinion from counsel would exculpate her, particularly with the criminal standard of proof.

CHAPTER 7

DISREPAIR AND THE LAW

INTRODUCTION

The recent Law Commission Report, No 238, *Landlord and Tenant: Responsibility for State and Condition of Property*, does not make any sweeping proposals for reform. It does, however, focus sharply on the problem: that a distressingly high percentage of properties in England and Wales are unfit for human habitation according to the statutory criteria as amended by the Local Government and Housing Act 1989. The private sector is particularly bad, in this respect, with more than one-fifth of English and one-quarter of Welsh private rented properties so unfit. The Commission also extracts from official surveys, such as the English House Condition Survey 1991, the finding that not only is the private sector disproportionately unfit, but, within the sector, it is characteristically the older properties of low value that are affected. Such properties are often occupied by people of comparatively modest means.

Readers of the White Paper, *Our Future Homes, Opportunity, Choice, Responsibility*, 1995, and of the Housing Act 1996 could be forgiven for thinking that the Law Commission is referring to another country. The White Paper celebrates various successes, such as the reduction in the number of council homes without central heating from 50%–23% between 1981 and 1991. Unfitness statistics hardly rate a mention. In the Housing Act 1996, there is some tinkering with local authorities powers and duties in relation to houses in multiple occupation, but no attempt to tackle more general problems of disrepair, save in minor projects, such as the Single Regeneration Budget Challenge Fund, which will have an effect on only around 50,000 homes in run down urban areas. The Housing Grants Construction and Regeneration Act 1996 merely abolishes the old mandatory renovation grant system and introduces new types of discretionary grant.

Periodically, there are discussions about how many billions of pounds would be required to put matters right in the private sector or, indeed, the public which is, by no means, immune. One typically demoralising statistic is contained in the 1994 National Housing Forum report, *Papering over the Cracks*. It estimates that £70 billion would be required to repair all privately owned and housing association properties to building society valuation standards. Whatever sums are quoted are beyond the reach of the politically feasible when housing has been an easy target for public expenditure cuts for decades. The Law Commission, as will be seen, envisages a gradual programme of improvement by the prospective phased introduction of a new improved covenant for fitness for human habitation across the spectrum of short term agreements analysed in this book. Before analysis of possible reforms, it will be necessary to explore the sad picture of inadequate and incoherent rules that currently constitute the law of repairs. It is appropriate, in view of the emphasis in this book, to confine the analysis to the problems of individual substandard houses, rather than to explore the range of options available on a group or area renovation strategy, although the micro- and macro-approaches are clearly linked economically. In fact, one of the criticisms of a system concerned to channel resources towards low income residents of individual unfit properties is that it starves neighbourhood renewal strategies of funds.

What are the main provisions currently governing repairs in short term lettings in the private and public sectors? It is not proposed to dwell on the meaning of the word 'repair' itself in the abstract, although, clearly, it is important to be able to distinguish it from other related concepts, such as renewal and improvement. One often quoted differentiation of repair and renewal is that of Lord Justice Buckley, in *Lurcott v Wakely and Wheeler* [1911] 1 KB 905, p 924:

> Repair is the restoration by renewal or replacement of subsidiary parts of a whole. Renewal, as distinguished from repair, is reconstruction of the entirety, meaning by the entirety not necessarily the whole, but substantially the whole subject matter under discussion.

The distinction between repair and improvement is less sharp edged, since, naturally, repairs will often involve the making of improvements. Ultimately, it is a matter of degree and sometimes remedial work is so extensive as to go beyond the natural meaning of repair. The Law Commission is content to leave such border disputes to judicial determination and is opposed to any codification of the current set of definitions.

Remedies in contract and tort

As might be expected, the common law has never been enthusiastic about implying repairing obligations into contracts. It is a general principle that a landlord will only be liable if any obligations have been expressly undertaken. Similarly, there is no general duty of care in tort owed by the landlord to the tenant. This reluctance to regulate the relationship has led to a variety of different statutory attempts to establish liability. Equally, a tenant, in the absence of any express agreement, is under no obligation to keep the premises in repair. What is incumbent on short term tenants, such as weekly tenants, is the duty to act in a tenant like manner. Lord Denning gave the authoritative account of the nature of the expectations in *Warren v Keen* [1954] 1 QB 15, p 20:

> The tenant must take proper care of the place. He must, if he is going away for the winter, turn off the water and empty the boiler. He must clean the chimneys, when necessary, and also the windows. He must unstop the sink when it is blocked by his waste. In short, he must do the little jobs about the place which a reasonable tenant would do. In addition, he must, of course, not damage the house, wilfully or negligently; and must see that his family and guests do not damage it: and if they do, he must repair it. But apart from such things, if the house falls into disrepair through fair wear and tear or lapse of time, or for any reason not caused by him, then the tenant is not liable to repair it.

The Law Commission propose to formalise this obligation to take proper care more briefly in statute, along with an updated version of the doctrine of waste.

STATUTORY REPAIRING OBLIGATIONS

Section 11 of the Landlord and Tenant Act 1985

One of the more important measures in this connection is s 11 of the Landlord and Tenant Act 1985, which has its origins in 1961 and is a clear encroachment on the *laissez faire* tradition that allowed landlords to impose heavy repairing obligations on short term tenants. It involves leases (not licences) of a term of seven years or less and, therefore, takes in the overwhelming majority of short term agreements in the private and public sectors. The obligation is to keep in repair the structure and exterior of the dwelling-house and to keep in repair and proper working order the installations in the dwelling-house for the supply of water, gas and electricity; also, those for sanitation and for space and water heating. Basins, sinks, baths and sanitary conveniences are included, but not other fixtures and appliances for making use of the services supplied. The scope of the statutory covenant was slightly extended by the Housing Act 1988 to cater for the common problem of disrepair in other parts of the building or installations not physically in the tenanted property, provided that the disrepair 'is such as to affect the lessee's enjoyment of the dwelling-house or of any common parts'.

The implication of the covenant cannot be excluded, save with the approval of the court. It can be used to counterclaim where there is, for example, a rent arrears action and can also be implemented through a decree of specific performance. In *Joyce v Liverpool City Council* [1995] 3 WLR 439, it has been established that specific performance can be ordered by a district judge, even in small claims arbitration. It has special value for council tenants, who cannot rely on the unfitness procedures under the Housing Act 1985.

However, there is a long list of putative disadvantages with the section. The landlord is not liable unless and until he has notice of any defect. In *O'Brien v Robinson* [1973] AC 912, the culmination of the preoccupation with notice was found when the House of Lords held that, even in the case of latent defects, notice was a prerequisite. The traditional justification for the requirement of notice is that the tenant has the means of knowledge because the landlord has parted with possession, but this, clearly, has no relevance to latent defects where it might be expected that the landlord should be put on inquiry. There is, incidentally, a further source of possible argument, in the absence of authority, where the defect is outside the premises in question; is it reasonable to adapt the principle applied to defects inside the premises, that is, the prerequisite of notice and a reasonable period elapsing before the landlord is liable? The arguments about means of knowledge are altered when the defect is external to the tenanted premises and, in *British Telecom plc v Sun Life Assurance Society* plc (1995) *The Times,* 3 August, the Court of Appeal held that there was a breach of repairing covenant immediately on the occurrence of the defect and the breathing space allowed the landlord, in the case of internal defects, could not be justified in the event of an external defect, such as bulging in brick cladding.

The standard of repair

Section 11(3) states: 'In determining the standard of repair required by the lessor's repairing covenant, regard shall be had to the age, character and prospective life of the dwelling-house and the locality in which it is situated.' In an era where the housing stock is ageing and not being replaced and the problems of unfitness are so pervasive, this section seems to offer a perverse incentive to let things slide. In *Newham LBC v Patel* (1978) 13 HLR 77, the Court of Appeal, however, concluded that it made economic sense to limit duties via such factors as life expectancy. The tenant was paying a low rent for the occupation of an unfit house in a redevelopment area. Similarly, in *Trustees of Dame Margaret Hungerford Charity v Beazeley* (1994) 26 HLR 269, s 11(3) came to the rescue of the landlords when the state of a roof that was well over a century old and in need of complete repair was held not to be in breach of the covenant. It was the practice of the landlords to replace individual roof tiles and pegs when informed of disrepair and they could not be expected to do more than that and replace the roof.

Another fundamental difficulty is that the definition of repair is such that many problems escape the ambit of the section because they relate to design defects or other factors which are not attributable to disrepair. The Law Commission introduce their latest report with a discussion of the most significant case in this area, *Quick v Taff-Ely Borough Council* [1986] QB 809.

Severe condensation caused damage to decorations and to bedding clothing and other fabrics. The house was virtually unfit for human habitation. However, the problems fell outside the notion of 'repair', as they stemmed from windows of a defective design and their interaction with the central heating system. There was no evidence of damage to the structure and exterior. The windows were in good physical condition. The house had been built in accordance with current standards and regulations.

What other possible causes of action were open to the tenant? Attempting to use the Housing Act 1985 procedures would be hopeless, as authorities cannot be made to take action against themselves. It was established, in *R v Cardiff City Council ex p Cross* (1981) 1 HLR 54, that the machinery in the 1985 Act is inapplicable where the authority is the 'person having control' of the premises in question. Using the Environmental Health Act 1990 procedures for statutory nuisance might have borne more fruit, as there is provision in the 1990 Act and its predecessor, the Public Health Act 1936, for action by aggrieved individuals to compel the person or body responsible for a nuisance to take action to abate it. As will be shown shortly, in more detailed analysis of the public health oriented procedures, there is a considerable tolerance in the content of any order abating a nuisance and it is not certain that replacement of design defects could be guaranteed. Another difficulty is that compensation for the losses incurred through the condensation will not normally be recoverable when taking this route. There are, however, recent instances of quite substantial damages being awarded for disrepair in general.

In circumstances such as those of *Quick,* where the problem seems in danger of falling into various gaps between grounds for liability, the Law Commission are currently pinning their hopes on a modernised version of s 8 of the Landlord and Tenant

Act 1985, which imposes statutory conditions for fitness for human habitation on houses let at very low rents. The current limits are annual rents of £80 or less in London and £52 a year elsewhere, since the limits have not been changed since 1957 and, therefore, the conditions are currently pointless. The merits of any scheme to resurrect such an implied term will be considered later, but it is clear that with different rent limits the council house in *Quick* would have been within the section.

The Defective Premises Act 1972

By virtue of s 4(1) of the 1972 Act, landlords are under a duty of care to 'all persons who might reasonably be expected to be affected by defects in the state of the premises' when they are under an obligation to the tenant for maintenance or repair. Unlike s 11 of the 1985 Act, occupational licences are also included under s 4(6). The substance of the duty is 'to take such care as is reasonable in all the circumstances' to ensure that persons to whom the duty is owed 'are reasonably safe from personal injury or from damage to their property caused by a relevant defect'. The duty arises if the landlord knows of the defect or ought, in all the circumstances, to have been aware of it. This objective assessment of awareness will favour tenants disadvantaged under the traditional rule for consensual and statutory covenants that notice from the tenant is a prerequisite for liability.

Although there has not been much litigation under the 1972 Act, it does, in principle, offer some prospects for certain tenants and others, but only where the problem is one of safety and protection of property from damage. Visitors can come within the scope of the duty of care, as was shown in *Clarke v Taff-Ely BC* (1980) 10 HLR 44, where the plaintiff was helping the tenant to redecorate and was injured when a defective floorboard gave way. It was held that the local authority were liable for the injury, since they should have anticipated accidents of this type and inspected their properties. Unfitness is not the criterion, so the common difficulty of cockroach infestation would not be covered and it is doubtful that condensation and dampness problems, as in *Quick*, would qualify.

Section 8 of the Landlord and Tenant Act 1985

This section has a long history, well documented in the latest Law Commission report. It is a potentially far reaching statutory condition of fitness for human habitation, currently implied only into certain tenancies at an extremely low rent, since the rental limits have not been altered for 40 years. In *Quick,* Lord Justice Dillon observed of its predecessor that 'it is not available to the plaintiff in the present case because his rent is too high, even though he is an unemployed tenant of a small council house'.

To be precise, s 8 states that, irrespective of any contrary stipulation, there is implied a condition that the house is fit for human habitation and an undertaking that the landlord will keep it so fit throughout the tenancy. To that extent, in positing a continued obligation and not discriminating between types of premises, it is a general advance on the long standing principle that furnished premises have to be fit for habitation at the start of the tenancy (*Smith v Marrable* (1843) 11 M & W 5).

Although, originally, the determination of criteria for fitness or unfitness was left to judicial discretion, for decades, statute has also specified a list of factors to be taken into account. To be unfit, a property must be 'so far defective' in respect of one such factor as to be not 'reasonably suitable for occupation in that condition'. The current criteria diverge somewhat from those formulated for the exercise of Housing Act 1985 powers by local authorities. The factors are: repair; stability; freedom from damp; natural lighting; ventilation; water supply; drainage and sanitary conveniences; and facilities for the preparation and cooking of food and for the disposal of waste water.

An element in the law which appears to give landlords a licence to dilapidate is the decision in *Buswell v Goodwin* [1971] 1 WLR 92 that the implied obligation is limited to cases where the house is capable of being made fit for habitation at reasonable expense. This is comparable to the provision in s 11(3) of the 1985 Act making obligations relative to such factors as the condition and life expectancy of the property. Against the argument that it gives landlords a vested interest in deterioration is the contention endorsed by the Law Commission that such dereliction of responsibility would entitle a tenant to terminate the tenancy and to expect substantial damages. This contention makes a number of optimistic assumptions: that tenants will have somewhere else to go and are well versed in the relevant legal complexities.

The Housing Act 1985

Rather than offer remedies for individuals, the next statutes to be considered operate more in the field of public law and are concerned, primarily, with the duties of local authorities. The amended s 604 of the 1985 Act contains a subtly different set of criteria to the unfitness criteria in the s 8 of the 1985 Act. The main disadvantages of the 1985 Act criteria, despite their greater detail than the implied term, are that they can only be operated if an authority is satisfied that a dwelling is unfit and they cannot be invoked by council tenants against their authority.

The current standards are set out in the 1985 Act, as amended by the Local Government and Housing Act 1989. A dwelling-house will be unfit if the authority deems it not reasonably suitable for occupation because it fails to meet one or more of the following requirements:

(a) it is structurally stable;

(b) it is free from serious disrepair;

(c) it is free from dampness prejudicial to the health of the occupants (if any);

(d) it has adequate provision for lighting, heating and ventilation;

(e) it has an adequate piped supply of wholesome water;

(f) there are satisfactory facilities in the dwelling-house for the preparation and cooking of food, including a sink with a satisfactory supply of hot and cold water;

(g) it has a suitably located water closet for the exclusive use of the occupants (if any);

(h) it has, for the exclusive use of the occupants (if any), a suitably located fixed bath or shower and wash hand basin each of which is provided with a satisfactory supply of hot and cold water; and

(i) it has an effective system for the draining of foul, waste and surface water.

If an authority is satisfied of unfitness, it must either serve a repair notice, a closing order or a demolition order. In determining which option to take, the authority has to have regard to guidance from the Secretary of State and is supposed to undertake two assessments; one of the economic merits of any decision; the other of any socio-environmental implications for the locality. The net result is that any directives are very vague and, even if an authority does decide to go down the 1985 Act route, rather than, say, opt for using the Environmental Protection Act 1990, it will be difficult to challenge any decision.

Proposed new housing fitness standard

In 1998, the government announced plans to change the fitness for human habitation criteria and issued a Consultation Paper, *Controlling Minimum Standards in Existing Housing*. The main motivation behind the proposed changes, which have not yet materialised, is to modernise the criteria to reflect a composite approach more sensitive to health and safety issues, instead of the present somewhat arbitrary list of possible defects. It was stressed that, currently, certain important aspects of home health and safety are not covered by the existing criteria – for instance, poor energy efficiency, susceptibility to hazards, such as radon gas, and design defects. The proposed new Housing Fitness Rating System would incorporate reference to all the important health and safety aspects of the home, would provide a means of comparing degrees of habitability and facilitate targeting of resources on the houses found to be most unfit under the modernised criteria.

The Environmental Protection Act 1990

The relationship between the Housing Act 1985 and the public health powers contained in the latest legislation, the Environmental Protection Act 1990, is a complex one. The public health legislation focus is not strictly on disrepair and the action possible may not be far reaching enough to prevent repetition of a nuisance. The clichéd example of public health intervention would be the replacement of leaking roof tiles, rather than a new roof, which might be achievable over a longer period via the Housing Act 1985. Another significant element of the public health law is that, unlike the Housing Act, it can be used against local authorities themselves. There is also the vexed question of a hierarchy of codes in this area. Can the undertaking of action under the Environmental Protection Act be a bar to any further action or are the various remedies separate and cumulative? What if an authority decides that the public health procedures are the most appropriate for use against a private landlord in default? Is there any way of compelling an authority to take Housing Act action, in such circumstances? The answers are that the remedies are supposedly separate and cumulative, but that it is virtually impossible to steer a local authority down one procedural channel rather than another.

Outline of the 1990 Act provisions

The concern of the legislation is 'any premises in such a state as to be prejudicial to health or a nuisance'. Prejudicial to health is helpfully defined elsewhere in the Act as 'injurious, or likely to cause injury, to health'. It has taken some time for expert opinion about the effect of such matters as dampness and condensation on health to be accepted. Not so long ago, only more obvious factors, like plaster falling on occupants' heads, would be accepted as a health risk. The health risk is a separate issue from that of nuisance, which has been defined as either a public or private nuisance and, therefore, traditionally, a nuisance cannot originate if the problem only affects the person(s) in occupation of the premises in question.

Where the local authority is satisfied that a statutory nuisance exists or is likely to occur or recur, s 80 of the 1990 Act requires it to serve an abatement notice requiring the abatement of the nuisance or otherwise prohibiting or restricting it and specifying the works necessary.

Section 82 preserves some of the force of the celebrated s 99 of the Public Health Act 1936, which afforded individuals the chance to lay any information before magistrates alleging the existence of a statutory nuisance on public or private sector property. Under the old law, the person or body responsible for the nuisance did not have to be given notice of the complaint, but, under the 1990 Act, three weeks notice is generally required, thereby giving the landlord time to negotiate or otherwise avert the action. As s 99 was a thorn in the side of local authorities, particularly, and carried the stigma of a criminal conviction, it was lucky to survive, even in modified form in the 1990 Act.

The scope of the environmental health provisions is, as elsewhere, limited by pragmatic considerations. What if there is block infestation in flats or, as in *Birmingham DC v McMahon* (1987) 19 HLR 452, the claim that a whole block constitutes a nuisance because of pervasive damp and mould? The court, save in exceptional circumstances, could only countenance action by individuals in respect of their own flats rather than a collective action, since 'the making of an order in relation to the entire block could heavily strain a local authority's finances and disrupt its housing department's programme for years to come'. This concern for the resources of authorities is echoed in other pronouncements where the courts stress that discretion and common sense are the keys to the formulation of a nuisance order.

The lack of adequate redress for occupants under the public health route is stressed by the Law Commission in focusing on another case, *Habinteg Housing Association v James* (1994) 27 HLR 299, which involved cockroach infestation. It took five years for the infestation to be eliminated after action under the public health legislation. The difficulties with the operation of various branches of the law are well seen in this case.

So far as the question of compensation was concerned, there were insurmountable difficulties blocking an action in tort for damages for nuisance. There was no proof that the infestation emanated from any property held by the landlord housing association. Since they had parted with possession completely and not retained the common parts of the premises, there was nowhere where the landlords could be said to be occupying for the purposes of the law of nuisance, even if the question of the causation of the infestation had been more clear cut. The situation was distinguishable from that in *Sharpe v City of Manchester* (1977) 5 HLR 71, where liability was conceded because the infestation did come from the retained common parts of a block of flats.

Given the traditional reluctance of the courts to imply terms into an agreement, what of the proposition that an action for breach of contract or covenant could be derived from the following term?

> The landlord shall take reasonable care to abate an infestation arising on the estate which could not be abated other than by the landlord taking timely action in respect of all or any of a group of dwellings on the estate.

Lord Justice Waite rejected the importation of any such term to make sense of the agreement, as was successfully argued in *Liverpool City Council v Irwin* [1977] AC 239, in connection with liability to maintain common parts. The difficulties with such an implication were that the formula itself was less than clear; it was not so obvious, as on the traditional test, to go without saying; and, in any case, the contract would still be effective without it, because if the infestation could be traced back to another property that might generate an action in nuisance.

What about a claim in negligence? The difficulty was in presupposing the existence of an extensive duty of care in circumstances of block infestation. It was not possible to invent a duty to act promptly to abate a nuisance which could only be eradicated by block disinfection, where a landlord, such as a housing association, could not take the action itself under common law powers, but had to rely on the invocation of public health legislation procedures. There could be no duty of care in such circumstances. The conclusion was that there was no ground for liability and it was acknowledged judicially that this was justified by the fact that a contrary decision would have probably bankrupted the association after an avalanche of claims.

The presence of liability gaps was re-emphasised in the case of statutory nuisances by the recent Court of Appeal decision in *R v Bristol City Council ex p Everett* (1999) *The Times*, 9 March. A dangerously steep internal staircase was held not to constitute a statutory nuisance as the terminology: 'in such a state as to be injurious, or likely to cause injury to health' in s 79 was thought inapplicable to physical injury or the risk of such injury from the staircase. The long history of 'sanitary' statutes, dating from the Victorian era, convinced the appellate court that the reproduction, over the decades, of the original formula 'injury to health', without any parliamentary amendment through legislation, indicated that physical injury through accidents had always been and should continue to be excluded from the definition of a statutory nuisance. This view endorses the approach taken in cases, such as *Coventry City Council v Cartwright* [1975] 1 WLR 845, which involved a large pile of building refuse and other materials. According to the then Lord Chief Justice, Lord Widgery, 'the underlying conception of the section is that that which is struck at is an accumulation of something which produces a threat to health in the sense of a threat of disease, vermin and the like'. Accordingly, obvious risks to children of injury from broken glass and other sharp objects in the refuse fell outside the ambit of the statute.

One aspect of the law underexplored in contexts such as this, until recently, is the scope of the covenant of quiet enjoyment. There is no need to go through the exercise of implying terms tailor made for various deficiencies in premises if the quiet enjoyment covenant is already broad enough to encompass matters, such as cockroach infestation. Why, if, as conceded in *Browne v Flower* [1911] 1 Ch 219, 'there must be some physical interference with the enjoyment of the demised premises' and flooding and smoke and vibration have, in the past, constituted breaches of the covenant, should cockroach infestation be outside its scope?

The scope of the covenant for quiet enjoyment has recently come under intense judicial scrutiny in two conflicting Court of Appeal cases: *Baxter v London Borough of Camden* (1998) 30 HLR 501; and *Southwark London Borough Council v Mills* [1999] 2 WLR 409. In both cases, the problem was one of inadequate sound insulation exposing flat dwellers to all the noises of everyday domestic activity in adjoining flats. As clearly understood by the judges, the practical importance of such a question is immense, since, if a landlord, such as a local authority, is to be liable for breach of such a covenant to tenants when normal and ordinary user is complained of, then the execution of the necessary work to improve the sound insulation would be extremely expensive. It was, naturally, argued for the landlords that the covenant for quiet enjoyment could not of itself be used to demand repairs or improvements and it was accepted by the judges in the *Southwark* case that such a demand was unwarranted, since damages were available for breach. However, as was pointed out by the dissenting judge, Lord Justice Peter Gibson, in terms of future liability, a landlord vulnerable to claims for damages may have no option but to keep the premises empty or take steps to improve the sound insulation.

In the *Baxter* case, the Court of Appeal, in the shape of Mr Justice Sumner, concluded that:

> ... the landlord will be liable for breach of the covenant of quiet enjoyment where the contemplated use for which the landlord let, for instance, the adjoining flat, was one which interfered with the reasonable enjoyment of the premises in question. The date of actual presumed knowledge is the letting to the plaintiff.

However, the majority of the appellate court in *Mills* rejected this line of reasoning, partly because they had the benefit of analysis of cases such as *Duke of Westminster and Others v Guild* [1985] QB 688. The majority view was that a tenant could not invoke the covenant for quiet enjoyment to gain 'some abstract standard of peace and quiet', but, rather, that a tenant should take the house as he finds it, complete with inadequate insulation. This issue of actual or constructive knowledge of levels of interference at the commencement of the tenancy was rather sketchily examined in these cases, although it does seem central to the argument. As Lord Justice Peter Gibson pointed out in his dissent in *Mills*:

> It would create serious practical problems for would be tenants, whose ability to rely on the covenant for quiet enjoyment would depend on their actual or deemed knowledge of the noise interference, at the date when entering into their tenancies, and the extent to which the measure of interference is subsequently exceeded. Should the prudent would be tenant insist on inspection by day and night at hours when any noise from neighbours might be expected to be at its most intrusive before taking the tenancy?

The House of Lords is expected to pronounce on this matter before long and will be forced to choose between the two conflicting Court of Appeal decisions. Another analytical loose end which may be tidied, somewhat, is the relationship between the law of nuisance and the criteria for breach of the covenant for quiet enjoyment, which seem to have been fudged by some of the judges.

THE LAW COMMISSION PROPOSALS FOR REFORM

It is worth examining the proposals and their justification in some depth and, on past experience, there will be plenty of opportunity for the fine tuning of any reforms before a move towards implementation. The Conservative government resisted pressure to include any proposals in the Housing Act 1996 and the Housing Minister said in Committee in the Commons that 'we need to consider particularly the impact on local authorities' ability under their strategic housing responsibilities to assess and prioritise needs in relation to their resources'.

After reviewing the state of the nation's housing stock and the law on disrepair, the Commission formulates the premise that there is a gap in the law where some civil remedy for short term tenants ought to exist in respect of properties unfit for human habitation. They identify the anomaly that there is a fitness term implied for furnished but not unfurnished premises and the absurdity that tenants have rights in the event of disrepair, but not if unfitness is not the consequence of disrepair.

The central proposal adopted is to refashion the covenant currently in s 8 of the 1985 Act to cover all leases of less than seven years, in tandem with the obligations under s 11. Against arguments that such a reform would be too costly and onerous on landlords, they intend to make the obligation prospective, and, therefore, in the case of local authority landlords envisage that it would take 15 years for all tenancies to be covered by the new covenant. The Commission think that private landlords can reasonably be expected to observe minimal standards in the deregulated climate following the 1988 Act and would expect any greater requirements to be 'reflected in the rent'. This expectation will not be welcomed at a time when housing benefit is under constant pressure.

The covenant is not to resemble the strict liability obligation advocated by some commentators. Instead, notice will be retained as a prerequisite, as will the rule in *Buswell v Goodwin* that liability will be limited to cases where the premises can be made fit at reasonable expense. The Commission regard the latter rule as a safety valve to prevent the imposition of an unrealistic burden on landlords, but it is not difficult to see that, for instance, private sector landlords will have little incentive to improve or renovate property in future, but will rely on a satisfactory return on an investment in dilapidated property.

Should local authority landlords be exempted from the new statutory covenant? The Department of the Environment made strong representations to that effect, arguing that authorities' plans for improvement would be impaired by meeting the costs of inevitable litigation. This concern echoes the claim currently made by some local authorities in the absence of such a covenant that pressure of litigation on disrepair is exhausting funds which would otherwise be used for renovation and that lawyers and surveyors are the main beneficiaries. However, the Commission holds out for a general covenant, since:

> ... a requirement that accommodation should be fit for human habitation is regarded by most people as a fundamental and basic one. In our view, it should in principle be enjoyed by all residential tenants holding under short leases as of right, subject to certain very limited exceptions of a pragmatic kind.

The statutory covenant and renovation grants

The Department of the Environment have also expressed concern that any modifications to existing law could imperil local authority strategic use of renovation grants. The Housing Grants, Construction and Regeneration Act contains measures for making renovation grants in cases of unfitness discretionary, rather than mandatory, to assist targeting of funds and the Commission cannot see any conflict between the two sets of reforms. It would, for example, be open to an authority to serve a repair notice on a landlord and to simultaneously refuse a renovation grant. In fact, if renovation grants were to become wholly discretionary, the Commission see this development as strengthening the case for the new statutory covenant to assist tenants under short leases.

Details of the proposed new covenant

It is envisaged that the criteria would be derived from s 604 of the 1985 Act, rather than from those currently attached to s 8. The general rule would be that there should be implied into a lease of a dwelling-house for less than seven years a covenant by the lessor that the dwelling-house is fit for human habitation at the start of the lease and that the lessor will keep it so fit during the lease.

Restrictions on the operation of the covenant would include items borrowed from s 11 of the Landlord and Tenant Act 1985. Thus, the implied obligation should not require the lessor to carry out any works or repairs for which the tenant is liable or to rebuild the house if it is destroyed by fire, tempest, flood or other inevitable accident. Tenant's fixtures are also exempted.

Moreover, the Commission exclude liability where the principal cause of unfitness is tenant breach of covenant or in the unlikely event of repairing obligations being excluded by court order under s 11 of the 1985 Landlord and Tenant Act. It is also proposed, for reasons already analysed, to restrict liability to circumstances where the property can be made fit for human habitation at reasonable expense. As stated, the standard to be applied is that contained in s 604 of the Housing Act 1985, as amended, rather than the existing criteria attached to s 8. This means that, unlike previous versions of the statutory covenant, basic amenities, such as baths or lavatories, are part of the definition of fitness for habitation.

Other proposals: abolition of the law of waste

As has been seen, the doctrine of waste crops up in unlikely contexts, such as certain grounds for possession against tenants. The Law Commission recognises its archaic nature and proposes to abolish it prospectively in relation to tenancies and licences, whilst retaining it for 'any person who occupies any property as a beneficiary under the terms of any will or trust'. The doctrine has always been much more suited to the intricacies of rights and duties of tenants for life and remaindermen under the Settled Land Acts.

The current covenant of tenant like user will also be abolished in favour of an implied statutory covenant or duty applicable to both tenants and licensees. The obligations would involve taking proper care of the premises, making good any damage wilfully done to the property by occupants and refraining from works 'the actual or probable result of which is to destroy or alter the character of the premises to the detriment of the interest of the landlord or licensor'. These provisions are not mandatory and can be varied by the parties. One of the main reasons for clarifying obligations in this area was uncertainty in the case of informal relationships, such as tenancies at will and licences, about the nature of the occupier's responsibilities. Tenancies at will are much more significant in relation to business tenancies than to residential tenancies. As the Commission put it, the objective of the reforms is to 'capture the essence of what the law of waste and the implied covenant of tenant like user are together intended to achieve and to restate them in clarified unitary form'.

Verdict on the proposals for reform

The present morass of overlapping and distinct private and public law measures for combating disrepair will still be distinctly recognisable after implementation of the proposed reforms. However, updating the statutory covenant in s 8 does make for a relatively clear statement of liability, even if the practical impact of the reform is blunted by the fact that implementation is prospective and inapplicable to existing agreements. Criticisms that lawyers find easy pickings in enforcing repair obligations and compelling local authorities to spend a disproportionate amount of their repairs budget on litigation will presumably be reinforced if there is something in the nature of a catch all fitness for human habitation requirement. At present, as demonstrated in some crucial cases, there are gaps in liability, but the proposals would make assistance in cases not strictly involving disrepair that much easier, since both *Quick* and *James* would be covered by the new statutory covenant.

The last word must be that conceptual clarification and updating of anachronistic statutory covenants is in itself, as the Law Commission would no doubt concede, unlikely to effect major improvements in the state of housing stock across the spectrum of the various tenures in the absence of any clear political and financial commitment from government to make the unfit more habitable. The whole question of access to justice in housing cases is also under review as part of a general overhaul of civil procedure.

CHAPTER 8

UNLAWFUL EVICTION AND HARASSMENT

INTRODUCTION

Problems associated with unlawful eviction and harassment of private tenants, particularly, go back for decades and the response from the law and from law enforcement agencies has traditionally been half hearted. There are also significant regional variations in the gravity of the response to harassment and unlawful eviction; in some areas, fines of only a few hundred pounds are imposed in serious cases which would attract the full measure of punitive damages elsewhere. As with the law of repairs, one difficulty is that the various legal principles are in such a chaotic state and the difficulties are compounded by the complexities of unravelling the precise legal status of occupants. Fundamental rights, such as a day in court – no eviction without due process of law – are by no means universal. Uncertainties about legal status are the more disturbing because there is stringent provision in the Criminal Justice and Public Order Act 1994 to ensure squatters are quickly evicted; legitimate occupiers may also find themselves subject to the procedures by mistake.

The Housing Act 1988 supposedly introduced a powerful deterrent to unlawful eviction in the shape of swingeing financial penalties. However, with the other hand it excluded certain categories of occupant from basic rights, thereby creating an impression of ambivalence by sending out conflicting messages about the exercise of self-help by landlords.

There is a bewildering variety of possible responses to the actions of unscrupulous landlords. So far as criminal prosecution is concerned, the punishments imposed are often light and there is no prospect of enjoining the landlord to refrain from further actions of this type or of reinstating the occupier. However, it is hoped that publicising more serious punishments for offences will eventually help to create a culture in which actions of this type are less common. Civil actions may be more fruitful when it comes to compensation and also as a means of preventing unlawful eviction by the use of injunctions. The measures in the Housing Act to combat antisocial behaviour could also make a contribution in this context.

THE CRIMINAL LAW

The criminal offences of unlawful eviction and harassment have their origins in the aftermath of the deregulation following the Rent Act 1957. Their most recent manifestation is in the Protection from Eviction Act 1977, as amended by the Housing Act 1988.

Residential occupiers

The focus of the legislation is on a broad category, 'residential occupiers', which, at a stroke, transcends the difficulties associated with border patrol of the lease/licence distinction. The definitions section is s 1(1) of the 1977 Act:

> In this section, 'residential occupier', in relation to any premises, means a person occupying the premises as a residence, whether under any contract or by virtue of any enactment or rule of law giving him the right to remain in occupation or restricting the right of any other person to recover possession of the premises.

Clearly, trespassers are outside the scope of this definition, but, otherwise, it is designed to include contractual arrangements of various types and their statutory continuation under Acts such as the Rent Act 1977 and the Housing Act 1988.

Unlawful deprivation of occupation

Section 1(2) of the 1977 Act states:

> If any person unlawfully deprives the residential occupier of any premises of his occupation of the premises or any part thereof, or attempts to do so, he shall be guilty of an offence unless he proves that he believed, and had reasonable cause to believe, that the residential occupier had ceased to reside in the premises.

It is clear from this that partial deprivation of occupation will suffice; it also covers the common situation where locks on the house or room are changed and belongings put in the street or in storage. Unhelpfulness on the landlord's part in not providing a replacement key when one is lost does not constitute an offence as a sin of omission, rather than one of commission. If it is clear that there is no intention permanently to deprive, but displacement for a few days only, then this might be thought to fall under harassment provisions instead, but the courts sometimes award damages for very short-lived unlawful eviction, as when, in *Uckuzular v Sandford-Hill* [1994] (unreported) CL, 4 November, £750 in total was awarded for exclusion for around 36 hours. 'Unlawfully' highlights the fact that other parts of the legislation stipulate that eviction without a court order is prohibited, save for a minority, albeit a significant minority, of occupiers.

Harassment

Not all actions by the landlord result in deprivation of occupation, and sub-s 1(3) of the 1977 Act covers the circumstances of harassment falling short of eviction. The burden of proof and the definition of offences were altered by the 1988 Act to meet anxieties that the differentiation between prior and subsequent occupiers' rights would encourage harassment by landlords. When the Housing Act 1988 was being debated in Parliament references to Rachman were rife.

Sub-section 1(3) now states:

> If any person with intent to cause the residential occupier of any premises:
>
> (a) to give up the occupation of the premises or any part thereof; or

> (b) to refrain from exercising any right or pursuing any remedy in respect of the premises or part thereof,
>
> does acts likely to interfere with the peace or comfort of the residential occupier or members of his household, or persistently withdraws or withholds services reasonably required for the occupation of the premises as a residence he shall be guilty of an offence.

Sub-sections 1(3A) and 1(3B) read:

> 1(3A) Subject to sub-s (3B) below, the landlord of a residential occupier or an agent of the landlord shall be guilty of an offence if:
>
> (a) he does acts likely to interfere with the peace or comfort of the residential occupier or members of his household; or
>
> (b) he persistently withdraws or withholds services reasonably required for the occupation of the premises in question as a residence,
>
> and (in either case) he knows or has reasonable cause to believe, that the conduct is likely to cause the residential occupier to give up the occupation of the whole or part of the premises or to refrain from exercising any right or pursuing any remedy in respect of the whole or part of the premises.
>
> 1(3B) A person shall not be guilty of an offence under sub-s (3A) above if he proves he had reasonable grounds for doing the acts or withdrawing or withholding the services in question.

The original sub-s 1(3) specified that any person, not just the landlord or agent, could commit the offence, but the prosecution would have to demonstrate the intention to evict or hamper the exercise of rights. In addition, 'likely' has replaced 'calculated' in an attempt to facilitate convictions, although 'calculated' means much the same. By contrast, the newer sub-s 3A focuses more narrowly on landlords and agents, but reasonable foresight of consequences and causation, rather than explicit intent, is sufficient.

It is also significant that the actions complained of do not themselves have to be unlawful or in breach of the terms of any tenancy agreement. In *R v Burke* [1991] 1 AC 135, preventing tenants from using outside lavatories and disconnecting the front door bell were held to suffice.

'Persistent' withdrawal of services requires more than one act and non-payment of bills leading to withdrawal of services is unlikely to be counted as intentional, although it would be vulnerable in relation to reasonable foresight.

Other aspects of the criminal law

The Criminal Law Act 1977 contains measures designed to discourage self-help. Under s 6, it is an offence to use violence without lawful authority to secure entry to premises. 'Displaced residential occupiers' or those acting on their behalf are exempted, provided they only use reasonable force. Another precondition is that there must be someone present on the premises who is opposed to the entry and the person deploying violence is aware of this.

THE CIVIL LAW

Statutory tort of unlawful eviction

It is convenient, at this point, to mention a feature of the 1988 Act, supposedly designed to act as a powerful deterrent against unlawful eviction and meet the anxieties about Rachmanism following deregulation. This is contained in ss 27 and 28 of the Act and the underlying proposition is that damages are based on the difference between sitting tenant and vacant possession values, so that the more a landlord stands to gain by eviction, the more he could lose. However, as the case of *Melville v Bruton* (1997) 29 HLR 319, discussed below, demonstrates, this assumption is an oversimplification where there are several occupiers, not all of whom are evicted. In general terms, there is emphasis on the effect eviction has on valuation, as the eviction of a protected tenant would attract, probably, the highest measure of damages because of the significance of the security of tenure. From the perspective of an assured shortholder, this may not be so heartening, as their insecurity will make for lower awards. Section 27 will have to be considered in some detail and there are other features in it which could make it less daunting than might initially be assumed.

The section began to operate after 9 June 1988 on actions of a landlord or any person acting on behalf of the landlord. It covers what might be called direct unlawful deprivation, such as lock changing and belongings removal, and also more indirect, where the residential occupier is driven out by acts of harassment of the type already identified in the 1977 Act. Liability in damages will not arise if the occupier is reinstated before proceedings are concluded or if the court makes an order to that effect at his instigation. Handing back a set of useless keys and suggesting resumption of occupation of a wrecked room does not constitute reinstatement (*Tagro v Cafane* [1991] 2 All ER 235, where over £30,000 was awarded):

> Further limitations are that damages may properly be reduced to reflect any reprehensible conduct on the part of the occupier or fellow residents, or the fact that the landlord in default offered to reinstate the occupier before commencement of the proceedings 'and either it was unreasonable of the former residential occupier to refuse that offer or, if he had obtained alternative accommodation before the offer was made, it would have been unreasonable for him to refuse that offer if he had not obtained that accommodation'.

The statutory tort operates independently of any criminal prosecution for the same offence and is not dependent on a conviction. By virtue of s 27(5), the right to pursue other causes of action is expressly preserved, but damages are not supposed to be awarded twice over for the same loss. The courts have had some difficulty juggling with this sub-section. However, it was established in *Kaur v Gill* (1995) *The Times*, 15 June, that separate damages can be awarded at common law for breach of the covenant of quiet enjoyment, in addition to the more substantial damages awarded under the statutory tort. As with the criminal offences, there are defences available: that it was reasonably believed that the premises had been vacated or, in the case of withdrawal of services, that such action was reasonable in the circumstances.

Agents

A further problem relates to the activities of agents. How far can ss 27 and 28 be invoked against an agent and is the focus solely on the landlord when it comes to assessment of damages? In *Sampson v Wilson* (1996) CL 39, the Court of Appeal pronounced on this question. The plaintiffs were tenants of property owned by Mr Clarke, who appointed Wilson as his agent while he was abroad. Wilson became ill and delegated the management to another, who committed various acts of harassment and ultimately drove the plaintiffs out. The Master of the Rolls rejected the proposition that Wilson could be liable in damages as a joint tortfeasor. The language of s 27 was indicative, in that sub-ss (1) and (2) spoke of acts of harassment by a landlord 'or any person acting on behalf of the landlord', but sub-s (3), in establishing liability in damages, referred only to the landlord in default and made no mention of 'any person acting on behalf of the landlord'. So, the landlord might be liable for his own actions or those of others, but only he was liable in damages. This restrictive interpretation was further justified by the fact that the basis for the calculation of damages in s 28 (supposedly the difference between sitting tenant and vacant possession values) appeared to be aimed at the Rachmanite landlord seeking to profit from harassment. Agents liability stemmed from their own personal torts such as trespass or nuisance.

What if eviction makes no difference to the value?

Further difficulties with interpretation have appeared in the case of *Melville v Bruton* (1997) 29 HLR 319. The issue was when it is appropriate in the calculation of damages to assume that vacant possession has been secured by the landlord in default. The 1988 Act, in ss 27 and 28, seems to offer the prospect of a simple minus sum, but what of the situation where there are other occupiers of the premises who have not been displaced by the landlord and vacant possession is notional rather than actual? If actual vacant possession is the criterion, we end up with the curious proposition that an occupier under harassment, in a property occupied by many, scoops the punitive damages pool by outlasting other occupants whose relative lack of fortitude deprives them of substantial compensation, even if, perhaps, they have endured worse treatment than the last one out. Is it likely that the mischief aimed at in the Act is confined to sole rather than multiple occupation? Or is it just a fact of life that someone evicted from a flat in a large block deserves less than someone driven from a house in sole occupation?

This last proposition seems implausible, but the Court of Appeal are reconciled to such an interpretation. In *Melville*, the landlord acquired a house subject to a restrictive covenant prohibiting use, save as a dwelling-house in single occupation. When the plaintiff moved in under an assured shorthold, there were already two other occupants of part of the premises, whose precise status was unknown, but they were either tenants or licensees. There was no dispute that the defendant landlord had unlawfully evicted the plaintiff a few weeks after the start of the agreement. At first instance, damages of £15,000 were awarded via ss 27 and 28, expressed to be the difference in the value of the property immediately prior to and after the eviction. On appeal, it was argued that the purpose of the Act was to deprive the landlord of any profit accruing from the unlawful act and that necessarily involved consideration of the actual/factual difference in value and not a hypothetical difference, otherwise landlords would be fined more than they would actually have gained.

The Court of Appeal were receptive to this line of argument and concluded that there was nothing in ss 27 and 28 to justify disregarding the existence of the other residential occupiers. On these facts, the eviction had made no difference to the value of the property as it was still encumbered. There was no reason, according to Lord Justice Hutchinson, to suppose that the purpose of the 1988 Act was so comprehensive as to provide damages for evicted tenants in all circumstances. Why should interpretation of the Act not reflect the fact that the eviction had not materially increased the value of the landlord's interest? The outcome was that the award of £15,000 was set aside and £500 substituted for inconvenience, discomfort and distress. The previous award of over £2,000 damages for conversion of the plaintiff's goods was not challenged.

What are the merits of that decision? Some bizarre implications have already been canvassed – that it could create a competition to be 'last out' if there is serial harassment. The aim underlying the statutory tort was to provide a clear deterrent to those engaged in Rachmanite activities. However, s 28 does not directly talk of the difference between sitting tenant and vacant possession values, which would introduce punitive damages whether or not there were other occupiers to affect valuation; instead, it settles for the circumlocutory formula that the basis for damage assessment is the difference between:

> ... the value of the interest of the landlord in default determined on the assumption that the residential occupier continues to have the same right to occupy the premises as before that time; and the value of that interest determined on the assumption that the residential occupier has ceased to have that right.

Because the differential varies with the type of tenancy and because protected tenants have a more profound effect on the valuation than, say, assured shortholders, it was natural to express the formula as just quoted. To that extent, the Court of Appeal seem to be correct in supposing that it is a factual matter, calculating how much a landlord has actually gained in the circumstances, depending on the nature of the occupier's interest. However, the drafting appears to be defective in that the deterrent effect is dissipated in the common circumstances of multiple occupation, where the departure of one sitting tenant after harassment may not have a significant effect on the overall value of the premises. The message to landlords, in these circumstances, is to make sure that the last in a line of occupants in a property is the most amenable to being bargained out. The traditional complaint about the operation of the law in this sphere, prior to the introduction of the statutory tort, was that the penalties likely to be incurred would be dwarfed by the gains on vacant possession, so that landlords had nothing to lose, but this case demonstrates that, in certain circumstances, they can still proceed with relative impunity.

The *Melville* approach has yet to be scrutinised in the House of Lords, but was reaffirmed in the Court of Appeal in *Tinker v Potts*, 30 July 1996. Perhaps, ambitiously, the displaced occupant sought damages, under ss 27 and 28, of £55, 000, after leaving a room in a house in multiple occupation after, apparently, just one day as an assured tenant under an oral agreement. Three other occupants remained, although the plaintiff had been driven out through threats and intimidation. The appellate court approved the reasoning of the trial judge, who rejected the claim for substantial damages under the Act because the house was still in multiple occupation after her departure and, hence, there was no substantial difference in the value as a result of the unlawful eviction.

Similarly, in *King v Jackson* (1998) 30 HLR 541, the award, under ss 27 and 28, at first instance, was rather generous: £11,000 for what was, in effect, the loss of six days of occupation, since the tenant had already served a notice to quit on the landlord, who was anxious to install a new tenant. The judge, for no apparently good reason, fixed the award by reference to one-fifth of the vacant possession value of the flat and the Court of Appeal reined in such generosity. In much the same fashion, the appellate court expressed surprise at an 'extraordinary assessment' by an ex-tenant's surveyor in *Ashton v Coleman*, 8 June 1998. The surveyor had unaccountably fixed on a figure of £10,000 for the difference between vacant possession value and the value with an incumbent assured shortholder, presumably, partly, through exaggeration of the likely difficulties to be experienced by a landlord attempting to evict such a tenant. Lord Justice Stuart-Smith endorsed the statement by Lord Justice Hutchinson in Melville, that 'In the ordinary way, where premises are let at a rack rent on a shorthold tenancy, it is difficult to see why there should be any significant difference'.

Invalid notice to quit and the 'reasonable cause' defence in s 27

As *Wandsworth London Borough Council v Osei-Bonsu* [1999] 1 WLR 1011, demonstrates, the statutory damages under ss 27 and 28 are, in some circumstances, available to tenants of social landlords as well. In this instance, a wife had obtained a non-molestation order and an ouster injunction against her husband and joint secure tenant. After he left the property, she served a notice to quit on the council, but it specified only a fortnight, less than the period defined in the tenancy agreement and stipulated by the Protection from Eviction Act 1977. It was not until three years later and some time after the discharge of the ouster order that the wife belatedly gave the requisite 28 days notice. In the circumstances, the court had to grant the husband's application for a declaration that he had remained a joint tenant of the property until the expiry of the proper notice to quit. At first instance, he was awarded the substantial sum of £30,000 in damages for trespass and unlawful eviction under ss 27 and 28.

On appeal, Wandsworth naturally contended that he should not get both the declaration and substantial damages and also invoked the defence in s 27(8) arguing that it had 'reasonable cause to believe that the residential occupier had ceased to reside in the premises in question at the time when he was deprived of occupation'. Although Lord Justice Simon Brown thought that some mistake on a point of civil law could, in principle, afford such an excuse, on the facts, he did not accept the defence of reasonable cause, as the council had treated the short notice as valid without taking any further steps, such as initiating proceedings for possession or asking for a declaration that the tenancy had ended. So far as the 'penny and the bun' problem was concerned, he held that taking the damages retrospectively ended the tenancy at the time of the unlawful eviction in 1990. However, he reduced the damages from £30,000 to £10,000, as he was unconvinced that the judge below had formed the correct view of mitigating factors as defined in s 27(7)(a).

Forfeiture under the 1977 Act

The law of forfeiture has been under a cloud for some time and the Law Commission (Termination of Tenancies Bill, Law Com No 221) has recently made recommendations to enlarge the scope of the right to a day in court beyond residential tenancies. Section 2 of the Protection from Eviction Act requires a landlord of residential premises who has reserved a right of entry or forfeiture in the lease only to exercise that right by court proceedings. This requirement of due process only operates 'while any person is lawfully residing in the premises or part of them', so that, for example, where premises have been totally sublet in breach of covenant and the breach has not been waived by acceptance of rent, self-help via peaceable re-entry is permitted.

Prohibition of eviction without due process of law

The elaborate frameworks of security of tenure for various private and public sector tenants have already been considered. The purpose of s 3 of the 1977 Act, which goes back a long way, was originally to extend basic rights to tenants unprotected by various codes, but still deserving of a day in court. An example might be tenants with board who had neither protected tenancies nor restricted contracts, but still deserved court supervision of their departure.

The opportunity has been taken to amend the section over the years to accommodate various deserving classes of licensee, such as 'restricted contract' licensees, and the culmination in the 1988 Act was to exclude certain categories of tenancy and licence from protection under s 3, but otherwise extend the ambit to tenancies and licences.

The section is now hideously complicated, with additions from both 1980 and 1988 clumsily grafted on to existing principles. The basic principle, as amended, is that, where there is a residential tenancy or licence, with the exception of statutorily protected tenancies as defined in the Act and 'excluded' tenancies and licences and the agreement has ended, but the occupier is still in residence, 'it shall not be lawful for the owner to enforce against the occupier, otherwise than by proceedings in the court, his right to recover possession of the premises'.

It is, therefore, crucial to determine which tenancies count as 'statutorily protected' for these purposes. A list is given in s 8 and the main qualifiers of relevance are those 'protected' within the 1977 Act and assured tenancies under the Housing Act 1988. These, as seen, contain their own procedures for achieving the same end – the operation of due process – and, hence, do not require assistance under s 3. However, the list is not comprehensive and does not include statutory tenancies under the 1977 Rent Act or secure tenancies under the 1985 Act. These two important tenancies are, therefore, governed by s 3.

The significance of s 3 for statutory tenants was brought out in *Haniff v Robinson* (1994) HLR 386, where the punitive damages in ss 27 and 28 of the Housing Act also came into play. In this instance, the statutory tenant was continuing to reside in the property after the landlord had obtained a possession order by falsely claiming to be a resident landlord. The tenant, Miss Robinson, had applied to have the order set aside, but the landlord became impatient and forcibly ejected her a few weeks before that happened.

The Court of Appeal upheld an award of damages of £28,300, including ss 27 and 28 damages, and were satisfied that the natural meaning of s 3 was that Miss Robinson would remain a statutory tenant so long as she continued in occupation of the dwelling-house. It was argued for the landlord that she had ceased to be a statutory tenant either when the possession order was first made, when it took effect or when the landlord applied for the warrant of execution, but the court took a generous view.

How far did the protection of s 3 extend? The crucial formula was 'it shall not be lawful for the owner to enforce against the occupier, otherwise than by proceedings in the court'. It was admittedly vague, but Lord Justice Woolf considered that their object was to provide continued protection until execution of a warrant by court bailiffs in the orthodox fashion. Therefore, the landlord, despite obtaining an order for possession, had no right to resort to self-help to recover possession. So, the 'death's door' protection for occupants under s 3 can be as substantial as other safeguards.

Another last gasp involvement with s 3 arose in *Mohamed v Malek and the Royal Borough of Kensington and Chelsea* 30 March 1995, where the delicate question of the interaction of homelessness and protection from eviction legislation surfaced. The basic issue was whether someone put in a bed and breakfast hotel, while the authority conducted initial investigations of status under Pt III of the 1985 Act, could claim the rights under the 1977 Act, in particular the entitlement to four weeks notice, when an adverse decision was made on priority need. Since the section covers all those non-excluded tenants and licensees who are occupying premises as a dwelling, why should not someone housed, albeit temporarily, be able to use the 1977 Act? The Court of Appeal, unsurprisingly, delivered a pragmatic judgment rejecting such a contention. Lord Justice Auld stated:

> A council's ability efficiently to perform its public duty as a local housing authority could be seriously affected if the protection of the 1977 Act were automatically to attach to every temporarily housed unsuccessful applicant for housing just because he had been able to satisfy the low threshold under s 63 for investigation of his application.

Excluded tenancies and licences

This category devised in the 1988 Act has the function of depriving certain occupants of their day in court and the normal notice to quit preconditions under s 5 of the Act; characteristically, four weeks notice. When is speedy, peaceable re-entry without recourse to the courts deemed appropriate? The common factors seem to be found mainly in situations of enforced proximity in the private sector and areas of housing management for local authorities where rapid turnover of occupiers has to be guaranteed. However, there are categories which seem open to abuse. Transitional provisions protect tenancies granted before the commencement of the 1988 Act.

Because of its importance, much of the text of sub-s 3A(2) will have to be given verbatim:

> (2) A tenancy or licence is excluded if:
>
> (a) under its terms the occupier shares any accommodation with the landlord or licensor; and
>
> (b) immediately before the tenancy or licence was granted and also at the time it comes to an end, the landlord or licensor occupied as his only or principal home premises of which the whole or part of the shared accommodation formed part.

Similarly, sub-s (3) excludes sharing with a member of the family of the landlord or licensor, provided that the building in question is not a purpose-built block of flats. Sub-section (5) defines 'accommodation' negatively by saying that it 'includes neither an area used for storage nor a staircase, passage, corridor or other means of access'. By sub-s (6), agreements are excluded if granted as a temporary expedient to 'a person who entered the premises in question or any other premises as a trespasser'. Holiday lettings and agreements 'granted otherwise than for money or money's worth' are excluded by sub-s (7). Various forms of hostel licences with social landlords are excluded by sub-s (8). Tenancies in hostels are not excluded, but are always going to be thin on the ground, particularly in the light of the reasoning in *Westminster City Council v Clarke* [1992] 2 AC 288.

Points to note about the various categories are that there is, in some instances, obvious dovetailing with non-secure tenancies under the 1985 Act. The sharing criteria applicable to the private sector are not couched in terms of living accommodation unlike, for instance, ss 21 and 22 of the 1977 Rent Act as interpreted. 'Accommodation' is extensively defined and, therefore, the sharing of a bathroom or lavatory will be enough to deprive occupiers of fundamental rights. It seems anomalous that people with exclusive possession and tenancies of their own rooms should lose notice and due process rights by virtue of such limited sharing, when licensees in a floating population, such as in the *Vaughan* case are to that extent better off. Resident landlord tenancies where there is no sharing or only inconsequential sharing of corridors or access are not within the excluded category.

'Rights to occupy the premises for a holiday only' may prove attractive to certain landlords anxious to circumvent even the minimal rights guaranteed in s 3 and seem more precarious than assured shortholds. It is also possible that landlords may be tempted to 'plant' family members in houses with tenants and ensure a rapid turnover by stipulating a modicum of sharing.

Notices to quit

There are long standing legal principles governing the operation of notices to quit in respect of periodic tenancies. Strictly speaking, to talk of notices to quit in the case of licences is inappropriate, as the licensor has the power, but not necessarily the right to terminate a licence prematurely. As elsewhere, the arrival of social legislation superimposed on common law principles has created analytical complications. The Housing Act 1988 altered the basic statutory principles in order to bring non-excluded licences into the fold, although, as already demonstrated, the list of excluded licences is extensive.

The basic framework of protection in s 5 of the Protection from Eviction Act 1977, as amended, is that no notice by landlord or tenant or licensor or licensee will be valid if premises are let or occupied as a dwelling, unless the notice is in writing, contains prescribed information and is given not less than four weeks before the date on which it is to take effect. Excluded tenancies dating from after the commencement date of the 1988 Act are outside this framework, unless entered into under a contract predating that commencement. Premises occupied under an excluded licence of whatever age are outside.

There is no set form of words for the prescribed information, but the gist of it is that, if the occupier does not leave the dwelling, the landlord must get a court order before he can be lawfully evicted and such an order can not be sought before the expiry of the notice to quit. No prescribed information has ever been produced for notice from tenants or licensees.

Civil remedies

Some possible avenues have already been identified in previous discussion. Sections 27 and 28 are likely to be the most lucrative in cases of unlawful eviction and there is the possibility, in some circumstances, of an action for breach of statutory duty in respect of breach of obligations under s 3 of the 1977 Act. There are many other possible causes of action which may be appropriate according to the circumstances of the individual case and these will be outlined now. For detailed exposition, see Arden and Partington, *Quiet Enjoyment*, Legal Action Group.

Breach of the covenant for quiet enjoyment

At this point, the lease/licence distinction reasserts itself, since only tenants of whatever description have such a covenant expressly or impliedly. Licensees are dependent more on the terms of their licence. 'Quiet' is not meant just in the acoustic sense, but in terms of undisturbed enjoyment of the rights of a tenant. Even if the landlord does not cross the threshold, threatening letters and visits may suffice, as in *Kenny v Preen* [1963] 1 QB 499. Cutting off essential services is another clear example. Breach of a covenant for quiet enjoyment will not, of itself, entitle a tenant to damages for mental distress. For recovery, in such circumstances, trespass or nuisance would have to be claimed.

Trespass

As well as trespass on land and trespass to the person (inflicting injury on the occupant), there is, as seen in the *Melville* case, trespass to goods also. This is a common phenomenon when goods are removed from the premises by the landlord.

Nuisance

The law of nuisance is still developing, but there are long established principles concerned with unlawful interference with use and enjoyment of land. Tenants are clearly covered, but those without an interest in land, such as licensees, have, until recently, been generally excluded from the law of private nuisance. However, in *Khorasandjian v Bush* [1993] QB 727, an injunction preventing further nuisance phone calls was granted to a person without any proprietary right to be protected, as she was living in her parents' house. In *Hunter v Canary Wharf* [1996] 2 WLR 348, where the issue was interference with television reception, the Court of Appeal adopted a similar approach and rejected the view that exclusive possession of property was a prerequisite for sustaining an action in nuisance. Some lower level test of occupation of property as a home would be sufficient basis for a claim.

The House of Lords, to no great surprise, reaffirmed the traditional view that the right to sue in private nuisance must be based on exclusive possession and proprietary right, rather than on some more opaque notion of residential occupation ([1997] AC 655). Although there was a powerful dissenting judgment from Lord Cooke, the majority repudiated the more generous approach, as exemplified by the following statement from Lord Justice Pill in the Court of Appeal, specifying that:

> ... a substantial link between the use and the land on which he or she is enjoying it is essential, but, in my judgment, occupation of property as a home does confer upon the occupant a capacity to sue in private nuisance.

Lord Goff's pronouncement in the House of Lords typified judicial disquiet about such a 'link':

> But, who is to be included in this category? It was plainly intended to include husbands and wives, or partners, and their children and, even, other relatives living with them. But, is the category also to include the lodger upstairs or the *au pair* girl or resident nurse caring for an invalid who makes her home in the house while she works there? In any event, the extension of the tort in this way would transform it from a tort to land into a tort to the person in which damages could be recovered for something less serious than personal injury and the criteria for liability were founded not upon negligence, but upon striking a balance between the interests of neighbours in the use of their land. This is, in my opinion, not an acceptable way in which to develop the law.

The majority were also convinced that the introduction of the Protection from Harassment Act 1997 had properly disposed of the *Khorasandjian* problem and left no room for further judicial development of the law in this sphere. Against this conservatism, it was argued, by Lord Cooke, that the traditional law of nuisance predated television and other technological developments and that clinging to proprietary right as a precondition could involve a court in the legal complexities surrounding the acquisition of a beneficial interest in the matrimonial home. He could have added that the notion of exclusive possession is a particularly awkward and opaque notion with which to patrol the boundaries of the law of nuisance against interlopers. What of the category of occupants discussed elsewhere in this book: family members or occupants under special arrangements who, nonetheless, are deemed to have exclusive possession? Are the vagaries and uncertainties of the notion not just as unsettling as the nightmare vision, conjured up by Lord Goff, of *au pairs* having legal rights in this domain? Lord Cooke also made the point that the emergent international recognition of the separate interests of children, as seen, for example, in the United Nations Convention, rendered the traditional view increasingly anachronistic.

The complexities of the law on nuisance have also surfaced in two contentious recent cases: one involving a campaign of racial harassment by council tenants; the other a history of acts of nuisance and trespass committed by travellers against neighbouring occupiers from a 'tolerated' base of council owned property. In the first case, *Hussain v Lancaster City Council* (1998) 96 LGR 663, the plaintiffs were joint owners of a shop and residence on a housing estate and the acts of harassment against them became a *cause célèbre* and attracted much media attention. They sued the council both in negligence and nuisance, relying, among other things, on the fact that Lancaster's standard form tenancy agreement required occupants to refrain from harassment of residents and the council were on record as committed to taking action 'against anyone who harasses others'. They succeeded, at first instance, in nuisance because the judge held that council occupation of the common parts of the estate, such as roads and walkways from which the harassment originated, was sufficient to ground a claim.

This rather tenuous proprietary link to the common parts of the estate was rejected in the Court of Appeal. This would be sufficient to dispose of any claim in private nuisance, but could, as noted in the later case involving the travellers, leave any claim in public nuisance untouched. So far as the alternative negligence action was concerned, the appellate court found that the claim foundered at the two criteria set by Lord Hoffmann in *Stovin v Wise and Norfolk County Council* [1996] AC 923, namely, that the plaintiff had failed to show that Lancaster had acted irrationally in failing to exercise its statutory powers to evict and, secondly, that no exceptional reasons had been established to justify the payment of compensation to those injured by such a failure. In addition, the claim failed the highly flexible 'fair, just and reasonable' test outlined by Lord Browne-Wilkinson in *X (Minors) v Bedfordshire County Council* [1995] 2 AC 633. It was inappropriate to single out the council in an area where the police had a major responsibility and a multi-disciplinary response was required.

The more recent case, *Lippiatt v South Gloucestershire Council* [1999] 3 WLR 137, might seem indistinguishable from the *Hussain* facts, but great judicial emphasis was placed on the fact that the acts of harassment in *Lancaster* were not initiated from an identifiable base, but, presumably, from a range of different locations. However, in the more recent case, a group of travellers had been allowed to congregate on a strip of land in large numbers and, as licensees of the council, had used the land as a base or springboard for multifarious acts of damages and trespass. The Court of Appeal had the benefit of citation of cases not mentioned in *Hussain*, such as *Attorney General v Corke* [1933] Ch 89 and *Smith v Scott* [1973] 1 Ch 314. In *Corke*, it was accepted that a cause of action arose in the case of licensees and the travellers and, in that case, were also stigmatised as 'things likely to do mischief if they escape' under the celebrated rule in *Rylands v Fletcher* (1865) 3 H & C 774. *Smith v Scott* was an endorsement of the traditional approach to liability in private nuisance in the context of landlord and tenant, that landlords are not responsible for the actions of tenants in the absence of express or implied authorisation of the offending actions. In that case, even though the council had housed a problem family next door to the plaintiff, they were not liable in nuisance.

In *Lippiat*, the collective view in the Court of Appeal was that all the preconditions for sustaining an action in private nuisance had been made out and the plaintiff's claim should not have been struck out at first instance. The travellers had been on the council's land for several years and their presence there could, arguably, constitute a nuisance to adjoining occupiers. According to Lord Justice Mummery, the prerequisites for liability in nuisance for the actions of licensees were as follows:

> Those circumstances were that the plaintiff's use and enjoyment of his rights in his land were interfered with by the continuing presence on the defendant's land of persons whose actual or apprehended activities included, to the knowledge of the defendant, harmful acts repeatedly committed by them on the plaintiff's land from their base on land occupied by the defendant.

Accordingly, the justification for allowing liability, or at least not excluding it, in the *Lippiat* case, is that it displayed two features absent from the *Hussain* circumstances; the presence of a clearly identifiable and fairly contiguous base from which to operate to the detriment of neighbouring landowners; and a relationship between licensor and licensees which, inevitably, imposes relatively greater responsibilities on the former, consistent with the greater degree of control exercised over licensees than tenants. However, to the victim of acts of nuisance or harassment, such distinctions may appear specious.

CHAPTER 9

LONG LEASES AT LOW RENTS

INTRODUCTION

We have already seen how various types of long lease have been excluded from frameworks of protection, such as the Rent Act 1977. What are the distinctive features of long leases and why has so much overelaborate statutory machinery been brought piecemeal into operation laboriously in recent years, culminating in the Housing Act 1996, to alter the balance of the relationship between landlord and tenant? At the time of writing, the whole long leasehold system itself is being earmarked for destruction, albeit by death by a thousand cuts, and being ultimately replaced by some commonhold system under which management and maintenance of blocks of flats, particularly, will be improved, at least in theory.

Leases can be for anything up to 999 years and beyond, but one of the most striking features of property law and urban development in England and Wales has been the use of the so called 99 year 'building lease', prominent from Georgian times. A variety of different legal techniques and transactions was employed to set up building leases, but they had various common features, as follows. The fragmentation of ownership interests involved was particularly suitable for landlords in a developing market. Under building leases, large tracts of land could be uniformly developed and the retention of the freehold reversion by the owner intrinsically meant that the leaseholder acquired a depreciating asset, although the initial premium involved on acquiring the lease would not be far different to the price of the freehold of the same property. From the perspective of the freeholder, leasehold estates had several advantages; uniformity and observation of covenants were better secured by the leasehold system, given the inability of the law to deal with the enforceability of positive covenants between freeholders. In addition to the initial premium paid by leaseholders, a steady annual income was guaranteed by the exaction of a ground rent for each property. Although the passage of time and inflation rendered some rents anachronistic, large scale landowners benefited from a substantial annual income. Commonly, because, after all, the freeholder had parted with possession for the duration of the lease onerous repairing covenants might be imposed on the leaseholder, including an obligation to render up the premises in good repair at the end of the lease. High reversionary values were guaranteed so far as the terms of the lease could stipulate. Accordingly, the freehold interest became increasingly important and valuable as the lease progressed.

It is, therefore, far easier to identify the benefits accruing to the freehold owner by such a system, than to see what the leaseholder gains, especially in a time of housing shortage, such as followed the Second World War, when options were limited. What the leaseholder or successive leaseholders on long leases acquired, according to traditional property law, can be described very quickly; the right to exclusive possession of the premises for the stipulated period, but no interest in the bricks and mortar and by definition no security of tenure. In many cases, in the author's experience, the incumbent leaseholders having paid the full market price, virtually indistinguishable from the freehold or, being assignees of the leasehold interest, would have great difficulty in penetrating the legal jargon and realising that they were not owner-occupiers in law. The predicament of some long leaseholders would be particularly striking when leases began to run out, with no prospect of renewal, but continuing obligations to keep in repair. The unattractively, but realistically labelled 'fag end' of a lease was scarcely a marketable asset and the insecurity of tenure was often damaging to the health of elderly persons who previously thought themselves owner-occupiers.

Pressure for reform of the long leasehold system is, therefore, not exactly a new phenomenon. At the end of the last century, there was great agitation for enfranchisement – that is, enabling leaseholders to acquire the freehold of their properties. However, the vested interests at stake are very clear and little progress was made until the Landlord and Tenant Act 1954 when the possibility of security of tenure was granted to many. As has been observed:

> In 1954, the security aspect predominated. The tenant's economic claims were not allowed to interfere with the ownership of property. Tenants were seen to want security, not owner-occupation and the supposed freedom of property ownership [Stewart, *Housing Action in an Industrial Suburb*, 1981, p 88].

It was not until the late 1960s that property ownership became more of a possibility, with the contentious enfranchisement of houses under the 1967 Leasehold Reform Act. 'This is, bluntly, confiscation', fulminated *The Times*. Because of the apparent injustices in the freeholder/leaseholder relationship, exacerbated, often, by monopoly conditions, the White Paper that preceded the Act formulated the interesting proposition that, because successive leaseholders had, in many cases, paid for the building several times over in rent and still had an obligation to maintain it to the vanishing point, they should be credited with the bricks and mortar when it came to assessing the price to be paid for the freehold. This notion that, in equity, the building should be seen as belonging to the leaseholder who would then only be concerned with site values attracted violent hostility, including from property lawyers anxious that the sacred name of equity should not be sullied by association with such a suspect principle of (re)distributive justice. According to Megarry and Wade, *The Law of Real Property*, 4th edn, p 1149, 'Whatever political or social expediency there was in this 'principle', it is difficult to perceive any equity in it, in any sense of that word'. Even the jurisdiction of the European Court of Human Rights was unsuccessfully invoked in 1986 on behalf of a Duke of Westminster, whose descendant, incidentally, left the Conservative party when the measures to enfranchise flats were passed in the Leasehold Reform, Housing and Urban Development Act 1993. It was unsuccessfully contended before the European Court of Human Rights, in 1986, that the policy was in breach of Art 1 of the First Protocol to the European Convention of Human Rights, which states: 'No one shall be deprived of his possessions except in the public interest.' The Court was satisfied that the supposed pursuit of social justice in allowing enfranchisement constituted a policy 'in the public interest'. It should also be noted that the policy behind the 1993 enfranchisement is far more oriented to market values than was the 1967 enfranchisement.

In property law terms, there are clear distinctions between house and flat ownership and one of the particular evils besetting flat dwellers has been the spectre of 'flying freeholds'; parts of a building, such as a block of flats in freehold ownership. The property law and conveyancing difficulties associated with flat ownership are partly attributable to the already mentioned difficulties of enforcement between freeholders of positive covenants, such as repair and maintenance. The drafting of the 1967 Act was careful to confine the rights to enfranchise to ordinary houses, but, when the ideological drive towards owner-occupation reached break neck speed in the 1980s, the pressure from flat dwellers for some distributive justice (or political or social expediency) to be accorded to them became unanswerable. The resultant legislation, the Landlord and Tenant Act 1987 and the Leasehold Reform, Housing and Urban Development Act 1993, have particular importance for flatdwellers and will be discussed in the next chapter. The saga of attempting to introduce a little social justice into the leasehold system never ends, as is shown by the very latest legislation, the Housing Act 1996, which is designed to amend some of the mistakes in 1993 and also alter significantly earlier unsuccessful legislation such as the Landlord and Tenant Act 1987.

The Landlord and Tenant Act 1954

The original aspiration behind this Act was to confer something comparable to Rent Act security of tenure on certain long leaseholders paying a low rent. A long tenancy is defined in the Act as 'a tenancy granted for a term certain exceeding 21 years, whether or not subsequently extended by act of the parties or by any enactment'. The basic qualifying condition is circuitously expressed in s 2(1) of the Act. It is that 'the circumstances (as respects the property comprised in the tenancy, the use of that property and all other relevant matters) are such that, on the coming to an end of the tenancy, at that time, the tenant would, if the tenancy had not been one at a low rent, be entitled, by virtue of the Rent Act, to retain possession of the whole or part of the property comprised in the tenancy'. So, in principle, subject to any modifications, the whole apparatus of the Rent Acts, with the exception of the low rent exclusions, becomes relevant for the purposes of establishing whether a lease falls within the 1954 Act. This, perhaps, saves time for the draftsman in the short term, but derivative or cross-referential drafting often creates difficulties in the longer term.

One obviously unintended consequence of this dependency materialised following the passage of the deregulatory Housing Act 1988, aiming, as already demonstrated, to phase out Rent Act protected tenancies. By a legislative sidewind, persons previously eligible to capitalise on the Rent Acts to claim 1954 Act security via the 1977 Act had their rights blown away; s 34 of the 1988 Act makes it clear that, after the commencement date, protected tenancies can only be created in exceptional circumstances and there was no saving clause for long leases at low rents. Therefore, long leaseholders whose tenancy dated from after the 15 January 1989 and who previously would have enjoyed the security of a statutory tenancy on termination of the lease were deprived of any such expectation, since, as a result of the 1988 Act, they would obviously not 'be entitled by virtue of the Rent Act to retain possession'. In consequence, the draftsman had to intervene in the Local Government and Housing Act 1989 to restore some equality of consideration for old and new leaseholders and these complexities will shortly be explored. This, in turn, means, as with other occupiers, that the dates of agreements become important and there is even a risk of certain categories falling into a jurisdictional gap between statutory codes!

What is a low rent?

For older agreements

If the lease predates 1 April 1990 or is derived from a prior agreement, then the test is that the rent must not exceed two-thirds of the rateable value of the property.

Leases dating from on or after 1 April 1990

Here, the relevant rent payable is separately regulated for the metropolis and the provinces. The level is £1,000 or less per annum if the property is in Greater London and £250 or less elsewhere. In addition, a convoluted formula introduced by the Reference to Rating (Housing) Regulations 1990 (SI 1990/434) in the shape of a new s 2(1A) has to be applied to those few tenancies not covered specifically by the 1989 Local Government and Housing Act.

The purpose of the tenancy

As already stated, the doctrine in the Rent Acts is to be applied, except where it is deemed inappropriate. In the case of the classic Rent Act requirement, dating from 1915, that the premises should be let as a separate dwelling, there are clearly, in the absence of time travel, difficulties in establishing the original purposes of lettings dating from before the institution of the Rent Acts. The solution adopted in the 1954 Act, to obviate too much historical speculation is contained in s 22(3):

> In determining ... whether the property comprised in a tenancy, or any part of that property, was let as a separate dwelling, the nature of the property or part at the time of the creation of the tenancy shall be deemed to have been the same as its nature at the time in relation to which the question arises, and the purpose for which it was let under the tenancy shall be deemed to have been the same as the purpose for which it is or was used at the last mentioned time.

The question of eligibility tends to arise at the time leases are expiring, so the statutory formula, in s 22(3), boils down to analysis of ultimate rather than original circumstances, and, far from requiring the long historical view, accommodates the short termist entrepreneur. This also demonstrates that, in the right hands, fag ends of leases can be valuable commodities. For example, in *Haines v Herbert* [1963] 1 WLR 1401, the last six weeks of a 99 year lease was acquired by the tenant who busily established a presence on several floors in a house split into apparently separate units of accommodation, claiming that she wanted to reconvert the house for her occupation. The Court of Appeal were satisfied that she was occupying the whole house as a residence and as a separate dwelling and was within the 1954 Act.

In *Herbert v Byrne* [1964] 1 WLR 519, the premises in question were typical, a large house on four floors let as a unit in 1863 at a ground rent of only £2 per annum for 99 years. Again, the fag end of the lease was purchased along with vacant possession of two floors, the other two being subtenanted. The whole property was held by the Court of Appeal to be within the 1954 Act, since it was plausible that the tenant intended to occupy the whole with his family on expiry of the subleases. Lord Denning summarised the proper judicial approach as follows:

> You are to look at the position at the end of the lease, and ask yourself whether the leaseholder would have been protected if it had not been a long lease at a low rent, but a short lease at a rack rent. If the leaseholder would have qualified under the old Rent Acts for protection on the expiry of such a short lease, he qualifies now, under the Act of 1954, for protection on the expiry of the long lease. There is, however, this difference – in determining whether he qualifies or not, you do not look at the terms of the old long lease itself as you would look at the terms of a short lease, but you look at the state of affairs as it actually existed at the end of the long lease. That is made clear by s 22(3) of the Act of 1954.

Similarly, in *Regalian Securities v Ramsden* [1981] 1 WLR 611, the House of Lords took a generously flexible view of the purpose of the letting. A flat and a maisonette were both let on a 42 year lease, and the tenant of the flat sublet the maisonette for the remainder of the term less one day. However, the subtenant did not vacate as agreed and stayed on after the 42 years expired, thwarting the tenant's plan of occupying the whole of the premises. Nevertheless, the court held that, on expiry, the whole was let to the tenant as a separate dwelling. This judicial attitude can be contrasted with the much warier approach to the acceptance of the existence of a separate dwelling in Rent Act cases, such as *Horford Investments v Lambert* [1976] Ch 39, where there was clear hostility to other forms of entrepreneurial endeavour.

Application for a declaration that the 1954 Act is inapplicable

In view of the ingenuity displayed by some tenants in last minute qualification for statutory rights under the 1954 Act, the same legislation in s 2(2) offers alert landlords a means of pre-empting any such tactics by taking certain action within the final year of a tenancy. It is possible to make an application to the court for a declaration that the tenancy in question is outside the 1954 Act and, crucially, the various qualifying conditions have to be met at the time of the application for the tenant to prevent the declaration. Against the tenant, the court is entitled to assume, by virtue of s 20, that there will be no change of circumstances before expiry of the lease and the onus is on the tenant to produce evidence to rebut that presumption.

More recent tenancies and the Local Government and Housing Act 1989

As already indicated, the phasing out of the Rent Acts threatened to phase out analytically derivative long tenancies as well. The solution propounded in the 1989 Act is not without its difficulties, the main one being the aforementioned legislative black hole into which long tenancies, created between 15 January 1989 and 1 April 1990 (the 1989 Act commencement date), appear to have disappeared. However, the basic outlines of the 1989 Act have to be sketched first. According to the Act, successful tenants can expect assured tenancies, rather than the obsolescent Rent Act statutory tenancy. The test formulated with typical obscurity of reference is found in s 186(2) of the 1989 Act:

> Schedule 10 to this Act applies, and s 1 of the Landlord and Tenant Act 1954 does not apply to the tenancy of a dwelling-house:
>
> (a) which is a long tenancy at a low rent, as defined in Sched 10 to this Act; and
>
> (b) which is entered into on or after the day appointed for the coming into force of this section, otherwise than in pursuance of a contract made before that day.

The relevant appointed day is 1 April 1990 and the test, in plainer English, is whether, apart from the fact of a low rent, a tenancy would otherwise qualify as an assured tenancy. The gap in legislative provision is now apparent, since tenancies postdating 15 January 1989 can only exceptionally fall within the 1954 Act and do not qualify for assured tenancy equivalence under the 1989 Act. The issue is not a live one until the likely expiry date of the relevant 'gap' tenancies, which will be in 2010, by which time a solution may be found. One suggested redemption of the gap tenancies is by a somewhat strained interpretation of another element in the 1989 Act, which is the next feature to be considered.

The phasing out of 1954 Act tenancies

Section 186(3) provides as follows:

> If a tenancy:
>
> (a) is in existence on 15 January 1999; and
>
> (b) does not fall within sub-s (2) above; and
>
> (c) immediately before that date was, or was deemed to be, a long tenancy at a low rent for the purposes of Pt 1 of the Landlord and Tenant Act 1954, then, on and after that date (and so far as concerns any notice specifying a date of termination on or after that date and any steps taken in consequence thereof), s 1 of that Act shall cease to apply to it and Sched 10 to this Act shall apply to it unless, before that date, the landlord has served a notice under s 4 of that Act specifying a date of termination which is earlier than that date.

In plainer English, this means that long tenancies covered by the 1954 Act will cease, at a certain point, to fall under that Act and will be transmuted into long tenancies under the 1989 Act, unless the wheels of termination have already been set in motion by the landlord. This transmutation is comparable to the metamorphosis of old style 'controlled' tenancies under the Rent Acts into regulated tenancies and avoids too much legislative clutter in an already congested area of law.

What of the question of whether some legislative home can be found for the stray tenancies? Condition (c) appears to be the difficulty, since it talks of belonging to the 1954 code, which is where the problem started. It is conceivable that there could be some mileage in the formula which was, or was deemed to be, a long tenancy, but that is somewhat optimistic.

Security of tenure and the 1954 Act

The basic principle is one familiar from the operation of statutory tenancies elsewhere, of automatic continuity unless and until the requirements for termination are met. According to s 3, a tenancy which subsists immediately before the 'term date' (time of expiry) will not come to an end unless it is ended according to the provisions of Pt 1 of the 1954 Act. Even if there is a change of circumstances such that the tenancy in principle fails to qualify, it will still be protected under the Act s 3(1).

When the tenancy continues, the rent and other terms are to be as before, with provision for apportionment of the rent if only part of the original premises have qualified for continuation.

Termination of tenancies

There is, naturally, no provision for either party to terminate an agreement before the term date of a tenancy. The tenant can terminate the tenancy under s 5 of the Act at any time after one month before the expiry of the tenancy by giving one month's notice.

The landlord can terminate the tenancy either at the moment of expiry or at any time thereafter by serving the appropriate notice. There are, basically, two options open to the landlord here. In either case, the landlord has to serve a notice in prescribed form not more than 12 and not less than six months before the proposed date of termination (which could be the contractual expiry date or any later date).

The first option is to attempt to convert the lease into a statutory tenancy. By virtue of s 4 of the Act, the landlord has to spell out basic proposals about rent and repairing obligations and also naturally state what premises are to constitute the dwelling-house in question. The notice must also ask the tenant if he is willing to give up possession. The tenant then has two months in which to assert the right to remain. If the tenant chooses to depart, then no statutory tenancy can arise, but, if he chooses to remain in possession, then the terms of the statutory tenancy are as agreed by the parties, with the county court settling them in the absence of agreement.

The second option available to the landlord is to rely on one of the grounds in the 1954 Act and seek to recover possession, rather than propose an agreement to be governed by the Rent Acts. In a notice to resume possession, the landlord must state that, if the tenant refuses to give up possession by the proposed termination date, the landlord will then apply for a court order on one of the grounds sanctioned by Pt 1 of the 1954 Act.

Under s 12 of the Act, there is only one mandatory ground for possession, as follows: the landlord has to demonstrate 'that, for purposes of redevelopment after the termination of the tenancy, the landlord proposes to demolish or reconstruct the whole or a substantial part of the relevant premises'. 'Proposes' is not as strong a term as 'intends', to be found elsewhere in the same Act for related purposes and the court must order possession if satisfied that the landlord has made such preparations for development as are reasonable in the circumstances.

Discretionary grounds

In Sched 3 to the 1954 Act, there are four grounds which bear a close resemblance to Rent Act 1977 grounds: being concerned with suitable alternative accommodation; failure to pay rent or insure; nuisance/annoyance and immoral or illegal user; or that the premises are reasonably required by the landlord for occupation by himself or a member of his immediate family.

If the landlord fails to obtain possession, it is open to him to serve a notice proposing a statutory tenancy. According to s 14, this notice has to be served within one month of the end of the proceedings for possession.

Forfeiture and long leaseholders

There is a risk that landlords, aware of the implications of the 1954 Act for security of tenure, could seek to prevent the operation of the Act by use of a pre-emptive forfeiture action when the lease still has some time to run. There is, therefore, provision in the shape of s 16 of the 1954 Act to confer additional rights on long leaseholders. However, s 16(4) naturally excludes action taken by the landlord in relation to failure to pay rent or rates, failure to insure the premises and immoral or illegal user.

The basic protection is found in s 16(3), under which, if the landlord is seeking an order for possession or damages and there are seven months or less left of the tenancy and the tenant has applied for relief, then the court cannot make an order. If there are more than seven months left and the court does make an order, that order will be suspended for 14 days to give the tenant the opportunity to apply for relief against forfeiture.

The Local Government and Housing Act 1989

It will be recalled that s 186(3) of this Act decrees that virtually all long tenancies governed by the 1954 Act, as of 15 January 1999, will be transformed into tenancies governed by the 1989 Act. The salient difference for those undergoing this transformation is that the framework of security of tenure and rent rights available for assured tenants under the new dispensation is significantly more landlord friendly than the terms under which statutory tenants hold after expiry of the term under the 1954 Act. Assured tenants have no rent rights to speak of and this has a natural effect over time on security of tenure, even though, notionally, assured tenants are, by definition, better off than shortholders. It is, perhaps, premature to speculate what impact the 1996 Act reforms could have in this regard, bearing in mind the dramatic effect of ill considered deregulation in the 1988 Act, as already described. Certainly, the very broad prospective provision in s 96 of the 1996 Act makes assured shortholds the norm. There is, however, some hope that the worst difficulties will be obviated by the fact that, in Sched 7 to the 1996 Act (creating a new Sched 2A to the Housing Act 1988), tenancies under Sched 10 to the Local Government and Housing Act are excluded from the category of assured shortholds.

Definition of a long tenancy

There are obvious correspondences with the previous legislation. A long tenancy is defined in the 1989 Act Sched 10, para 2(3) as:

> ... a tenancy granted for a term of years certain exceeding 21 years, whether or not subsequently extended by act of the parties or any enactment, but excluding any tenancy which is, or may become, terminable before the end of the term by notice given to the tenant.

The qualifying condition for a long tenancy

This is a necessarily amended version of the previous law tied to the Rent Acts. Instead, the focus is on assured tenancies, as constituted by the 1988 Housing Act. The basic condition is that 'the circumstances, as respects the property let under the tenancy, the use of that property and all other relevant matters are such that, if the tenancy were not at a low rent, it would at that time be an assured tenancy within the meaning of Pt 1 of the Housing Act 1988' (Sched 10, para 1(1)).

Security of tenure

Termination by the tenant

The tenant is entitled to terminate the tenancy on the expiry date or at any time, thereafter, by giving the landlord at least one month's notice.

Termination by the landlord

Mutatis mutandis, the provisions here closely resemble the earlier Act and the procedural niceties affecting notices in due form have yet to be resolved, as the draftsman has virtually until the millennium to produce the appropriate formulae. As before, there are two options for the landlord, on this occasion, to serve a notice proposing an assured tenancy or a notice to resume possession. In either eventuality, the landlord must wait until on or after the term date of the tenancy in question and give not more than 12 and not less than six months' notice of the specified date for termination.

Notice proposing an assured tenancy

According to Sched, 10 para 4, the landlord's notice must propose an assured monthly periodic tenancy and propose a rent for the new tenancy, a rent 'such that it would not be a tenancy at a low rent'. The notice must also indicate either satisfaction with the existing terms of the long lease or the desire to impose new terms. The tenant then has two months to respond and, in the absence of agreement, the rent assessment committee has jurisdiction to settle dispute. When assessing a suitable rent, the committee is required to aim for the going market rate; what might reasonably be expected to be the return in the open market for a landlord on an assured tenancy.

Under the 1989 Act, there is one innovation enabling the landlord to receive a market oriented rent as soon as possible. An 'interim monthly rent' can be imposed at any stage between the date of the service of the initial notice and the specified termination date. Again, the rent assessment committee will have jurisdiction in the event of disagreement, but may not be too receptive to a reference by a tenant dissatisfied with the operation of 1999 market forces.

Notice to resume possession

The relevant grounds for possession are in Sched 10, para 5 of the 1989 Act and can be summarised as follows:

(1) reliance on Ground 6 in Sched 2 to the Housing Act 1988 – where the landlord intends to demolish or reconstruct the whole or a substantial part of the dwelling-house. This is a mandatory ground for possession and an important prerequisite is that the work cannot reasonably be carried out with the tenant in possession;

(2) virtually all of the discretionary grounds for possession in Pt II of Sched 2 are available to the landlord. The only exception is ground 16, relating to employees and hence irrelevant;

(3) the landlord, for the purposes of redevelopment, proposes to demolish or reconstruct the whole or a substantial part of the premises after the tenancy has been terminated;

(4) the premises are wholly or partly required by the landlord for occupation by him or any son or daughter over 18 or his spouse's father or mother and, if the landlord is not the immediate landlord, that he or she will be at the specified termination date.

As with the 1954 Act, a landlord unsuccessful with a possession action has a month following the end of the proceedings to serve a notice proposing an assured tenancy.

In the next chapter, more substantial rights involving enfranchisement and lease extension will be considered. Long leases within the 1954 Act and the 1989 Act can, other things being equal, qualify for enfranchisement, as under the Leasehold Reform, Housing and Urban Development Act 1993. The prolongation of security does not seem to have caused problems sufficient to warrant intervention in the Housing Act 1996; the downside of this is that the legislative black hole already identified still exists.

CHAPTER 10

LEASEHOLD ENFRANCHISEMENT AND ASSOCIATED RIGHTS

THE LEASEHOLD REFORM ACT 1967

The problems and pressures associated with long leases have been documented in the preceding chapter. Here, the first task is to give an outline of the provisions of the Leasehold Reform Act 1967 and subsequent amendments. It should be admitted, at the outset, that the legislation supposed to enfranchise houses meeting certain qualifying conditions has not yielded a high take up, particularly at the more modest end of the market where the problems affecting leaseholders already mentioned are more heavily concentrated. This lack of response, in part, explains why the Act has never been repealed by governments ideologically opposed to any expropriation of private landlords. A number of reasons have been adduced for the relative failure of the 1967 legislation and the following seem the most plausible. First, ignorance of the law and the lack of any publicity campaign comparable to that heralding and promoting the right to buy for council tenants. Secondly, opposition from local professionals, such as solicitors and valuers, who often incline to the view that the Act is unjustifiably confiscatory. Thirdly, the economics of enfranchisement do not add up for many long leaseholders at the bottom end of the market, unable both to purchase and keep in repair their properties and likely to have difficulty in raising the requisite finance from institutional lenders. Fourthly, the lack of any simple mechanisms in the Act itself for determining basic questions, such as the price payable for the freehold. In the absence of a straightforward 'back of the envelope' formula of the sort implemented without difficulty in comparable legislation in Scotland and Ireland, the price of the freehold becomes a matter for the inexact science of valuation. Leaseholders are often well advised to bargain outside the Act, rather than pay everyone's costs and haggle extensively and expensively over the nebulous statutory formula, since an offer from the freeholder outside the Act is usually pitched at a level that makes further dispute unattractive. Fifthly, in certain areas such as Birmingham, there is frequently a problem of intermediate interests between the leaseholder in occupation and the freeholder and all these intermediate interests have to be identified and bought out at no little expense to the qualifying leaseholder.

As with other legislation in this sphere, the Housing Act 1996 makes some adjustments to the 1967 Act and these will be dealt with more fully at the appropriate point in the text.

In summary, the 1996 Act introduces a new element in s 105 to cater for the fact that the traditional characterisation of rateable values in the 1967 Act formulae did not include reference to a rateable value *other than nil*. The second more significant change via s 106 is the introduction, in Sched 9 to the Act, of new rights to enfranchisement for tenancies failing the low rent test. This is consistent with the general drive towards owner occupation – not necessarily at a massive discount – for all but short term residential tenants in the private sector.

The aims of the Act

As already stated, the purpose of the 1967 Act is to offset the perceived injustices of the leasehold system and s 1 affirms the intention 'to confer on a tenant of a leasehold house, occupying the house as his residence, a right to acquire on fair terms the freehold or an extended lease of the house and premises'. As could be anticipated from the previous survey of judicial attitudes to the Rent Acts, it is unlikely that the judiciary would welcome such a project unreservedly. The traditional, somewhat grudging, approach to the legislation is encapsulated in the often quoted statement from Lord Justice Roskill in *Methuen-Campbell v Walters* [1979] 2 WLR 113, p 128:

> I do not think it right to describe the 1967 Act as confiscatory legislation; it is a statute which obliges a landlord to enfranchise the tenant at a price fixed by the statute. Rather, it is in the nature of a compulsory purchase. But, where someone is seeking to exercise such a right given by statute, it seems to me that it is for the person seeking to exercise that right to show that on the facts found that he can properly bring his claim within the language of the statute which confers that right on him.

In other words, as with the Rent Acts, the gates do not open wide to all comers. An impressionistic survey of decided cases reveals that, often, the building and the subject matter in question is towards the more affluent end of the spectrum, partly because the average terraced house enfranchisement is not going to create legal, as opposed to financial, difficulties because the facts required by the qualifying conditions will be clear cut.

The prerequisite of a house

In keeping with the inability of English property law to cope with flying freeholds in flats, the Act is anxious to confine eligibility to houses of such a type as to avoid difficulties, such as enforcement of positive covenants. An elaborate, but necessarily inconclusive definition is provided in s 2 of the Act:

> (1) For the purposes of this Part of this Act, 'house' includes any building designed or adapted for living in and reasonably so called, notwithstanding that the building is not structurally detached, or was or is not solely designed or adapted for living in, or is divided horizontally into flats or maisonettes; and
>
> (a) where a building is divided horizontally, the flats or other units into which it is so divided are not separate 'houses', though the building as a whole may be; and
>
> (b) where a building is divided vertically the building as a whole is not a 'house', though any of the units into which it is divided may be.
>
> (2) References in this Part of this Act to a house do not apply to a house which is not structurally detached and of which a material part lies above or below a part of the structure not comprised in the house.

The use of horizontal and vertical is not very illuminating in this context, but the former appears to exclude the possibility of flats and maisonettes qualifying and the latter covers the familiar case of a row of terraced houses. Clearly, the whole street is not a house, but the individual terraced houses in a street are, in principle, eligible. Sub-section (2) covers the relatively rare set of circumstances where the building in question projects above or below adjacent dwellings, as in *Parsons v Viscount Gage (Trustees of Henry Smith's Charity)* [1974] 1 WLR 435, where part of the building lay over the next door garage. Although 'nothing propinqs like propinquity', it is not clear why the law should set its face against such fact situations which are different to the obvious flying freehold within the confines of one building. At any rate, the House of Lords confirmed the view of the first instance judge that the encroachment was by a material part of the dwelling. Enfranchisement was, therefore, not possible in that instance. It should also be noted that, since the definition concedes that the building need not be solely designed for living in, buildings with flats above shops can also qualify. It is also immaterial, in such circumstances, if the upper floors are sublet, so long as the mixed user building can still reasonably be called a 'house'. It was stated in the House of Lords, in *Tandon v Trustees of Spurgeon's Homes* [1982] AC 755, that the question of the reasonableness of the label 'house' is a matter of law and is not to be analysed solely in factual terms.

The significance of 'the house and premises'

Clearly, it is not just the dwelling house itself which will be the subject matter of a claim. The Act specifies that included in the transaction will be premises, defined as – 'any garage, outhouse, garden, yard and appurtenances which, at the relevant time, are let with the house and are occupied with and used for the purposes of the house'. Demarcation disputes are, therefore, inevitable and the courts have, in keeping with the judicial pronouncement quoted earlier, been curmudgeonly in admitting various claims to associated 'premises'. In the same case as the quotation, *Methuen-Campbell v Walters* [1979] 2 WLR 113, a paddock which had been included in the original lease was considered not part of the 'appurtenances' for qualification purposes and was not even deemed part of the curtilage of the house. In *Gaidowski v Gonville and Caius College, Cambridge* [1975] 1 WLR 1066, the claim to a strip of land failed because it had not been originally let by the landlord along with the house, but had been subsequently leased. Although the terminology of 'let with' could be argued either way, Lord Justice Ormrod decreed that it connoted 'some reasonably close connection between the transactions of letting the house and letting the strip'.

A long tenancy

Although, as already described, the classic building lease that generated pressure for reform was 99 years, a mere 21 years is the minimal qualifying period. According to s 3 of the Act, the stipulation is for a term of years certain exceeding 21 years, irrespective of whether the tenancy is or may become terminable before the expiry date by notice by either party or by re-entry, forfeiture or otherwise. If a tenant has had a long tenancy at a low rent and is granted another tenancy, whether expressly or by operation of law, then the second tenancy will be considered to be a long tenancy, irrespective of the new terms (s 3(2)). Similarly, when a long leaseholder takes another long tenancy of the same property or part of it at the end of the first tenancy, the two tenancies are regarded as one single long tenancy by virtue of s 3(3).

Special difficulties are associated with long leases stated to be terminable by notice on death or marriage. Prior to the implementation of the Leasehold Reform, Housing and Urban Development Act 1993, such tenancies were not considered to be qualifying long tenancies, despite the fact that s 149(6) of the Law of Property Act 1925 converts them into 90 year terms terminable on the specified event. Section 64(1) of the 1993 Act inserts a new s 1B in the 1967 Act and brings most of them into the statutory fold.

Low rent

To distinguish the tenancies in question from the short term agreements occasionally covered by the Rent Acts, the specification of a low rent is the obvious solution, but over the years, the requirement has been subject to the most preposterous legal complexities. No attempt will be made here to grapple with all the complexities, but a basic summary of the crucial dates and amounts will be provided.

Tenancies predating 1 April 1990

If the tenancy predates 1 April 1990 (or was granted after that date because of a prior agreement and the property had a rateable value on 31 March 1990), then the rent payable must not be equal to or in excess of two-thirds of the rateable value of the property on the appropriate day or, if later, the value on the first day of the lease (s 4(1)).

Tenancies entered into on or after 1 April 1990

If the lease was granted on or after the 1 April 1990 (otherwise than, where the property had a rateable value on 31 March 1990, in consequence of a prior contract), the rent per annum must not exceed £1,000 in Greater London and £250 elsewhere.

Tenancies originating between August 1939 and April 1963

As though there were not enough dates to contend with, the revaluation conducted in 1963 transmogrified what were, at the outset, market rents into low rents in principle within the scope of enfranchisement. In consequence, a lease granted between the dates must also satisfy the following condition: the rent payable at the start of the tenancy must not exceed two-thirds of the letting value of the property. Letting value has been defined as 'the best annual return obtainable in the open market for the grant of a long lease on the same terms whether this be achieved by letting at a rack rent or letting at a lower rent plus the payment of a premium'. (Lord Griffiths, in *Johnston v Duke of Westminster* [1986] 3 WLR 18, p 23). Therefore, the premium element in any transaction can legitimately be taken into account in decapitalised form, thereby pushing many tenancies outside the scope of enfranchisement. The onus is on the reluctant landlord to displace any assumption that the actual sums involved do not properly represent the letting value for the purposes of the special condition.

Alternative method of enfranchisement in the 1993 Act

Those falling outside the qualifying conditions already outlined can still hope for enfranchisement (but not extension of the lease) as a result of modifications in the 1993 Leasehold Reform Housing and Urban Development Act, s 65, which inserts a new s 4A in the 1967 Act. Whereas, characteristically, a claimant under the 1967 Act has to satisfy the low rent condition for the full qualifying period of three years, the focus in the 1993 reform is merely on the first year. The alternative test is as follows:

> A tenancy will qualify, other things being equal, if no rent was payable in the first year or the total payable during the year is less than the following amounts:
>
> For tenancies predating 1 April 1963, two-thirds of the letting value of the property on the date of commencement of the tenancy.
>
> Where the tenancy postdated 1 April 1963, but predated 1 April 1990 or was entered into on or after 1 April 1963 in execution of a prior agreement and the property had a rateable value at the start of the tenancy or at any time before 1 April 1990, two-thirds of the rateable value on the relevant date.
>
> In any other case, £1,000 for Greater London properties and £250 for properties elsewhere.

THE 1996 HOUSING ACT

As part of the general trend to increase opportunities for enfranchisement, Sched 9 to the Act creates a new s 1AA to help those disqualified from purchase of the freehold because they do not meet any of the low rent criteria. The new sub-s (2) of s 1AA states:

> A tenancy falls within this sub-section if:
>
> (a) it is granted for a term of years certain exceeding 35 years, whether or not it is (or may become) terminable before the end of that term by notice given by or to the tenant or by re-entry, forfeiture or otherwise.

Other eligible tenancies are perpetually renewable leases, unless the lease in question is itself a subletting from a non-qualifying tenancy, and tenancies not originally granted for 35 years, but attaining that age by renewal under a covenant for renewal without payment of a premium.

Excluded are tenancies if the house at issue is in an area designated for the purposes of the reform as a rural area by order of the Secretary of State.

The occupation conditions

As will be seen, the occupational time limits set for entitlement for enfranchisement or extension of the lease are a world away from the ideal type justification for the Act based on 99 years of exploitation. Instead, a fairly minimal approach is taken and the current three year specification has itself been reduced from five years since the 1967 Act was implemented. Another illustration of the remoteness of the legal criteria from the classic justification is that the benefit of the occupational conditions can be assigned on a transfer of the leasehold, to facilitate freehold purchase.

Section 1(1)(b) provides:

> At the relevant time (that is to say, at the time when he gives notice in accordance with this Act of his desire to have the freehold or to have an extended lease, as the case may be), he has been the tenant of the house under a long tenancy at a low rent, and occupying it as his residence, for the last three years or for periods amounting to three years in the last 10 years.

It is also stipulated that the occupation must be in the right of the tenancy in question, so occupation, for instance, under a licence would not qualify. In addition, it is stated that the tenant must occupy the house as his only or main residence, irrespective of any user for other purposes.

Partial subletting does not disqualify a claimant if the other conditions are satisfied, but the time of subletting the whole house cannot count towards the qualifying period. This is demonstrated by the case of *Poland v Earl Cadogan* [1980] 3 All ER 544, where, after a short period of occupation, the tenant went abroad and instructed agents to sublet the whole property. The claim included the time when the subletting had happened and the Court of Appeal concluded that the occupation conditions had not been satisfied, since, in the words of Lord Justice Megaw, 'a tenant cannot be said to be occupying a house as his residence during a period of time in respect of which he has no intention of occupying it or residing in it because of his belief or expectation, whether it is accurate or not that he has given up his legal right to occupy or reside in the house'.

The occupational conditions are, therefore, almost as generous as those for the right to buy council dwellings under the 1985 Housing Act. There is one other important provision, in s 7, which allows for a member of a tenant's family who has been living at home to add in the period of occupation by the deceased predecessor to the occupation period he has accumulated since the death.

Rateable value limits

An initially convenient mechanism for regulating eligibility, here, as with other legislation such as the Rent Acts, is the use of rateable value limits as a criterion. However, over time, with revaluations and changes of policy, a hideously complicated accretion of different rules can arise and the 1967 Act is no exception. The Leasehold Reform, Housing and Urban Development Act 1993 has typically added a further layer of complication on top of previous modifications to the system. The purpose of the 1993 intervention is to amplify the scope of enfranchisement (but not lease extension) to those previously disqualified occupiers of high value houses, but appropriate compensation has to be paid to the landlord. No attempt will be made here to give all the possible relevant facts and figures and appropriate days for valuation purposes, but a general summary will be attempted. An outline of the limits applicable prior to the 1993 reforms will be given first.

Tenancies predating 1 April 1990

The value of the premises is determined by a statutory formula and the rateable value must not exceed certain limits, as follows:

Where the appropriate day is on or after 1 April 1973 and the lease was created on or before 18 February 1966, the value must not exceed £1,500 in Greater London and £750 elsewhere. If the lease was created after the 18 February 1966, the relevant limits are £1,000 and £500 respectively.

Where the appropriate day predates 1 April 1973 and the rateable value on the appropriate day was more than £400 in Greater London and £200 in the provinces, and the tenancy predates 18 February 1966, then the appropriate day is deemed to be 1 April 1973 and the relevant limits are £1,500 and £750.

Where the appropriate day is before 1 April 1973 and the tenancy postdates 18 February 1966, the rateable value on the appropriate day must not exceed £400 in Greater London and £200 elsewhere.

Tenancies granted after 1 April 1990

In the case of such tenancies, there is a statutory formula for determining the value of the premises and the formula is to be applied at the date of the contract for the grant of the tenancy or, failing that, the date the tenancy was entered into.

Impact of the 1993 Act

As already stated, the notion behind the reform, in this instance, is that no leaseholder should be disqualified from enfranchising by reason only of high rateable value limits, but the formula for determining the price is different to the norm and the landlord is entitled to compensation. It therefore makes sense to go through the possibilities of qualifying without invoking the 1993 alternative, as the original formula will work out cheaper for the leaseholder. The 1993 Act s 63 inserts s 1A into the 1967 Act and it says that, where a leaseholder is excluded from the operation of the 1967 Act procedures because of the limits already outlined, the right to enfranchise nevertheless exists.

Exclusions from the 1967 Act

Unlike some legislation previously examined, the list of specific exclusions from access to the statutory rights is not lengthy. The main exclusions are shared ownership leases, granted by such bodies as housing associations. This exclusion is derived from the Housing and Planning Act 1986, s 18 and Sched 4. Also, outside, are agricultural holdings, as defined in s 1(3) of the 1967 Act. Houses are outside the scope of enfranchisement, but not of extension if the landlord is a charitable housing trust and the house is provided in furtherance of charitable objects.

How to use the Act on qualification

The details of the various procedural hoops that have to be gone through will not be belaboured here. The starting point is that, if the leaseholder satisfies the conditions already outlined, he is, under s 8, entitled to be granted the house and premises for an estate in fee simple – that is, buy the freehold. Alternatively, a qualifier can demand a new tenancy of the house and premises for a term ending 50 years after the expiry date of the current tenancy – an extension. If a tenant opts for an extension, which is the cheaper and less popular option, then the right to enfranchise is still available up to the point of expiry of the original lease.

Summary of the procedure

It is an established criticism of the procedural requirements of the Act that the timetable and other regulations are not stringent enough to prevent prevarication and delay by reluctant leaseholders. The leaseholder naturally initiates the process by serving notice of his 'desire' to purchase the freehold or extend the lease. The notice must be in prescribed form and state which option is preferred. According to the perverse logic of s 5 of the Act, this unilateral act by the tenant has the same effect as a freely entered bilateral contract. Another consequence of the notice is that the landlord then has to have permission from the court to commence proceedings to terminate the tenancy. However, the court, in such instances, will not look favourably on a tactical exercise by the leaseholder to counter the threat of forfeiture by serving a notice under the Act.

The landlord has two months after receipt of the leaseholder's notice to reply in prescribed form and state whether the claim is accepted or contested. Generally speaking, there is little that can be done, if the qualifying conditions are met, to defeat any claim. There are, however, two possibilities; the first of using s 18 of the Act and establishing through a court order the right to repossess on the grounds that all or part of the property is reasonably required for occupation by the landlord or an adult member of his family as their only or main residence. Clearly, this can only avail the individual, rather than the institutional landlord. The second option is confined to opposition to an extension, rather than to enfranchisement, and is found in s 17. The landlord may apply for a court order requiring repossession of the property on the grounds that he proposes to demolish or reconstruct the whole or a substantial part of the premises for the purposes of redevelopment.

Addition or exclusion of certain property

Since the landlord may have an interest in adjacent property not actually part of the premises in question or may be concerned about part of the premises underlying or overhanging his own property, there is further elaborately drafted legislative machinery in s 2(4) and 2(5) of the Act to achieve the basic purposes of forcing the leaseholder to take in additional property on enfranchisement or excluding certain otherwise eligible property. As with the general response, the landlord has two months from the date of the tenant's initial notice to reply and, if agreement cannot be reached on inclusions and exclusions, the court has jurisdiction to settle the matters. The test for additional property is simply if the court is satisfied that it would be unreasonable for the landlord to retain the shed, or whatever, in the circumstances. Conversely, with retained property under the threat of flying freeholds, the test is whether any hardship or inconvenience likely to result to the tenant from the exclusion is outweighed by the difficulties likely to beset a landlord if the property were included.

The price of enfranchisement

As already indicated, large sums in solicitors' and valuers' fees would have to be foregone if a simple statutory formula for calculating the freehold price were operative. Instead, as with other aspects of the 1967 Act, the criteria are unnecessarily complicated and there are several different modes of calculation applicable in different circumstances. In all the complexity, the basic proposition underpinning the White Paper preceding the Act, that the bricks and mortar belong in equity to the leaseholder, is sometimes in danger of disappearing from view.

The criteria in s 9 of the Act

Where the rateable value limits are relatively low, there are various elements in the statutory criteria to keep the price of the freehold moderate. The relevant limits are £1,000 in Greater London and £500 elsewhere and there are several assumptions to be made. The most significant are that it is taken that the current tenancy has been extended for 50 years, thereby, where the lease has some time to run, reducing the reversionary value considerably and making it sensible merely to capitalise remaining ground rent. It is assumed that the tenancy does not confer a right to acquire the freehold and, importantly, that the tenant and family members living in the house are not interested in buying it. This last hypothesis is valuable for claimants because occupiers seeking the freehold may have to pay more than 'outside' purchasers who would necessarily purchase with a sitting tenant.

Where the rateable values are above the limits just itemised, a different set of criteria initiated in the Housing Act 1974 applies. The significant differences in the statutory assumptions are that there is no assumption that an extension is operative, merely that the leaseholder will have the right to remain in occupation under the 1954 and 1989 Acts analysed in the preceding chapter. In addition, the assumption that the tenant and family are not interested parties is displaced by the more realistic view that the 'marriage value' of leasehold and freehold cannot be ignored. These altered assumptions have had the desired effect of increasing the price of enfranchisement and shifting the ground from the equitable justification in terms of bricks and mortar.

In those circumstances already described, where the 1993 Act comes to the rescue of high rated properties, the dice are further stacked against the leaseholder by new assumptions that the tenant is only entitled at best to 50% of the marriage value and that the landlord can claim compensation for any reduction in value in other property interests.

Extension of the lease

This option is seldom taken up by leaseholders; the equivalent, under the 1993 Act, is likely to prove more popular. The criteria involved in the 1967 Act are, for once, relatively straightforward. Naturally, the rent payable is as contractually agreed up to the point of expiry of the lease. Thereafter, the rent for the extended lease is a modern ground rent reflecting the letting value of the site and this ground rent can be revised after 25 years. The only other points worthy of mention are that, after the extension has commenced, the leaseholder loses the right to enfranchise and, at the end of the extension, there are no rights under the 1954 or 1989 Acts to continue the tenancy.

Estate management schemes

One of the anxieties at the time of the implementation of the 1967 Act was that leasehold estates would lose their character as houses were gradually enfranchised. It is, arguably, in the interests of both landlord and tenants for the appearance and amenity of estates to be preserved. In s 19 of the 1967 Act, there was, therefore, scope for landlords of large estates to retain management powers to maintain the quality and character of the original development.

Two years were allowed in the first instance for schemes to be submitted. Obviously, with the passage of time, there could be grounds for further intervention and the Leasehold Reform, Housing and Urban Development Act 1993 makes provision both for alteration of existing schemes by leasehold valuation tribunals and for the creation of new schemes within two years of the commencement of the Act, with some discretion to accept late submissions.

THE LANDLORD AND TENANT ACT 1987

It is apparent, so far, from this approximately chronological survey of leasehold legislation, that there are grave problems with the long leasehold system and that, although the legislative remedies are not worse than the disease, they are often flawed. One intractable problem is bad management by freeholders of long leaseholders and, recently, there has been much agitation in the media about the antics of certain property companies buying the freehold of blocks of flats relatively cheaply and then proceeding to enforce repairing covenants and service charges in a highly aggressive and expensive fashion. No legislation is yet extant to deal effectively with such entrepreneurial activities, although the 1996 Act, in s 81, does offer some respite to leaseholders faced with forfeiture for failure to pay service charges, but the next Act to be considered, the Landlord and Tenant Act 1987, does, at least in principle, offer some tenants an escape by way of the right of first refusal when the landlord plans to sell on the freehold. This right of first refusal is confined to the private sector and is not available to tenants of social landlords. The Act was rushed through Parliament and has come in for heavy criticism from academics and the judiciary and was characterised by Sir Nicholas

Browne-Wilkinson VC in *Denetower Ltd v Toop* [1991] 3 All ER 661, p 668, as 'ill drafted, complicated and confused'. Only a relatively brief summary of the Act will be offered here.

Yet again, there are provisions in the 1996 Housing Act making substantial alterations to such elements as the right of first refusal and introducing a penal element in the shape of a new criminal offence of contravening various vital sections of the Act without reasonable excuse. Schedule 6 to the Act consists of revamped and enlarged ss 5–10 of the 1987 Act and those reforms will be analysed in due course. Provisions of this type are not listed in the Act as coming into force immediately or two months after the passage of the Act, so are dependent on an order by the Secretary of State.

The qualifying conditions

Part 1 of the 1987 Act sets out the preconditions for the exercise of the right to first refusal. It applies to premises consisting of the whole or part of any building which must contain two or more flats held by qualifying tenants. So, some form of multiple occupation of a building is required. The number of such flats held by qualifying tenants must amount to more than half the total number of flats in the premises (s 1(2)).

Excluded premises

To focus properly on residential occupation, there is provision in s 1(3) for premises to be excluded if those parts of the premises occupied or designated for non-residential purposes constitute more than half of the internal floor area of the premises. For these purposes, the internal floor area of any common parts is to be disregarded.

Also excluded are premises where there is a resident landlord – 12 months residence is required – and where the freehold is held by an exempt landlord. The most significant categories of exempted landlords are social landlords – local authorities and housing associations.

Which tenants qualify?

Rather than state simply and affirmatively what classes of tenant are eligible the Act in s 3(1) places the emphasis on those disqualified, leaving the gaps to be filled in. Those ineligible are protected shorthold tenants, business tenants within the Landlord and Tenant Act 1954, Pt 2, tenants with tied tenancies terminable when employment ceases, and assured (including shortholders) and assured agricultural occupants. The common denominator between these types of tenancy is that, almost by definition, the interests of the landlord are regarded as outweighing any proprietary aspirations of the tenants. It would be bizarre if assured shortholders, for instance, could be elevated from the lowest form of tenant life to owner-occupation on some 'relevant disposal'.

There is also provision for the tenant with several flats. By virtue of s 3(2), a tenant will not qualify if he holds a tenancy of three or more flats in the same premises. There is no residential qualification for tenants built into the Act, so in other instances absentee tenants can qualify. In the case of the three flat tenant, subtenants become eligible on his disqualification.

This leaves the question of who does qualify? Characteristically, long leaseholders at low rents in the private sector will be eligible, as will, perhaps surprisingly, Rent Act regulated tenancies. The inclusion of these last would come as a surprise to most landlords and tenants and it is unlikely that the Act is in practice often observed on disposal. This is one of the perils of essentially negative drafting. To compile only a list of those excluded is a hostage to fortune, as new tenancy types are constantly being created and, unless s 3 of the 1987 Act is updated with ceaseless vigilance, there is a danger of unlikely candidates qualifying at birth.

What is a relevant disposal?

The nub of Pt 1 is the obligation on the landlord to serve an offer notice on qualifying tenants if he intends to make a disposal caught by the Act. In general terms, a disposal is relevant, as defined by s 4, if it involves parting with any legal or equitable estate or interest in the premises, including disposal of the common parts. Disposals under the terms of a will or in consequence of intestacy are not 'relevant', nor are the grants of tenancies where the premises consist of a single flat.

There is a list of further exclusions from the category of relevant disposal given in s 4(2). It covers such matters as family arrangements and disposals in connection with settled land, trusts and bankruptcy, rather than traditional market transactions. Disposals to the Crown are also excluded.

The Housing Act 1996, in s 89, enlarges the scope of relevant disposals by inserting a new s 4A into the 1987 Act. The purpose is to apply the right of first refusal to contracts to create or transfer an estate or interest in land, whether conditional or unconditional and irrespective of enforceability via specific performance.

Procedural formalities and time limits

As stated, s 5 imposes a duty on a landlord about to make a relevant disposal as defined to serve notice on the qualifying tenants. The notice has naturally to give details of the transaction, affirm that the notice constitutes an offer by the landlord to sell on these terms if the offer is acceptable to the requisite majority of tenants and specify various periods for the processing of the offer. According to s 5(4) the landlord does not have to contact all qualifying tenants. It is sufficient if the notice is served on at least 90% of them or if there are fewer than 10, on all but one. Alert tenants who detect a relevant disposal in the offing without due notice are able to stay the landlord's hand by applying for an injunction.

The Housing Act 1996 in Sched 6 attempts to delineate more accurately the types of disposal which fall within the Act. New ss 5A–E are created and the offer notice must reflect the different transactions. The general outlines in terms of time limits and percentages of qualifying tenants entitled to offer notices remain much the same as in the existing Act. The relevant subdivisions are: 5A, where the disposal consists of entering into a contract to create or transfer an estate or interest in land; 5B, disposal by means of a sale at a public auction; 5C refers to the grant of an option or right of preemption; 5D covers the the circumstances where the 'disposal is not made in pursuance of a contract, option or right of pre-emption binding on the landlord'; 5E covers the rare occurrence of disposal for non-monetary consideration. It remains to be seen whether the more accurate specification of types of disposal coupled with criminal sanctions for non-compliance have any effect on the notorious neglect of the statutory duties in this sphere. The history of the 1987 Act does not encourage optimism.

Acceptance by the tenants

Unanimity would be too much to hope for in many instances, however mismanaged the property in question. Acceptance has merely to be forthcoming from the 'requisite majority' as defined in s 5(6) of the 1987 Act. One flat, one vote, is the underlying principle, and at least half the qualifying tenants must accept within the time allowed at least two months. If there is the requisite majority in favour, an acceptance notice then has to be served on the landlord and a 'person' (usually a company) nominated to take over the freehold.

The landlord is then effectively paralysed in dealing with the property until the end of the 'relevant period' specified in s 6(1). This period is three months on top of the time allowed for consideration of the original offer. If the tenants fail to nominate the appropriate person in due time, the landlord can then dispose of the interest elsewhere.

Counter-offers

It may be that the tenants are not satisfied with the original terms of the offer and elect to serve a counter-notice on the landlord. The landlord is not obliged to accept this counter-offer and, if it is rejected, he can dispose of the property elsewhere, subject to the proviso that the price must not be less than that contained in the original offer.

Inaction by the tenants

If the qualifying tenants fail to act in time, again, the landlord is entitled to sell the freehold elsewhere on the same terms as the original offer.

What happens if the landlord ignores the Act?

Although in many cases landlords dispose of reversions rapidly without let or hindrance, there is, in theory, in the 1987 Act, some machinery enabling the requisite majority to enforce their rights, even after the disposal has happened. Section 11 gives the qualifying tenants the right to obtain information about any extra-statutory transfer and s 12 allows them to serve a purchase notice on the new landlord, compelling him to transfer the freehold to the 'person' nominated. That, at least, is the theory, but the drafting of the section is not precise enough to afford an easy answer to the basic question, whether a duty to sell to the tenants exists. The Court of Appeal recently in *Green v Twinsectra Ltd*

[1996] 1 WLR 1587 struggled to make sense of this area of the statute and apply the spirit rather than the letter. Similarly, in *Mainwaring v Trustees of Henry Smith's Charity* [1998] QB 1, the then Master of the Rolls, Lord Bingham, made the following comments about s 5:

> It is a noteable feature of the section that, although it lays a clear mandatory duty on a landlord, there is apparently no sanction against a landlord who fails to comply: in practice, neglect of the statutory duty has been common and has given rise to considerable litigation.

The 1996 Act seeks to remedy this.

The central issue in the case was whether the requirement not to dispose of the freehold without conferring the right of first refusal became operative on exchange of contracts or on completion. The Master of the Rolls, perhaps surprisingly, opted for completion, and said of the Act:

> With any other Act we should think it extraordinary that doubt should exist on a point so fundamental as this. We have to say that we do not find the answer indicated with an acceptable degree of clarity in the language of the section itself or elsewhere in the Act.

These provisions complained of have been 'strengthened' in the Housing Act 1996, in Pt II of Sched 6, and must be an improvement on the original. So far as the new criminal offence is concerned, s 91(1) of the 1996 Act inserts a new s 10A in the 1987 Act making it an offence to make a relevant disposal without reasonable excuse without having first complied with the requirements of s 5 in respect of notices or in contravention of any requirement in ss 6–10. Where the offence is committed by a body corporate, a director or other similar functionary is liable to prosecution for deliberate connivance or for neglect. This reform is not retroactive and does not apply to a disposal made prior to the commencement of s 91, which could be some time away, most probably the beginning of 1997.

THE LEASEHOLD REFORM, HOUSING AND URBAN DEVELOPMENT ACT 1993

This is the last measure to be considered in this context and is chiefly concerned with conferring rights of collective enfranchisement on flat dwellers and the option of individual lease renewal as an alternative. The arbitrariness of excluding flatdwellers from the putative joys of owner-occupation available to the vast majority of tenants became increasingly pressing. The election manifesto preceding the Act spoke of the need to emancipate around 750,000 flatdwellers, but it is unlikely that significant numbers of leaseholders will use the collective rights under the Act. Although the emphasis in the Act is anything but confiscatory and the calculation of the freehold price is more market-orientated than the 1967 Act, it attracted great opposition during its parliamentary passage (including the Duke of Westminster's departure from the Conservative party) and experienced some amendments, such as a residence qualification, which go some way to undermining some of the manifesto promises.

As with the 1967 Act, the only consensus is that the Act is very badly drafted and, yet again, unnecessarily complicated. The very complexities are likely to discourage tenants from seeking to invoke the Act and the criteria for determining the freehold price have already had to be amended in the Housing Act 1996, which contains some other reforms to the Act. In keeping with the tenor of this chapter, the emphasis in exposition of the Act will be on substantive issues and likely difficulties, rather than on procedural matters. This is not to deny that, as with the 1967 Act, the inbuilt procedural complexities can operate as a powerful disincentive to those contemplating using the Act.

COLLECTIVE ENFRANCHISEMENT

Qualifying premises

Section 3 is the first of the crucial definitional sections to be examined and it is linked to the definition of a flat in s 101. According to s 3(1), as originally drafted, the premises must 'consist of a self-contained building or part of a building and the freehold of the whole of the building or of that part of the building is owned by the same person'. However, s 107 of the Housing Act 1996 deletes reference to the same person owning as a prerequisite, to make allowances for multiple freeholders. The amendment is intended to combat the ingenious practice of freeholders selling off the freehold of one or several flats within the premises to a company created for the purpose and defeat any hope of enfranchisement because the freehold is not owned by the same person. This subdivision of the freehold was anticipated when the 1993 Act was debated, but the opportunity for avoidance/evasion was left intact.

The premises must contain at least two flats held by qualifying tenants and the total number of such flats held must not be less than two-thirds of the total number of flats in the premises.

Section 3(2) contains an elaborate definition of a 'self-contained building'. A whole building is self-contained if it is structurally detached and a part of a building is a self-contained part if it enjoys an independent existence as follows:

(a) it constitutes a vertical division of the building and the structure of the building is such that that part could be redeveloped independently of the remainder of the building; and

(b) the relevant services provided for occupiers of that part either:

- (i) are provided independently of the relevant services provided for occupiers of the remainder of the building; or
- (ii) could be so provided without involving the carrying out of any works likely to result in a significant interruption in the provision of any such services for occupiers of the remainder of the building.

The definition of a flat

Section 101(1) states:

> ... flat means a separate set of premises (whether or not on the same floor):
>
> (a) which forms part of a building; and
>
> (b) which is constructed or adapted for use for the purposes of a dwelling; and
>
> (c) either the whole or a material part of which lies above or below some other part of the building.

It may be that flats, like elephants, are difficult to define, although you know one when you see one, but this conventional definition does not, perhaps, adequately distinguish, for instance, between bedsits with an annex doubtfully described as a kitchen and flats properly so called. 'A separate set of premises' begs too many questions.

What premises are excluded?

Section 4 outlines the main exclusions, again in tortuous language. The first exclusion is designed to eliminate mixed user premises where non-residential user, actual or prospective, accounts for more than 10% of the internal floor area of the premises. Garages and storage areas used in conjunction with flats are counted as residentially occupied and the common parts of the building are naturally left out of the equation.

Premises with a resident landlord are also excluded if they do not contain more than four units. 'Unit', according to s 38, means a flat, any other separate set of premises which is constructed or adapted for use for the purposes of a dwelling or a separate set of premises let, or intended for letting, on a business lease. Purpose built blocks of flats are outside the exclusion and the occupational conditions in s 10 are that the freeholder or an adult member of the freeholder's family occupies a flat in the premises as his only or principal home and has done so for at least the previous 12 months. This gives the smaller landlord plenty of scope for installing relatives to prevent enfranchisement.

Qualifying tenants

The basic proposition in s 5 is that a person is a qualifying tenant of a flat if he is tenant of the flat under a long lease at a low rent. Thereafter in the section, the picture becomes murkier. Section 5(2) excludes certain situations, such as business tenancies and lettings by charitable housing trusts as part of charitable purposes. Also excluded are circumstances where the lease in question was granted in breach of covenant out of a superior lease which was not a long lease at a low rent and the breach has not been waived. Although there could be many leasehold interests in the same flat, s 5(3) avoids double counting by asserting that no flat shall have more than one qualifying tenant at any one time. The case of joint tenants is resolved by counting them as one single qualifying tenant.

To qualify, a tenant does not have to occupy the flat as a residence and could sublet, but aggregate residence qualification is important for eventual qualification for enfranchisement *en bloc*. Where there are several leases involved and the subtenancy otherwise qualifies, then s 5(4)(a) disqualifies the superior landlord. Multiple qualified tenants who could claim for three flats or more in one building are literally disenfranchised, as s 5(5)(b) says there will then be no qualifying tenant of any of those flats.

Residence condition for qualifying tenants

The significance of any residence condition is spelt out in s 13 which states cumbersomely that at least two-thirds of qualifying tenants must be in favour of enfranchisement that they must represent at least half the total of flats in the building and that at least half the qualifying tenants serving notice of their right to buy must satisfy the residence condition! To be fair to the draftsman, he was not attempting to construct a Mensa puzzle, but responding to the late insertion of the residence requirements into the Bill. When cross-examined in Parliament about the justification for this late modification of expectations, the Minister responsible claimed that few blocks of flats would, in reality, be disenfranchised by the alteration and that, in any event, the amendment would 'exorcise the spectre of control by an absent majority'. As already shown, residence requirements figure more prominently in other enfranchising legislation, but they can be correlated with the discount prices available, whereas the 1993 Act is much more mindful of open market values.

The requirements in s 6 can, for once, be simply stated. According to s 6 the condition is that 'the tenant has occupied the flat as his only or principal home for the last 12 months or for periods amounting to three years in the last 10 years, whether or not he has used it also for other purposes'. The section also affirms that it is immaterial whether the tenant's occupation was under the relevant long lease and it clearly allows for long periods of subletting. However, occupation by a company does not satisfy the residence condition. Section 111 of the Housing Act 1996 makes minor modifications to the residence conditions in relation to trusts.

Long leases

The definition of a long lease is closely modelled on that in the 1967 Act and s 7 specifies a lease granted for a term of years certain exceeding 21 years, whether or not it is or may become terminable prematurely by notice from the tenant or by re-entry, forfeiture or otherwise. The definition is generous enough to encompass those granted a further tenancy of whatever description on expiry of the original long lease and also includes fixed term leases of less than 21 years which are renewed so as to accumulate 21 years. Perpetually renewable leases, not surprisingly, also qualify, along with leases granted in pursuance of the Housing Act 1985 right to buy.

Low rent

The focus is on the initial year of the lease and the usual convolutions reflecting different criteria for different dates are to be found in s 8. The relevant ceilings are as follows:

For leases predating 1 April 1963, two-thirds of the letting value of the flat on the date of the commencement of the lease. Letting value is to be calculated using the criteria already described in the Leasehold Reform Act 1967.

Where the lease was entered into either on or after 1 April 1963, but before 1 April 1990 or on or after 1 April 1990, in pursuance of a prior contract, and the flat had a rateable value on commencement of the lease or at any time before 1 April 1990, then the ceiling is two-thirds of the rateable value of the flat on the appropriate date. According to s 8(2)(b), the appropriate date means the the date of the start of the lease, or, if the flat in question did not then have a rateable value, the date on which it was first rated.

For later leases, the limits are the more straightforward: £1,000 for Greater London; and £250 for the demetropolitanised.

The right to collective enfranchisement

Just as with other types of enfranchisement, the purchase of the freehold is often complicated by the need to accommodate ancillary matters, such as appurtenant property and the common parts of a building. Section 1 of the 1993 Act goes into some detail about the type of property owned by the freeholder, but not necessarily comprised in the claim, which the enfranchisers can, nevertheless, expect to acquire. Appurtenant property, such as garages, outhouses and gardens, is a case in point, provided it is property demised by the lease held by one of the qualifying tenants. Equally, property which any tenant is entitled to use in common with occupiers of other premises can also be acquired, irrespective of whether the common parts are in the premises claimed or not. However, the freeholder can prevent exercise of this latter right by creating such permanent rights in favour of the enfranchisers that the closest approximation to the status quo is achieved (s 1(4)).

The converse proposition also holds. Section 21(4) enables a landlord to offload on the purchasers property which would be useless for all practical purposes or impossible to manage or maintain.

How to claim

If all the conditions previously outlined have been satisfied, a claim to exercise the right to enfranchise can proceed in accordance with s 13 of the Act. As already indicated, the thresholds are that two-thirds of the total number of tenants in the flats must be qualifying tenants and the quota of qualifiers must be at least half the total number of flats involved. The discrepancy between the fractions is explained by the fact that some flats may not have qualifying tenants at all. The initial notice must be given to the 'reversioner' of the premises, since there are possibly chains of intermediate interests involved and the freeholder will not always be the person chosen to negotiate. The tenants are obliged to nominate someone – an individual, a group or a company – to conduct all proceedings arising from the initial notice on their behalf, defined in s 15 as the 'nominee purchaser'.

Prior to the service of any initial notice, qualifying tenants are enabled by ss 11 and 12 of the Act to extract from the freeholder or other suitable person vital information about other interests in the property. This preliminary information gathering is often indispensable, as the initial notice is required to go into some detail about the premises claimed the proposed purchase price the possibility of compulsory leaseback for certain tenancies and other related matters.

The reversioner then has two months from the date of the notice to reply and serve a counter-notice, governed by s 21. Basically, there are three possible responses: accepting the entitlement; disputing the claim; or, in any event, announcing the intention of an 'appropriate landlord' to apply for an order under s 23(1), disallowing the claim on the grounds of intended partial or total redevelopment of the premises. Because this, as with other redevelopment grounds, could be partly camouflage used to defeat a claim, there are stringent conditions in s 23(2) which must be satisfied before a claim can be rejected. The conditions are that at least two-thirds of all the leases of the flats are due to expire within five years and the more familiar criterion that the landlord intends on termination to demolish or reconstruct or carry out substantial works on the premises and needs possession in order to do so.

Where the claim is disputed, the nominee purchaser can apply to the county court for a declaration that the tenants are entitled to exercise the right to collective enfranchisement. If the claim is conceded, then further negotiations about the terms of the acquisition can proceed and, if there is no agreement after a specified period, either side can apply to a leasehold valuation tribunal to determine the matters in dispute under s 24 of the Act.

The price of the freehold

It is not just the freehold, but any intermediate interests which will also have to be valued and acquired. The criteria for calculating the value of the various interests are set out at prodigious length in Sched 6 to the 1993 Act and no attempt will be made to summarise them here. The gist of them, in connection with freehold purchase, is to calculate the market value of the freeholder's interest, plus a certain percentage of the marriage value and allow for compensation for the freeholder for consequential loss from enfranchisement. Marriage value is one of the more contentious aspects of the calculation, as it can generate additional costs for the leaseholder, particularly if the freeholder is held to be entitled to more than 50% of the value. However, one of the more important interventions by the Housing Act 1996, in this area, is to amend the valuation principles in s 109, apparently because the original criteria betrayed a misunderstanding of the different nature of marriage value computations as between houses and flats. Section 108 of the 1996 Act also removes the requirement (in s 13(6) of the 1993 Act) that qualifying tenants have to obtain a professional valuation of the interests involved before proceeding to serve their initial notice.

The individual right to acquire a new lease

This second and, apparently, subsidiary right for an individual tenant of a flat to acquire a new lease is likely to prove more important and less cumbersome to operate, in practice, than the vagaries of the collective enfranchisement rules. However, yet again, there appear to have been deficiencies in the original drafting, particularly as regards the formulae for determining the premium and other grants payable by the tenant on the grant of a new lease and s 110 of the 1996 Act has weighed in with lengthy alterations to the original criteria, covering such matters as valuation of intermediate interests and assessing the value of the interest of the tenant under the existing lease.

Qualifying tenants

The criteria here are very close to those for collective enfranchisement. Sections 5, 7 and 8 are again applicable, although sub-ss 5 and 6 of s 5 are omitted. Therefore, the basic conditions about long leases and low rents are familiar, as is the precondition that the tenant has occupied the flat in question as his only or principal home for the last three years or for periods amounting to three years in the last 10 years, irrespective of whether the flat has also been used for other purposes. Since the exclusions operative in s 4 for enfranchisement are not applicable, resident landlords are no bar to qualification, any more than a level of non-residential user in the building.

What sort of new lease is acquired?

According to s 56 of the Act, the qualifying tenant gets the right to a new lease of the flat at a peppercorn rent for a term expiring 90 years after the term date of the existing lease. This is in substitution for the existing lease and dependent on payment of the premium payable under Sched 13 to the Act. The terms of the new lease are to be the same as the existing lease except to take account of circumstances, such as alterations to the property, since the grant of the existing lease (s 57). According to s 59, although the leaseholder has no rights under the Landlord and Tenant Act 1954 or the Local Government Act 1989 to a continuation after expiry of the new lease, it is open to the leaseholder to use the 1993 procedure again and again.

The price of the new lease

As already indicated, the 1996 Act has modified the criteria in the 1993 Act, but not affected the basic structure of the valuation criteria. The new criteria are applicable to any claim made after the 19 January 1996 by service of the requisite notice, unless the amount payable has been determined, either by agreement or by the leasehold valuation tribunal before the day on which the Act was passed (24 July 1996).

In broad outline, the criteria in Sched 13 state that the premium payable in respect of the grant of a new lease is to be the sum of three factors: the diminution in value of the landlord's interest in the flat; the landlord's share of the marriage value; and any compensation payable for losses arising out of the grant of the new lease.

The major impact of the 1996 reforms appears to be in giving details about the calculation of the value of the interest of the tenant as a component in the complicated statutory equation establishing marriage value. A new para 4A is inserted after para 4 of Sched 13 to the 1993 Act giving detail about the factors relevant to calculation of the tenant's interest. In the original, it was simply stated that the value of the interest of the tenant fell to be determined as at the valuation date.

Summary of the procedure

The qualifying tenant has to serve an initial notice in accordance with s 42 of the Act. The notice must be served on the landlord and any third party to the tenant's lease and contain the details of the subject matter of the claim. As with enfranchisement, there is provision in s 41 for the tenant to extract information from his immediate landlord about the nature of any superior interests. The landlord then has two months to serve a counter-notice. The responses are analogous to those available in the case of enfranchisement, save that there is more scope for rejecting the claim on the grounds of intended redevelopment in the case of individual leases, as the landlord only has to show that the one lease will expire within five years, as opposed to two-thirds of all the leases in the premises for collective enfranchisement.

A question that surfaced in relation to the initial notice under s 42 in *Cadogan v Morris* (1998) *The Times*, 24 November was whether s 42(3)(c), stating that the tenant has to specify the premium he proposes to pay for the grant of a new lease, requires the tenant to come up with a realistic figure, although no such word as genuine or *bona fide* appears in the statute. The 99 year proposed lease in question was valued at somewhere between £100,000 and £300,000 and the tenant, somewhat hubristically, proposed the paltry sum of £100 as the premium. The Court of Appeal were satisfied that the freeholder, Earl Cadogan, deserved better than a nominal sum; a more realistic figure had to be specified, even if it were not the tenant's final proposal.

Conclusion

This morass of overlapping legislative detail does not appear to contain any clear principles. The initial effort to assist leaseholders of houses in the 1960s has not, by and large, benefited the intended recipients. The legislation of the last two decades has drawn most leaseholders into the net of enfranchisement, but bad drafting and other difficulties have again reduced the level of response. At the Committee stage of the Housing Act 1996 in the House of Commons, the Labour spokesman produced the following polemical, but accurate summary of recent legislative efforts in this field:

> The history of leasehold reform over the past 10 years or more has been a sorry story of failure. Leasehold is an inherently unsatisfactory tenure. It is a tenure that has enabled freeholders to amass substantial fortunes by selling and reselling their land, obliging the leaseholder to bear all the costs of maintaining the property. In many cases, the leaseholders have even built the property in the first place, but it is the freeholder who benefits from the reversionary interests. That is a type of tenure that has benefited the few, not the many.

With the advent of the Labour government in 1997, the impetus for reform in such a well trodden area seems to have gathered some momentum. At the end of 1998, the government produced a consultation paper, *Residential Reform in England and Wales*. The main proposals are: to assist the collective purchasing of the freehold of flats by leaseholders; to find ways of minimising disputes over the price of a freehold; to introduce a new right to manage for those reluctant to exercise the right to buy; to improve the standards of management by freeholders and property managers; to stop the use of the threat of forfeiture as a means of extorting unreasonable service charges; and to introduce – at long last – commonhold. According to the Housing Minister, 'We plan to strengthen leaseholders' rights, while striking a fair balance with landlords' legitimate interests' – a difficult, if not impossible, balancing act!

INDEX